PRAISE FOR

ROBERT J. MRAZEK

TO KINGDOM COME

"[The] personal accounts of surviving the horrors of deadly aerial combat to return to base, escape capture in France, or become POWs are riveting, giving readers the real flavor of the war." —*Library Journal*

"With power and passion, Robert J. Mrazek tells the story of one of the most calamitous American bombing missions of World War II. . . . Mrazek writes about the ill-fated Stuttgart Raid as though he had gone into the heart of the Reich with the audacious American bomber crews . . . a great book with 'hold on to your seat' suspense."
—Donald Miller, author of *Masters of the Air: America's Bomber Boys Who Fought the Air War Against Nazi Germany*

"Mrazek has uncovered the moment of profound exigency for the bomber crews, when the course and consequence of the air war converged, and rendered it in vivid clarity."
—Hugh Ambrose, *New York Times* bestselling author of *The Pacific*

"[A] work of cinematic sweep and pace."
—Richard Frank, author of *Downfall* and *Guadalcanal*

"Through superb historical research and powerful narrative writing, the author brings back to life a pivotal, heartbreaking episode."
—Tami Biddle, professor, U.S. Army War College, and author of *Rhetoric and Reality in Air Warfare*

A DAWN LIKE THUNDER

"Strap yourself in as Robert Mrazek takes you on a heroic flight into history."   —James Bradley, author of *Flyboys* and *Flags of Our Fathers*

continued . . .

"A spectacular achievement."

"A remarkably vivid tale of valor, fate, and young men dying young. Mrazek's epic story, reconstructed with breathtaking research and recounted with a novelist's keen eye for detail, is a worthy monument to Squadron Eight."

"A stirring, truly heroic book that is destined to become a classic."

"Fast-paced and yet personal, Mrazek's narrative carries the reader to Midway quickly. . . . He melds a good story with solid and skeptical research."

"A must read for any World War II buff . . . A *Dawn Like Thunder* is gripping like few history books are, with the immediacy of Mrazek's prose making you feel like you're part of the action."

"Robert Mrazek has, with a raw, unsparing telling, given grace and life to so many who died so young, so everyday, so gallantly."

"A compelling account."

TO KINGDOM COME

AN EPIC SAGA
OF SURVIVAL
IN THE AIR WAR
OVER GERMANY

ROBERT J. MRAZEK

NAL
CALIBER

New American Library
Published by New American Library, a division of
Penguin Group (USA) Inc., 375 Hudson Street,
New York, New York 10014, USA
Penguin Group (Canada), 90 Eglinton Avenue East, Suite 700, Toronto,
Ontario M4P 2Y3, Canada (a division of Pearson Penguin Canada Inc.)
Penguin Books Ltd., 80 Strand, London WC2R 0RL, England
Penguin Ireland, 25 St. Stephen's Green, Dublin 2,
Ireland (a division of Penguin Books Ltd.)
Penguin Group (Australia), 250 Camberwell Road, Camberwell, Victoria 3124,
Australia (a division of Pearson Australia Group Pty. Ltd.)
Penguin Books India Pvt. Ltd., 11 Community Centre, Panchsheel Park,
New Delhi - 110 017, India
Penguin Group (NZ), 67 Apollo Drive, Rosedale, Auckland 0632,
New Zealand (a division of Pearson New Zealand Ltd.)
Penguin Books (South Africa) (Pty.) Ltd., 24 Sturdee Avenue,
Rosebank, Johannesburg 2196, South Africa

Penguin Books Ltd., Registered Offices:
80 Strand, London WC2R 0RL, England

Published by NAL Caliber, a division of Penguin Group (USA) Inc. Previously published in an NAL Caliber
hardcover edition.

First NAL Caliber Trade Paperback Printing, March 2012
10 9 8 7 6 5 4 3 2 1

NAL Caliber Trade Paperback ISBN: 978-0-451-23575-6

THE LIBRARY OF CONGRESS HAS CATALOGUED THE HARDCOVER EDITION OF THIS TITLE AS FOLLOWS:

Mrazek, Robert J.
To kingdom come: an epic saga of survival in the air war over Germany/Robert J. Mrazek
p. cm.
Includes bibliographical references and index.
ISBN 978-0-451-23227-4
1. World War, 1939–1945—Aerial operations, American.   2. World War, 1939–1945—Campaigns—
Germany, Stuttgart.   3. Bombing, Aerial—Germany—Stuttgart—history—20th century.
4. B-17 bomber—history.   5. Bomber pilots—United States—Biography.   6. United States. Army
Air Forces. Air Force, 8th—Biography.   7. Survival after airplane accidents, shipwrecks, etc.—Germany—
Stuttgart—History—20th century.   8. World War, 1939–1945—Personal narratives, American.
9. World War, 1939–1945—Casualties—Germany—Stuttgart.   I. Title.
D790.M7220110
940.54'2134715—dc22   2010040928

Set in Electra
Designed by Ginger Legato

Printed in the United States of America

For Carolyn Rae, always

Out there, we've walked quite friendly up to Death;
Sat down and eaten with him, cool and bland . . .
Oh, Death was never an enemy of ours!
We laughed at him, we leagued with him, old chum.

—Wilfred Owen

Apparently the Gods were with us.
Otherwise we would have been blown to Kingdom Come.

—Second Lieutenant Vern Moncur
B-17 Pilot, *Wallaroo*

This is the story of an aerial bombing mission to Stuttgart, Germany, that resulted in a shattering defeat of the U.S. Army Air Forces in the Second World War. It is told through the eyes of some of the men who fought in the battle.

It was not lost through want of courage.

CONTENTS

Slipstreams

Epilogue   295

TO
KINGDOM
COME

PRELUDE

Hap

G eneral Henry "Hap" Arnold awoke in darkness. It had become his habit to rise before dawn since the war began. By the time his aide Clair "Pete" Peterson arrived at the house to take his baggage to the airfield, he had bathed, shaved, and was dressed in full uniform.

It was the fourth year of the most horrific slaughter in human history. Across the globe, more than 20 million people had died in the titanic struggle to defeat the Axis powers of Japan and Germany.

For the past eighteen months, Hap Arnold had lived on Fort Myer's "General's Row," a few doors from George Marshall, the U.S. Army's chief of staff. Marshall had wanted all his senior officers to be quartered in the same protected military reservation. As the commanding general of the U.S. Army Air Forces, Arnold now led an organization of more than 2 million men equipped with fifty thousand aircraft.

The large brick house overlooked the Potomac River and enjoyed a magnificent view of the Capitol. Its spacious rooms were quiet since his wife, Eleanor "Bee" Arnold, had left him. On the few occasions they were together in the months before she moved out, she was always brimming over with complaints. Long ago, they had shared a deep romantic bond, celebrating the date of their anniversary every month. She remained proud of her husband's accomplishments, but had become increasingly bitter about his failure to make time for her. He understood it and regretted it.

The morning had dawned hot and humid, the kind of Washington tropical heat that sucked the energy out of a man, especially one who was still recovering from his second major heart attack in four months.

The first coronary occurred following an exhausting trip back from the Casablanca meetings in February 1943, after a series of tension-filled conferences with Roosevelt and Churchill over the future of his air force.

In the wake of the attack, he refused to allow a doctor to examine him, much less go to the hospital, out of fear of losing his job. According to army regulations, no senior officer could continue to serve on active duty if he had a serious illness. Only President Roosevelt had the authority to overrule the decision, and he had done so in Arnold's case. The general was considered too important to the war effort.

He was fifty-seven years old.

On this last morning in August 1943, he would leave behind the sweltering heat of Washington, as well as all the political infighting among the American war chiefs, to make an inspection tour of the Eighth Air Force command in England. The first stop on his transatlantic flight was Gander, Newfoundland, where it would be thirty degrees cooler than the U.S. capital.

Arnold's doctors had strongly urged him to cancel the trip. After his second coronary in May while attending the Trident meetings in Washington, he was still experiencing shortness of breath, his stomach ulcers were back, and his weight had ballooned, the product of too many old-fashioneds and rich desserts. At five feet eleven inches, he was still stocky and broad-shouldered, but no longer the trim 185 pounds he had been at West Point.

At the Point, he had earned the nickname "Happy," later shortened to "Hap," because of his seemingly perpetual grin. The grin was no more than a hereditary facial characteristic that belied his intense and often melancholy nature.

Much of the intensity stemmed from an austere childhood. His father, Herbert Arnold, had been a humorless Baptist doctor firmly set on his personal path to salvation. A rigid disciplinarian, he had raised his five children under the ascetic principle of all toil and no play. Young Henry had been put to work for a neighboring farmer at the age of seven. He hadn't stopped working since.

At 0820, General Arnold's command car arrived in front of Quarters Number 8 to take him to the airfield at Gravelly Point, a few miles down the Potomac River. His transport aircraft was waiting for him on the tarmac.

It was a four-engine Douglas C-54 Skymaster, and had been outfitted for a general's comfort. The plane carried twenty-six passengers in plush leather seats that were positioned in group settings. It was equipped with a full galley, as well as comfortable sleeping compartments for long ocean crossings. The president had one almost exactly like it. With a cruising speed of 200 miles per hour and a range of four thousand miles, it was perfect for the globe-trotting Arnold.

Four army generals and several other staff officers were traveling in Arnold's party that morning, including David Grant, the army air forces' chief surgeon, and Arnold's personal doctor.

Arnold and the other passengers were given a briefing in lifeboat drill before the pilot took off from Gravelly Point at precisely 0900. Off to their left, the white dome of the Capitol shimmered in the steamy haze as they headed north along the Eastern Seaboard. Eight hours and sixteen hundred miles later, they landed at Gander, Newfoundland. It was raining and cold, with low clouds and light fog.

Most of the buildings at the airfield were newly constructed corrugated steel Quonset huts, surrounded by vast stores of supplies and equipment set out haphazardly in mountainous piles as far as the eye could see. Small caravans of fuel trucks moved slowly around the base like weary caterpillars. The airfield's runways, aprons, and revetments were jammed with aircraft, including B-24 Liberators, Douglas B-18 Bolos, British Hurricane fighters, and transport planes of every hue and vintage.

Waiting to take off when Arnold arrived were several squadrons of B-17 Flying Fortresses on their way to join the Eighth Air Force as replacement aircraft. Arnold's C-54 would be following one of the squadrons across the North Atlantic later that night.

After an inspection tour of the military base, Arnold was scheduled to confer with Air Chief Marshal Sir Frederick Bowhill, the Royal Air Force's commander in chief of the ferry command, to discuss safer routes for his B-17 bomber crews on their flights from the United States to England. Bowhill was flying to Gander especially to meet him.

While the Skymaster was being refueled, Arnold embarked on his tour with the local army commander, periodically making notes in his confidential diary as they visited each installation on the post. The tone of his observations quickly became mocking.

"More men needed for the band," he recorded tartly at one point, and then, "Our men poach on Canadian preserves." At the hospital he wrote, "Inspected hospital . . . saw mostly injured from volley ball."

When he arrived for his conference with Air Chief Marshal Bowhill, he learned that the RAF commander had been briefly delayed by bad weather. Arnold waited fifteen minutes before deciding that was long enough. He ordered Captain Niswander, the pilot of his C-54, to prepare the plane for immediate takeoff to Prestwick, Scotland, their next destination.

Impatience.

It was the trademark of Arnold's life, both his blessing and curse.

He was no armchair general. In 1911, Hap Arnold had been one of the first two pilots to become a qualified army aviator in the newly formed branch of military aviation. He had been personally trained to fly by Orville and Wilbur Wright.

In the early and dangerous days of military aviation, army pilots flying largely untested aircraft were dying every month. Arnold had survived multiple crashes in unstable crates made of canvas and wood.

His first accident occurred in an early-model floatplane that crashed into the ocean off Plymouth, Massachusetts. Severely injured, he had been rescued by the coast guard while clinging to wreckage that was floating out to sea.

An even more harrowing incident left him unnerved, and he refused to fly again, deciding to transfer to the infantry instead. Four years later, he was able to conquer his fear of flying through sheer willpower because of his fervent desire to return to military aviation.

A disciple of the legendary airpower advocate General Billy Mitchell, Arnold devoted twenty-seven years of his life to helping build a modern air arm; he was intimately involved at every level with the development of faster aircraft, bombers with greater load capacity, up-to-date air facilities, and improved training methods.

Few of his contemporaries ever dreamed that he would one day command the army air forces. A maverick from the start, Arnold made a habit of leaving outraged superior officers in his wake. Contemptuous of the army bureaucracy, and unyielding in his pursuit of his objectives, he often risked his career by criticizing and opposing his more senior officers when he thought they were wrong. On more than one occasion he narrowly avoided court-martial proceedings.

In spite of his headstrong personality, he rose steadily through the officer ranks for one simple reason. He was a man who made things happen in an organization filled with officers who avoided risk. He thought faster and he acted faster. With his single-minded focus, he could always be counted on to get things done. Above all else, he became known in the air service as a doer, an achiever, always working toward meeting his next goal. A day that passed without advancing one of them was a wasted day.

Occasionally, he could be cajoled into playing golf or going fishing, but it was almost impossible for him to relax. One of his aides said, "His idea of a good time was to work all day, then fly all night to California, and visit five aircraft plants, telling the chief executives, 'I need another hundred miles an hour out of your plane.'"

He was a man who placed duty above all things, including family. In the summer of 1923, his two-year-old son, John, died of a ruptured appendix, leaving his wife bereft. Arnold's other son, Bruce, lay in critical condition at the base hospital with scarlet fever.

On that same morning, General John Pershing, the army's chief of staff, was due to arrive for an inspection tour of Arnold's San Diego military base. Arnold spent the day escorting Pershing around the installation.

Wealth meant nothing to him. After twenty-seven years of military service, he couldn't afford the down payment on a $5,000 house. Years earlier, he had turned down the presidency of Pan American Airways.

He lived for the air force, and in 1938 he was finally given its top command, which then consisted of several hundred outmoded aircraft and a complement of less than twenty thousand men.

With war on the horizon, his real work was about to begin.

Arnold's days were soon filled with a dizzying array of command responsibilities: hectoring congressional committees for larger allocations, developing new prototype aircraft, improving the existing planes, pushing the aircraft manufacturers to speed up their assembly lines, meeting new recruitment goals, building airfields all over the world, setting up training regimens and flight schools, and selecting the best officers for promotion.

"He had enthusiasm," said Robert Lovett, the assistant secretary of war for air. "To him, there wasn't anything that couldn't be done."

The same impatience that had served as a blessing in his professional career proved to be a curse to his physical health and his marriage, contributing to his burgeoning stomach problems and his two heart attacks.

His legendary impatience had also led to the bitter estrangement from his wife. If he came home from work in time for dinner, the phone would begin ringing as soon as he arrived. He was impervious to her pleadings to cut back on his workload. Finally, she left.

On the night of August 31, Arnold's C-54 Skymaster took off from Gander, Newfoundland, at 2130 in a heavy rainstorm. The flight plan called for them to fly twenty-one hundred miles across the Atlantic before making landfall over Northern Ireland. As the big plane sped across the dark ocean, the generals smoked and chatted.

Part of the time, Arnold worked on the speech he was planning to deliver in London on September 4. It would mark the recent launching of his new heavy bomber air offensive against Germany. It was the culmination of everything he had worked for in building a modern air force.

Hap Arnold ardently believed that the quickest way to defeat Germany was to annihilate its capacity to wage war. In his mind's eye, he could envision thirty-mile-long armadas of his heavy bombers, a thousand or more blotting out the sky, thundering across Europe to reach their military targets in Germany, where the lead bombardiers would use their top secret Norden bombsights to drop payloads with pinpoint accuracy on the enemy's most important industrial targets, destroying the manufacturing plants that produced Germany's planes, tanks, and heavy guns. If given a free hand, he was confident that the Allies would never have to invade Europe.

The weapon of Germany's destruction would be the Boeing B-17, the heavy bomber that had become known as the Flying Fortress. It was big, handsome, and lethal, the first long-range bomber with the load capacity to fully deliver on Arnold's cherished doctrine.

With a crew of ten men, the plane bristled with Browning .50-caliber machine guns, and Arnold was convinced that the Fortresses could protect themselves from enemy fighters by flying in tight formations that gave the machine gunners in each "combat box" interlocking fields of fire.

In the draft of the speech he would be delivering in London, he had written, "I do not envy the prospects of a German fighter pilot these days. Say he chooses to attack the lead squadron to break up the whole group. The forward firing guns of every fort in the lead squadron, 8 guns to a fort, 48 in all, are bearing down on him—if he zooms over the flight, some 50 top turret, waist, and radio hatch guns of that flight, plus the ball turret, waist and tail guns of the high squadron get a crack at him. . . . The life of a young German in the Luftwaffe will not be a happy one from now on for of only one thing can he be certain—death."

With enough Fortresses, he was sure that the Eighth Air Force could bring Germany to its knees. And that was the problem. So far, he hadn't been permitted to put together the critical mass of bombers he needed to prove his case.

After almost two years of war, he was deeply weary of the Washington infighting with his fellow chiefs, as well as the concessions he was being forced to make to the British. Now that the bombers were finally coming off the assembly lines in sufficient numbers to carry out their planned purpose, the other chiefs were trying to take them away from him like a pack of carnivores, devouring his air force limb by limb.

The British were the worst. At the beginning of the war, they had tried daylight bombing and failed. Now they bombed only at night, setting German cities on fire under the cloak of darkness, waging war on civilians. Terror bombing would never break the will of the Germans, Arnold concluded, just as it hadn't worked when the Germans blitzed London every night for months. It had only strengthened the will of the British people.

The British, led by Prime Minister Winston Churchill, had strongly opposed Arnold's plan for the daylight precision bombing campaign against Germany, telling Roosevelt and the other American war chiefs that it would only lead to disastrous losses of planes and crews. If the British couldn't do it, how could the Americans succeed?

Churchill had assured Roosevelt that the British could put Arnold's B-17s to far better use, and requested five thousand of them for the Royal Air Force. After Arnold successfully rebuffed this demand, Churchill asked Roosevelt to give him two hundred fifty Fortresses to use as U-boat killers in the North Atlantic. With deft stalling tactics, Arnold parried this move as well.

It wasn't just the British. The American war chiefs were almost as bad. Admiral Ernest King, the chief of naval operations, was requesting that Arnold send hundreds of heavy bombers to the Pacific for the war against Japan. The navy planned to use many of them for long-range patrolling flights. It was ridiculous. Even General Douglas MacArthur, who commanded U.S. forces in the Southwest Pacific, had gotten into the act. He was demanding hundreds of B-17s, too.

Arnold fought them every step of the way. He had learned to play the Washington game as well as he knew how to fly, and was ready to undertake any step to advance the cause. At one point he received a handwritten note from President Roosevelt concerning his son, Elliott, who had joined the army air forces.

"I am a bit concerned because Elliot has a rather bad chronic case of haemoroids (sic) that need to be operated on," wrote the president. "He rightly insists on going through with his new assignment . . . but I hope you can give him enough time off in Texas to have them taken out." Arnold made sure it happened.

By April 1943, Arnold had expected to have three thousand bombers and fighters in England for his Eighth Air Force to conduct its day-light bombing campaign against Germany. Instead, a third of them had been sent to the Pacific for the war on Japan, and another third had been diverted to other theaters.

Utilizing all his political and organizational gifts, Arnold had managed to slowly build up the Eighth Air Force in England, bomb group by bomb group, against the ongoing opposition of Churchill and the others.

He had promoted General Ira Eaker, one of his most trusted subordinates, to command the Eighth's bomber force. In 1942, Eaker began the first daylight bombing raids against targets in France with his new and untested crews. They did well.

However, when President Roosevelt made the decision to invade North Africa in November 1942, the majority of the bombers, maintenance crews, and experienced flight crews were transferred to the Twelfth Air Force in Algeria.

In April 1943, Arnold was able to send four new bomb groups to England, bringing Eaker's B-17 strength back to more than four hundred combat crews. Over the summer, the buildup continued.

Arnold's new goal was to have at least a thousand heavy bombers attacking Germany every day that the weather cooperated, deploying fleets so huge that the Luftwaffe would be engulfed, overwhelmed, and given no chance to recover.

But time was running out to prove his case. With the recent Allied invasion of Sicily in July, and the continuing demands of King and MacArthur in the Pacific, there was ever-growing pressure on him to divert his air resources from the Eighth Air Force to other commands and combat theaters. It was now or never.

The early morning of September 1 was black with rain as Arnold's C-54 Skymaster finally reached landfall over the Irish coast after flying more than two thousand miles. His navigator established their position, and Captain Niswander turned onto the compass heading for Prestwick, Scotland, which was thirty miles southwest of Glasgow along the Firth of Clyde.

When the weather worsened, Niswander was forced to fly solely on instruments. As they approached Prestwick, he contacted ground control and was told that due to heavy rain and fog, the ceiling was less than two hundred feet.

A waiting line of military aircraft was stacked up and circling the fog-bound field at different altitudes, including more than fifty B-17s and B-24s that had flown out of Gander ahead of Arnold's Skymaster. Many of the pilots and crews were new, and they were running out of fuel.

With its four-thousand-mile range, the Skymaster had enough gas to circle the field for hours. This was one of the rare occasions when Arnold's impatience was tempered by the knowledge that men's lives were at stake. He ordered Niswander to wait until all the Fortresses had landed before attempting his approach.

A ground control officer at Prestwick radioed Niswander to urge him to divert to another airfield, but Lieutenant Fisher, the plane's navigator, couldn't locate the airfield on his map, and the ground control officer couldn't tell him where it was.

Arnold asked Captain Niswander to set the Skymaster's radio to the frequency being used by the B-17 and B-24 pilots, and to pipe the feed into his compartment. One after another, he heard the pilots calling in.

"Number twenty-six . . . one hundred eighty gallons of gas left," radioed one officer as Arnold recorded his words in his diary. "Number thirty-two . . . sixty gallons left."

The planes were being brought down by the controllers one by one.

As the C-54 continued to circle in the dense fog, several of Arnold's staff officers became visibly nervous. He set them at ease by casually regaling them with stories of his own past crashes.

Minutes later, one of the B-17s crashed trying to land. All aboard were killed, and the runway needed to be cleared before the controllers could resume landings. Soon after, a second B-17 went down after running out of fuel. Its crew was lost as well.

Then Arnold heard another pilot over the radio.

"This is number sixty-two," came the laconic voice. "You won't have to worry about us anymore. I'm plumb out of gas. So long."

At 0930, with the rest of the bombers safely on the ground, Captain

Niswander brought the Skymaster in for his landing. They had been in the air more than twelve hours.

Arnold was deeply angered by the communications and radio control failures that had led to the loss of the bomber crews before they ever flew a combat mission. He was convinced that it was just one of many systemic problems in the Eighth Air Force, and he was ready to shake things up at the highest level, if necessary.

At the highest level was its commander. Major General Ira Eaker.

Ira

M ajor General Ira Eaker stood at the foot of the ramp as Hap Arnold emerged from the C-54 Skymaster and came down the steps to meet him. They shook hands and greeted each other without genuine warmth.

Outwardly self-assured, Eaker privately viewed Arnold's inspection tour with foreboding. The two generals had been openly feuding for the previous three months, and it had seriously eroded a bond of mutual trust and friendship that went back more than twenty years.

Eaker thought that Arnold might be coming to relieve him of his command. It was the most important combat command in the air force, and he had come to relish its myriad challenges. He was prepared to do everything in his power to keep it, short of acceding to orders he was convinced could lead to its destruction, along with the destruction of the lives of thousands of young men whose fate rested on his decisions.

Arnold and Eaker enjoyed a complicated relationship.

Born in 1896, Ira Eaker began life in a six-family rural settlement in southwest Texas. His father, Y. Y. Eaker, was a proud and hardworking farmer, but continuing droughts in Texas made economic survival for the family a constant challenge.

15

Like Hap Arnold's father, Y. Y. Eaker was remote and uncommunicative. In Ira's case, it led him to seek out more responsive father figures as he grew older. His mother became the chief influence on his life.

Possessing only a grade school education herself, Dona Eaker was somehow convinced that of all her children, Ira was destined to accomplish great things. Early on, she imbued him with the drive to aim high in his goals.

In 1914, the family moved to Durant, Texas. It was their first home with electricity and running water. After Ira finished high school, his mother encouraged him to enter a nearby teachers' college, where he subsequently achieved the highest grades of any student who had ever attended the school.

Fastidious in his personal habits, he always dressed for classes in a suit. It was the only one he owned, and each night he cleaned and pressed it before going to bed. He made no time for a social life, although he did join numerous athletic teams and extracurricular clubs, excelling in every activity. It was as if he had embarked on a lifelong mission to succeed. In what, he didn't know, although his mother hoped he would someday become a distinguished judge.

On April 6, 1917, the United States entered the First World War. On the following day, Ira drove with friends to Greenville, Texas, and enlisted in the army. Because he was about to graduate from college, he was sent to an officers' training camp.

At twenty-one, he was not an impressive physical specimen, standing five feet eight and weighing 115 pounds, but he met all the physical and mental challenges. After completing officers' training, he was commissioned a second lieutenant and received orders to attend flying school.

The war ended before he earned his wings, but in the years afterward he came to love flying and became a gifted pilot, setting a number of flight endurance and distance records while also serving in a variety of staff and operational posts.

In 1922, he married the high-spirited Leah Chase, the daughter of an aerial flight surgeon. The marriage lasted only seven years. Like Hap Arnold, Eaker was devoted to his career. Leah Eaker found her pleasure in an active social life.

In the 1920s, Eaker served on the staffs of two senior generals in the air service, having an almost father-son relationship with each one as he continued his rise up the promotion ladder.

The ultimate father figure in Eaker's life appeared in the form of Hap Arnold.

Eaker first met Arnold while serving under him at Rockwell Field in San Diego. Arnold was impressed with Eaker's brains and grit. Eaker admired Arnold's willingness to risk his career to build an independent air force, and signed on as an eager protégé.

In the years that followed, Eaker persevered to help Arnold achieve his goals. Like his mentor, Eaker came to believe in the sacred doctrine that daylight precision bombing alone could defeat any of America's future enemies.

In 1942, Eaker had been Arnold's first choice to command the Eighth's heavy bomber force, and to prove its value in the skies over Europe. When the first bomb groups arrived in England in the summer of 1942, Eaker broke them in by attacking lightly defended military targets in France. He led the first mission himself.

On each succeeding daylight mission, American and British fighters escorted the Fortresses to and from the targets, defending them from enemy fighters. The losses in planes and crews averaged less than 3 percent, which Eaker considered acceptable.

In December 1942, he was promoted to command the entire Eighth Air Force, and over the next six months he slowly began to extend the range of the bombing targets into Germany, well beyond the capability of Allied fighters to accompany them. In these deeper-penetration raids, losses grew from 3 percent to nearly 10 percent of the crews.

These results caused Eaker to slowly change his mind about the Arnold mantra that the Fortresses could reach targets deep inside Germany without the support of long-range escort fighters. He had seen the debriefing reports in which returning crews repeatedly asserted that even superb air discipline hadn't prevented the loss of many crews to concerted enemy fighter attacks.

He began a quietly aggressive campaign designed to convince Arnold to expedite the delivery of long-range fighters, and he requested a delay in further deep attacks into Germany until his current fighters could be equipped with jettisonable belly tanks to extend their range.

Arnold, who had just suffered his second heart attack, began to privately question Eaker's toughness. He wouldn't be able to deliver long-range fighters for months. By then, it might be too late to save the daylight bombing campaign. How could he hold off MacArthur and Admiral King from poaching his planes if he couldn't show positive results?

He cabled Eaker a new series of demands, including an order to replace Eaker's senior commanders with more aggressive officers who understood the urgency of the situation. Why weren't they sending the new groups to Germany? he demanded to know. Why were so many of them grounded due to combat damage?

Eaker cabled back his own stinging reply.

"We get nowhere with recriminations," he wrote.

On July 25, 1943, a beleaguered Eaker announced the launching of the Eighth Air Force's long-awaited bombing offensive against Germany. Over the next week, seven different industrial and military complexes were attacked, including Hamburg, Hannover, Warnemunde, and Kassel. The bombing results were good, but bomber command lost a staggering total of one hundred Fortresses and a thousand men in the raids, 20 percent of its available planes and crews.

Eaker suspended the attacks on Germany until new replacements arrived.

The air offensive was resumed on August 17, 1943, when 146 Fortresses bombed the Messerschmitt factory complex in Regensburg, Germany, while 230 Fortresses hit the ball-bearing factories at Schweinfurt, Germany.

It was the most intensely fought air battle of the war up to that time. Both targets suffered extensive damage, but the Luftwaffe shot down sixty American bombers, thirty-six in the Schweinfurt attack and another twenty-four in the Regensburg force.

Although Eaker publicly hailed the Schweinfurt-Regensburg mission as a decisive victory, he privately wondered how long they could go on taking such enormous losses. With bomber command's morale shattered, Eaker canceled all further attacks for ten days.

Two weeks later, Arnold arrived in England.

On the afternoon of September 1, they flew together from Prestwick to London. Eaker briefed Arnold on the details of his schedule for the next five days, which included inspections of airfields, bomb groups, fighter units, maintenance facilities, military hospitals, hospitality centers, and meetings with the top British and American commanders.

On the morning of September 2, Arnold flew from London up to Eaker's Eighth Air Force headquarters, which was located at High Wycombe Abbey, formerly a school for well-bred girls, in the Chiltern Hills northwest of London. When Arnold arrived at the castlelike grounds, a brass band was on hand to mark his arrival, and he was greeted with a formal escort of honor.

Inside the sprawling mansion house, Arnold met the officers on Eaker's staff and was briefed on Eaker's method of operations, the types of air formations he was using, and the number of serviceable aircraft he had available after the recent battering over Regensburg and Schweinfurt.

After lunch with the senior commanders, the afternoon was devoted to a conference in which Arnold and Eaker could "discuss the employment of the Eighth Air Force, its present status, and its ultimate objectives."

Arnold pulled no punches.

He told Eaker that at the recent meetings in Quebec between Roosevelt and Churchill to finalize plans for the invasion of Europe, the British had taken the opportunity to strongly criticize Arnold for his stubborn adherence to daylight precision bombing. Now, General George Marshall was beginning to waver in his support for the campaign. Proposals were in the works to shift the assets of the Eighth Air Force to other theaters. Time was running out.

In two days Arnold would be holding a press conference to proclaim the success of the Eighth's new air offensive against Germany. What would he tell them? That they were going to attack France again?

On the previous day, Eaker had sent his Fortresses to bomb airfields near Paris.

Arnold told Eaker he would have to renew the air offensive against Germany with the assets he had. It was time to prove the effectiveness of daylight precision bombing once and for all. The Fortresses would have to protect themselves by using tight group formations. Battle cohesion would make the difference.

After serving under Arnold for twenty years, Eaker knew that the biggest mistake he could make would be to tell him that something he wanted done couldn't be done. Instead, he tried a different approach. As long as he commanded the Eighth Air Force, Eaker said, he would conduct operations in such a way that "we will always be growing . . . not diminishing." Arnold stood up and ended the conference.

On his way back to London, he wrote in his diary, "Couldn't take any more."

Over the next two days, Arnold inspected the Fourth Bombardment Wing, which included many of the groups that had bombed Schweinfurt and Regensburg a few weeks earlier. He praised the performance of Colonel Curtis LeMay, who had led the Regensburg mission, and General Robert Williams, who had commanded the force that went to Schweinfurt.

Later, he witnessed a scramble of P-47 Thunderbolt fighters, and asked to meet with some of the P-47 pilots. They assured him that the plane was a match for the newer-model Luftwaffe fighters.

On the afternoon of September 4, Arnold held his press conference on the importance of the bombing offensive against Germany. More than a hundred reporters packed the headquarters of the European Theater of Operations (ETO) in London.

"It has long been our firm conviction that the way to shorten the war against Hitler is to first win the air battle with Germany," he told them. "We weaken the punch of our enemy by hitting him directly over his heart. Cautiously, but without once wavering from our conviction that daylight precision bombing of German targets will work, the Eighth Air Force has pushed deeper and deeper into the so-called Nazi 'Fortress of Europe.' There were doubters of daylight bombing, here and at home in the past—but no more now."

Ira Eaker sat in the audience, listening. He had no doubts about the potential success of daylight bombing, either, once he got the long-range fighters that were needed to protect his bombers. Without them, it would be a bloody passage.

Arnold spoke for nearly thirty minutes, talking about the bravery of the Fortress crews as they "fought through Nazi fighter and flak defenses to bomb precision targets within eighty miles of Berlin, right into the heart of Germany." He cited the dire prospects of German fighter pilots who still attacked the Fortresses in their combat box formations. "The other day we intercepted the frantic question of one Focke-Wulf pilot . . . translated, in effect what he said was: How the hell do I bust into this formation? All I can see is tracers reaching for me!"

The British and Americans were now seizing "complete supremacy in the air over Germany," Arnold concluded before opening the floor to the assembled reporters. When the press conference was over, he wrote in his diary that he had successfully "dodged all of the embarrassing questions."

That evening, Eaker hosted a dinner for Arnold and a dozen of his old army friends. Eaker had arranged a special event for the after-dinner entertainment. It was a newly completed motion picture in which Arnold had been filmed talking about the growth of the air force and his pride in the men who served in it.

Due to a glitch in the projector, the sound of Arnold's voice was not synchronized with the movement of his mouth. Sometimes his mouth would move and there would be no sound. At other times, his mouth would be closed and the words would flow out.

No one laughed.

The next morning, Sunday, September 5, Eaker met with his staff at High Wycombe Abbey to plan the Eighth Air Force's next bombing mission. There was little doubt in his mind that if he didn't soon resume the attacks on Germany, he would be relieved of his command.

Although it was raining across southern England, the meteorological report for the following day suggested clear skies over most of Western Europe. It would be General Arnold's last day in England.

Arnold had spent September 5 visiting battle casualties at a hospital near Oxford. Late in the afternoon, he returned to his suite at Claridge's Hotel in London, and enjoyed a quiet dinner with two senior army commanders in the hotel dining room. He was back in his suite preparing for bed when the communication arrived.

It was what he had come to England for.

Eaker had ordered a "maximum-effort" strike for the following day, Monday, September 6. It would be the biggest attack of heavy bombers ever sent against a single target in Germany.

The twenty-mile-long armada of nearly 350 Fortresses would bomb the ball-bearing and aircraft complexes at Stuttgart, Germany, while another force of sixty-nine B-24 bombers would fly diversionary raids across the North Sea to France and Holland, designed to draw the Luftwaffe fighter squadrons away from the main force. It was the first time in the war that more than four hundred bombers would participate in a single mission.

The seven groups of the Fourth Bombardment Wing would lead the attack on Stuttgart. The nine groups of the First Bombardment Wing, led by Brigadier General Robert Travis, would hit the targets in Stuttgart right behind them.

Arnold was asleep at Claridge's when the Teletype machines at High Wycombe began clattering out the operational orders to the bomb groups based across southern England that would participate in the mission.

The telexes contained the takeoff times for each group, the assembly points for the groups after takeoff, the routes to be followed to the target, communications procedures, the size of the bomb loads, the projected weather over Europe, and the anticipated enemy response in terms of the numbers of enemy fighters and antiaircraft installations.

"URGENT SECRET . . . FIELD ORDER NO 53," began the opening line to the Fourth Bombardment Wing.

THE WARRIORS

Reb

Sunday, 5 September 1943
384th Bomb Group
Grafton Underwood, England
Sergeant Olen "Reb" Grant
2350

There were some very good reasons why Sergeant Olen "Reb" Grant was happy that the 384th hadn't been alerted for a bombing mission the following day. The most agreeable one was lying next to him in the ancient church cemetery in Leicester.

With the rough-hewn good looks of a rodeo bronc buster, the twenty-year-old from Eldorado, Arkansas, particularly enjoyed dating British factory girls. Many of them worked brutally long hours in monotonous jobs, and they looked at making love as a form of relaxation and release, just like the boys in the combat crews after they returned from a tough mission. Underneath the girls' ill-fitting clothes, some of them were truly stunning.

He had hitched a ride that evening with one of the truck convoys that carried fuel and freight between the American air base at Grafton Underwood and Leicester, the nearest large city, about thirty miles away. It was an important manufacturing center, and the armament plants all had big barrage balloons tethered in the sky above them to discourage low-level air attacks. To Reb, they looked like floating elephants.

Once in the city, he usually stopped at a roadside stand to buy a newspaper-wrapped portion of fish and chips. The greasy food seemed to lessen the effects of a hangover from the beer and whiskey he usually drank.

If the war hadn't come along, Reb would have already been married. After making sergeant for the first time, he had asked his girlfriend Dorothy to marry him, and she had said no. Her reason was that he might get killed, or even worse, crippled, and she couldn't stand the thought of it. In the wake of her rejection, he made up his mind not to get serious about any woman for the rest of the war.

That was before he met Estella. Just eighteen, she was Irish, and had a fresh-scrubbed innocence to her, along with a spirited personality and an easy sense of humor. She took pleasure in mimicking his Southern drawl. And like him, she had the resilience to take the tough breaks that life had handed out, including the loneliness of being far from home. It didn't hurt that she was a ripe-bodied redhead with a wonderful Irish lilt to her voice.

He had been dating her almost a month, ever since he had pried her loose from another flier who was trying to score. That first night, Reb decided not to use her for a one-night stand, even if she was willing. After they had gone out several times, she told him that she knew a safe spot where they could finally be together.

Due to the blackout restrictions, the city was always as dark as pitch, and there were few places for an American soldier to take a girl where they could be alone. The local parks had become the most common trysting grounds, but every bench was usually occupied.

They had walked across a good piece of Leicester before she led him through an iron gate that was cut into the middle of a high stone wall. It was dark and mysterious inside. Then he blundered into the first tombstone.

"The dead cannot see," she said to him when he realized where he was.

The next thing he knew they were lying together in the tall, unmown grass. After they were together the first time, she had asked him about his life back in the United States.

Reb decided not to spin a line. He told her they shared the same Irish heritage. His forebears had arrived in North Carolina after fleeing the Irish potato famine in the 1840s. From there, later generations of the Grant family had moved west.

He had grown up dirt poor in the horse-and-buggy town of Eldorado, Arkansas, close to the Louisiana border. It was an oil town with one big refinery that ran twenty-four hours a day. His father, Eli Sullivan Grant, loved being a roustabout in the oil fields, but after the Depression hit, he took work where he could find it.

For several years, the family lived in a small house so close to the refinery that the stench of hot petroleum was constant. At night in his bedroom, the floodlamps around the facility made it seem like daylight.

Reb went to school during the day. In the evenings, he sold his uncle's eggs door-to-door, six for a nickel. He wore the same blue bib overalls until the knees wore out. Then his mother would trim the leg portions off above the knees and hem the edges. He rarely wore shoes.

One day, his dad heard they had struck oil near Longview, Texas. He put the three kids and everything the family owned in his old car and drove there. He was offered a job, and the family moved into a squatters' shantytown outside Longview with the other new workers.

Their home was a single room under a tin roof with canvas walls, and a separate tent for the kitchen. There was no running water. Reb's principal chore was to go fetch a five-gallon can of it from a well every morning.

Estella had been brought up in an Irish family that was as impoverished as Reb's. Her father had worked most of his life as a tenant farmer on a large estate. After the Depression hit, the owner of the estate stopped paying wages to his tenants. Fortunately, the families were allowed to share some of the farm produce they grew. Estella hoped that someday she would be able to earn enough money to go to school.

Her background struck a resonant chord with Reb, and the two lovers formed a deepening bond as the weeks passed. This would be the last night they would spend together for several weeks. Estella had received permission from her factory manager to travel home to Ireland to see her ailing father.

It had rained most of that Sunday, and the unmown grass of the church cemetery remained soaked. Reb had spread his raincoat over one of the low granite tombstones. A thick fog settled over the ground, making the graveyard even more ghostly than usual. Lying together on the slab, they stayed up talking late into the night. Reb fell asleep in her arms.

It was well past two in the morning when they headed back to their favorite pub for a nightcap before he walked her home. They were approaching the blacked-out street entrance when someone on the sidewalk switched on a powerful flashlight and pointed it at his face.

It was an American military policeman. He demanded Reb's name and unit. Reb gave him his identification card and produced his overnight pass from the 384th Bomb Group headquarters. The MP scanned a clipboard in the beam of his flashlight.

"I've been looking for you for hours," said the exasperated MP.

"You wouldn't have found me," said Reb.

"Get in the back of the jeep," said the policeman. "You're flying a mission tomorrow."

The teletyped alert had arrived at his base in Grafton Underwood shortly after Reb had left for Leicester. The military police had been given a list of the crewmen who were off base and scheduled to fly, and the men had fanned out in all the nearby towns to find them. Reb's name was on the list.

He asked Estella to write to him from Ireland. She promised she would. As he rode through the silent, fog-shrouded villages on the way back to Grafton Underwood, Reb wondered what the target might be. Since the new air offensive had begun against Germany, more than half the men in his barracks had gone missing. He hoped it wouldn't be another mission like Schweinfurt.

The MP had no idea where the group was going, but he said it was definitely a maximum effort. Every plane that could pass inspection was going out. He had never seen so much activity at the base.

Maybe it would be another milk run to France.

After almost two years of service, Reb Grant had come to love the army. He had joined right after graduation from high school in 1941, and quickly felt like he was living rich. Good food, new uniforms, and clean sheets on his bed. He turned out to be a natural at handling weaponry, and within a year had been promoted to sergeant in the armament section of the 384th Bomb Group.

Except for the freshly minted junior officers who acted like they were the second coming of Eddie Rickenbacker, and who took pleasure in dressing down sergeants who didn't salute with sufficient flair, life was good.

With his growing expertise in the B-17's defensive weapons systems, Reb was awarded the fifth stripe of a technical sergeant and personally selected by Colonel Budd Peaslee, the group commander, to become the armament inspector of the 384th Bomb Group.

Each group was comprised of four squadrons. A full complement for a squadron was twelve bombers, giving the group a potential of forty-eight planes and 480 men.

In April 1943, the 384th was at Wendover Field in Utah, about to leave to join the Eighth Air Force in England. Many of the Fortresses in the group required their one-hundred-hour inspection, in which all the systems in the plane were checked, including the engines, hydraulics, radio communications, and armament, before the aircraft could be declared ready for active service. Reb's job was to personally inspect each B-17's motorized gun turrets and its eight Browning .50-caliber machine guns.

The base commander at Wendover had issued a strict order that no live ammunition could be loaded aboard a bomber until it had passed the final armament inspection. On the morning before the group was scheduled to leave, Reb was crouched in the ball turret of a B-17 to inspect its twin .50-caliber machine guns. He needed to check the firing mechanism, and since there was no electricity in the parked aircraft, he used his screwdriver to activate the solenoids behind the gun switch.

Instead of hearing the distinctive click of the firing pin, the machine guns began spewing .50-caliber rounds. The gun barrels were pointed down at the tarmac, but the lead slugs ricocheted off the concrete and tore a number of big holes in the horizontal stabilizer of the plane.

Some idiot in the armament section had loaded live ammunition in the guns in violation of the base commander's standing order. Before Reb could find out who had done it, he was ordered to report to Colonel Peaslee, the 384th's commander, who was ripping mad that he might lose one of his planes the day before the group left for Europe.

Without giving Reb a chance to explain what had happened, he busted him from sergeant to private, and ordered him transferred from group headquarters to the 545th Squadron, where he said Reb would be assigned every shit detail that could be found for him.

Later that day, Reb managed to discover who had armed the machine guns on the plane, but by then he had been formally charged in a court-martial proceeding. This led to a major complication for the group.

If Reb pleaded not guilty to the charges, a court-martial board had to be appointed, and the proceeding would be convened after Olen was given time to prepare his defense. Under army regulations, the 384th could not depart for England until the court-martial board had rendered its verdict, which meant that the group would miss its deployment window, and probably be sent back to Gowen Field in Idaho for another month's training. This had already happened to the 100th Bomb Group, and they had been cooling their heels and growing stale for weeks.

After learning that Reb was innocent of negligent conduct, a chastened Colonel Peaslee told him that if he pleaded guilty to the charges, he would personally see to it that Reb was restored to the rank of sergeant and given back his previous assignment in the group. Reb was dubious. The only way he could receive a promotion was if there was an available billet above him, and every position was filled.

Trust me, said the old man. Reb did.

In England, Colonel Peaslee made good on his pledge. Every time a new promotion list came out, Reb found his name on it until he made sergeant again. In June 1943, he was working in the armament section, inspecting the Fortresses' guns.

His best friend in the unit was a forty-year-old sergeant named Woody Cabot. Woody was the guy who had started calling Olen "Reb," short for Southern rebel. The name had stuck. One morning, he told Woody that he had decided to volunteer to become a machine gunner. He decided that being a member of the ground crew was too tame an occupation in the middle of a shooting war.

Don't be a fool, Woody told him. Only one crew out of three was successfully making it through the twenty-five missions they were required to fly before they could go home.

Reb went in to see the old man anyway. After Reb told him why he was there, Colonel Peaslee got up from behind his desk to shake his hand. Battle losses had badly depleted the group's reserve of spare gunners, he said, and then told Reb he was impressed that he had the moxie to volunteer.

"Same ole rebel," Woody had said afterward. "If the whiskey and women don't kill you, the Jerries will."

"I've got a guardian angel," Reb assured him, and Woody laughed.

Within days, he was at gunnery school on the "Wash," a remote estuary along the eastern coast of England. The men trained hard all day, firing .50-caliber machine guns from ground emplacements at moving targets. To Reb, it felt like he was holding on to a wild boar by its hind legs. At night, they would get drunk on vanilla extract pinched from the mess hall.

When the training ended, he returned to the 384th. Reb hoped he would be assigned to a permanent crew in one of the group's four squadrons, but instead he was sent to a replacement barracks at a far corner of the air base. A crudely written sign over the entrance read, "House of the Bastards."

Twenty men lived in the barracks, but that number dropped precipitously after the air offensive began against Germany. Following each mission, the personal effects of the lost gunners would be quickly removed. It was like they had never been there.

Except for their meals at the mess hall, Reb and the others rarely came into contact with the regular combat crews until they were assigned to one of the Fortresses for a mission.

He was pleasantly surprised to discover that combat crewmen enjoyed a different lifestyle than the ground personnel. At the mess hall, his food was served on a white tablecloth with real dishes instead of mess kits and canteen cups. Instead of powdered eggs and Spam, the combat crews enjoyed fresh eggs and bacon on the morning of each mission.

Now, he was going out again.

As dawn began to pale the sky on September 6, Reb arrived back at Grafton Underwood. He was too late to eat his combat breakfast. He had also missed the mission briefing that took place right after breakfast, and had no idea where the group was going, or which crew he would be flying with that day.

It was a maximum effort, all right. The roads on the base were choked with vehicle traffic. With the blackout in effect, and headlights mostly painted out, the fuel trucks and bomb carriers moved across the landscape like a fleet of fireflies. From every direction, Reb could hear the roar of 1,200-horsepower radial engines.

He watched the crews heading out to their planes on jeeps, bicycles, and trucks.

The military policeman took Reb directly to the parachute hut. A noncom told him it was going to be a high-altitude mission, and he needed cold weather flight gear. Reb had stripped down to his skivvies when he suddenly realized that he was missing his dog tag, then quickly remembered he had put it on the shelf over his bunk before heading over to the showers to get ready for his date with Estella.

It was too late to go get it now, he concluded, as he put on a blue heat suit with matching boots and gloves. The suit was honeycombed with tiny wires that would be plugged into an electrical outlet aboard the plane once they were airborne. Over the heat suit, he put on green gabardine flying coveralls, followed by an inch-thick, sheepskin-lined leather jacket, pants, helmet, and boots.

He was already sweating when he walked outside into the mild autumn air. The same military policeman was waiting in the jeep to run him out to the plane he had been assigned for the mission. It was a Fortress in the 546th Squadron called the *Yankee Raider*.

Yankee Raider. An odd fit for a good ol' Arkansas rebel, he thought.

When he arrived at the hardstand where the plane was parked, he could see the men in the crew surrounding the plane. A few of them were sitting on the ground. They stared up at him as he climbed out of the jeep.

He could imagine what they were thinking.

Here comes our new waist gunner, a guy whose marksmanship

might be needed to save our lives from an attacking fighter, and he is being delivered by an MP. It definitely didn't inspire confidence.

An officer detached himself from the group and came toward him. It was the pilot, a second lieutenant. He was a big, lanky guy, better than six feet tall, built like a linebacker. The lieutenant reached out to shake his hand.

Jesus, he looks even younger than me, thought Reb.

The Greek

Sunday, 5 September 1943
388th Bomb Group
Knettishall, England
Second Lieutenant Demetrios Karnezis
2200

T he officers' club at Knettishall Airfield did not share the same amenities as the Dorchester bar in London, and its décor wasn't quite as atmospheric as Manhattan's Stork Club.

The bare interior walls were fiberboard panels trimmed with batten board strips. Heat was provided by a coke-burning stove in the center of the room. Tables and chairs dotted the floor space. The bar's countertop was constructed of wooden planks. Behind it, an off-duty GI cook served drinks.

It was spartan, but the fliers of the 388th Bomb Group were happy to have it.

In September 1943, the officers' club drink menu wasn't expansive. One could order gin. The gin was served straight up or splashed with grapefruit juice from the cartons of number-five juice cans stacked along the wall behind the countertop. A newly arrived replacement might grouse about the lack of scotch or bourbon or soda water. After a few drinks, it didn't matter.

The Greek drank his gin with grapefruit juice. After knocking off two or three, he would feel the alcohol begin to cauterize his brain, which was good, particularly after the group's recent missions. So far, he had survived nine of them, including Regensburg.

For many of the combat fliers, the nights after rough missions brought vivid nightmares, usually related to the horrific things they had witnessed in the sky. One pilot called them heartbreak dreams, the ones about the friends who were never coming back, or of B-17s exploding in the sky like skeet in a shooting gallery.

There were plenty of bad dreams after the 388th's mission to Hannover at the beginning of the German air offensive. Antiaircraft flak had been terrifyingly accurate over the target. When the seventeen planes of the 388th reached Hannover, Johnny Denton's *Mister Yank* was hit by two shell bursts, one on the left wing and a second on the right. The plane exploded. Earl Horn's *A Little Horne* was hit a few moments later. His plane blew up, too. While the group was still over the target, Bill Beecham's *Impatient Virgin* collided with Ed Wick's *Wolf Pack* after Beecham was wounded by a cannon burst. As the group fought its way back to England, three more planes in the group, Aubrey Bobbitt's Fortress, along with *Wee Bonnie* and *La Chiquita*, had been shot down by German fighters.

The night after the mission, one of the group's pilots left the air base without authorized leave. When they brought him back, he refused to fly again. For those who stayed to fight, there was self-medication. Although regulations prohibited drinking alcohol within twenty-four hours of a mission, the rule wasn't enforced.

Along with gin, the officers used gallows humor to deal with their fears. Sid Alford, a Jewish bombardier from New York, flew in the Greek's squadron. Alford had been wounded on five missions, giving him a silver cluster to his initial Purple Heart medal. On the fifth mission, Alford had been manning the nose gun of his Fortress when an inward propeller on the Fortress went out of control. Its red-hot dome spun off, chopped through the metal bulkhead of Alford's compartment, and sliced off a section of his buttocks.

Sid had just returned from the hospital, and the rest of them were toasting his return to active duty. Alford stood up to receive the toast, pulled his pants down, and said, "I want to show you all what a half-ass bombardier looks like."

It was close to midnight and the Greek was feeling pretty mellow when one of the operations clerks walked into the club and came over.

"Lieutenant Karnezis, you're up for tomorrow's mission, and the squadron commander suggests that you get some sleep. It's going to be an early call."

He had been born Demetrios Karnezis in Norfolk, Virginia, and was the son of Greek immigrants from Tripolis. His father operated a food concession stand at the entrance to the Norfolk Ferry Terminal.

Growing up, he was fascinated by electronic gadgets, often rummaging through the trash barrels of a radio shop near his father's concession stand for discarded radio parts. One of his first inventions was a crude radio alarm clock that he gave to his amazed parents. At fourteen, he built a shortwave radio station in the attic. It had a long-range antenna that allowed the family to listen to the BBC in London and Adolf Hitler barking out his speeches to the Reichstag in Berlin.

By high school, he knew he wanted to become a career military officer, and decided to seek an appointment to West Point, focusing on achieving the grades and test scores that would make his selection a certainty. After earning the highest marks in the state on the entrance examination, he met his local congressman at a church function, and told him of his desire to attend the academy.

"Boy," said the congressman, "don't think that the young men who pass those exams are the ones selected to go." When he spoke to his high school counselor about it, she said, "Well, that is the way of the world."

Unable to afford college, he applied for work at the Bell Telephone Company. Impressed with the eighteen-year-old's knowledge of electronics, they hired him to troubleshoot the breakdowns of the complicated switchboard devices at the Norfolk naval base. When the Japanese attacked Pearl Harbor, his supervisor told him that he didn't have to worry about being drafted. He would be deferred due to the important nature of his work.

A friend who was in the army air corps came home on leave and told Demetrios how exciting it was to fly. That did it. His eyes had always been in the sky anyway, watching the planes taking off and landing at the air bases that surrounded Norfolk.

He applied and was accepted. At primary training school, he turned out to be a superb flier. After completing advanced flying school, he was one of the graduates chosen to go into fighters.

Along the way, he inherited the inevitable nickname "the Greek."

In February 1943, he was informed that the air force had a surplus of fighter pilots waiting for overseas assignments, and that instead he would be sent for training on B-17s. For six weeks, he flew around the clock to catch up to the men who had undergone multiengine training. In May, he joined a crew and was sent to England, where they were assigned to the 388th Bomb Group in Knettishall.

The morning mission would be his tenth. Only fifteen to go after this one.

An early call meant it would probably be Germany again. Following the advice of his squadron commander to get some sleep, he left the officers' club to walk back to his billet.

The Greek shared a large room in one of the Quonsets with nearly two dozen other officers, all of them pilots, copilots, navigators, and bombardiers in the same squadron. At night, the silence in the room would usually be punctuated by loud snoring. That didn't bother the Greek. Occasionally, a man in the grip of a nightmare would scream out. That was harder to ignore.

At 0300, he was sleeping soundly in his bunk when a flashlight beam was shined in his eyes, and a voice said, "Briefing at 0330, Lieutenant Karnezis."

It was a grim way to be woken up. Another twenty-four-hour life cycle. Birth, combat, survival or death. The Greek got up and went to the shower room. Like most of the other pilots, he shaved before each mission so his oxygen mask would fit tightly on his face when they climbed above ten thousand feet.

After showering, he put on a pair of gabardine twill uniform pants, a clean uniform shirt, and GI brogan shoes. Over his uniform, he wore flying coveralls and an A-2 horsehide leather flying jacket, with its light brown silk lining, knitted cuffs and waistband.

For good luck, he always carried a small Greek Orthodox icon in one of the zipper pockets of his coveralls. His mother had given it to him on his last leave before going overseas. It had a tiny painting of St. Demetrios, his patron saint, riding a horse.

On the base, he rode a bicycle instead of a horse. Enlisted men got their bicycles free. An officer had to buy one. If his plane went down, someone else would claim it and kick some money into the group morale fund.

At the mess hall, he had his breakfast eggs with English bangers, the spicy sausages he liked slathered with English mustard fortified with horseradish. It definitely opened his nasal passages.

The briefing hut for the officers of the 388th was another large, windowless hut with poured concrete floors. It had a small stage at the back facing more than a hundred folding chairs. The chairs were set up in two rows, with space down the middle for the group commander and his staff to enter and depart.

Shortly before 0330, the pilots, copilots, navigators, and bombardiers surged into the briefing hut from the mess hall. The Greek lit his first cigarette and waited for the room to warm up from the heat of their bodies.

As usual, the noise level was high as they speculated on what the target might be. On the stage, a pair of thick curtains hid a big map of Europe. Before the briefing began, the curtains would be drawn back by an intelligence officer. That's when the men would find out where they were going.

Their previous mission on September 4 had been a milk run to Meulan in northern France, and all nineteen planes in the group had come back safely. The Greek hadn't even seen an enemy fighter.

The big room quickly filled with cigarette smoke. Most of the men smoked to calm their nerves. The Greek enjoyed Raleighs, the coupon type he bought for ten cents a pack.

At 0330, the men were called to attention as Colonel Bill David, the commander of the 388th Bomb Group, came into the hut and strode to the stage with his staff trailing behind. The group operations officer drew back the curtain on the map. It produced a small roar of sound.

A line of red yarn connected their base at Knettishall to Stuttgart,

Germany, deep inside southern Germany. The yarn almost ran off the far edge of the map. The operations officer told them that they would be attacking a critically important strategic target, the SKF instrument-bearing plants. Next to the ball-bearing factories at Schweinfurt, it was the most important target in Germany, he said.

The Greek wasn't particularly interested in the strategic importance of the target. He assumed they wouldn't be sending them there unless it was important. What he wanted to know were the more practical details, like the group's relative position in the massive formation, and whether any diversions had been planned to keep the German fighters off their necks.

The operations officer told them it would be the longest mission ever undertaken by the Eighth Air Force. The route to Stuttgart was along a heavily defended enemy fighter belt, but diversionary flights had been planned in which four groups of B-24 bombers would draw off the German fighters on a mission over the North Sea, while another eight groups of B-26 medium bombers attacked enemy airfields in France and Holland.

The weather over the target was expected to be mostly clear. The group would bomb from twenty-three thousand feet. From takeoff to return, they would be in the air about seven hours. A group of American P-47 fighters would escort them into France, and nine squadrons of British Spitfires would be waiting to escort them home on the route back.

For communication with the P-47s, the VHF radio call sign for the bombers would be PHONEBOX, and for the fighters, HAYBANK. For radioing the Spitfires, the call sign for the bombers was WINDBAG, and the fighters, CROKAY.

Since the Schweinfurt-Regensburg raid, a joke had begun circulating at the briefings. "Now we have fighters with us all the way," it went. "Our P-47s take us as far as France. The Messerschmitts and Focke-Wulfs take us to the target and back. Then the P-47s pick us up again in France."

For the Stuttgart mission, they would be on their own for over four hours.

After takeoff, the 388th would join up with the 96th Bomb Group over Gravesend and then assemble with the rest of the 157 Fortresses of the Fourth Bomb Wing over Dungeness in Kent before heading across the English Channel. The Fourth Wing was leading the whole attack, with the 96th Bomb Group first in line. The 388th would be tucked into the low position of the first combat box.

That wasn't good news. The low group in the lead formation was referred to as "coffin corner," because the enemy fighters often focused their head-on attacks on the low group, starting with its lowest squadron at the base of the multigroup combat box and working their way up.

Staring up at the blackboard on the front of the stage, the Greek saw that the 388th was putting up twenty-four bombers for the mission. His own Fortress, *Slightly Dangerous II*, was in the second element of the lead squadron, just above the low squadron.

When the operations officer finished his briefing and opened it up to questions, one of the pilots asked what they could expect as far as enemy fighter activity around Stuttgart.

"The target area is practically void of fighters," the ops officer assured him.

Andy

Monday, 6 September 1943
306th Bomb Group
"The Reich Wreckers"
Thurleigh, England
First Lieutenant Martin "Andy" Andrews
0230

He awoke with the battered copy of *War and Peace* lying across his chest. The lamp was still on next to his bunk. He could hear the voice of the ops clerk as he slowly came down the hallway, waking the officers who were scheduled to go on the mission.

Most of the squadron's officers, all second lieutenants, lived in the big communal room that took up most of the Quonset hut. As a first lieutenant, Andy had been assigned one of the single rooms along the hallway at the end of the building.

There was a low knock at the door.

"Briefing at 0300, Lieutenant Andrews."

He called out an acknowledgment.

First Lieutenant Martin Andrews. All his life, he had been called Martin or Marty, but shortly after being assigned his new B-17 crew, the navigator, Lieutenant Gordon Bowers, had begun calling him Andy. It quickly took hold with the others.

In England, their crew had been assigned to the 306th Bomb Group. It was the oldest operational unit in England, and the first one to lead an attack on a target inside Germany.

After washing at the small sink in his room, Andy put on his flight suit, boots, and a fleece-lined leather jacket. He drew a white silk scarf around his neck and tucked it into his flying suit before heading over to the officers' mess hall. Before a mission, he always forced himself to eat a big meal, knowing that he wouldn't have another for six hours or more.

After finishing breakfast, he headed to the 306th's briefing hut with the other officers. Sitting down, he glanced at the blackboard in the front of the room. The group was sending up twenty-one B-17s for the mission. Each plane was identified with the pilot's name, showing its place in the group formation. Andy would be leading one of the high elements in the group.

When the group commander gave the word to begin the briefing, the operations officer pulled back the curtain covering the big map of Europe. As in every briefing hut across southern England that morning, a length of yarn connected the group's base to the city of Stuttgart, Germany.

The 306th was going to destroy the Bosch Magneto Works, he announced to the chorus of groans that invariably erupted when the target was Germany. Magnetos were critically important to the German war machine. The 306th was going to make sure there were a lot fewer of them by the end of the day.

Stuttgart would be the group's longest mission ever, he added.

Fuel would have to be conserved. Although the newer-model B-17s in the group were equipped with "Tokyo tanks" under the wings, which added more than a thousand miles to their range, most of the planes in the group didn't have them.

Andy's B-17 was an older model and didn't have the extra fuel. He remembered their July 28 mission to Kassel, when his Fortress had nearly run out of gas on the way home. After reaching the French coast, he was forced to shut down his two outboard engines and put the plane into a power glide with the remaining two in order to reach the base.

This would be his thirteenth mission. Lucky thirteen. He wasn't supposed to be flying it. After twelve missions, his crew had been scheduled to spend a week at a rest camp in Cornwall. Those orders were changed when another pilot in the squadron began exhibiting mental problems after four men in his crew were killed over Schweinfurt. He and his remaining crew members had been sent to the rest camp instead.

For Andy, the toughest part of combat wasn't facing the enemy. It was getting up in the middle of the night to fly the missions. He had been having trouble sleeping ever since the 306th's July 4 raid to Nantes, France, in the Loire Valley.

It was supposed to be a milk run. On America's national holiday, the Eighth Air Force had decided to deliver a statement by sending its groups to attack enemy airfields in occupied France. The 306th was ordered to bomb a German air installation near Nantes.

As a boy, Independence Day had been one of Andy's favorite holidays. Every year, he would ride his bicycle with red, white, and blue crepe threaded between its wheels in the Milwaukee parade. Afterward there would be ice cream and fireworks. Now he would be celebrating it by dropping several tons of high explosives.

What happened on that mission was seared into his memory. The 306th had encountered no fighter opposition on its way to the target. As they approached Nantes, the lead squadron in the formation flew straight and level for almost two minutes as the lead bombardier drew a bead on the target. The lead plane's bomb bay doors had just swung open when Andy saw the first bursts of antiaircraft fire coming up from the ground below.

Within seconds, the greasy smoke from exploding shells filled the sky directly ahead of them. The Germans were using their famed 88s, the finest antiaircraft cannons in the world, which hurled a twenty-pound shell five miles straight up in the air with deadly accuracy.

During training, the pilots had been taught to avoid flak by taking evasive action. But that was impossible. To reach the target at Nantes and drop their bombs, they had to fly through the umbrella barrage.

Suddenly, a plane ahead of Andy's blew up, literally vaporizing before his eyes. A few moments later, a plane on his left was hit by another cannon burst. Its right wing sheared off and the front half of the fuselage spiraled down. The rear section of the shattered Fortress continued flying forward several seconds as one man escaped the wreckage. He was on fire as he hurtled out of sight.

At the same time, Andy heard the excited voice of his tail gunner on the plane's intercom, calling out that the plane behind them had just exploded, too. Miraculously, no one in Andy's crew was killed or wounded. As they flew home, Andy pondered the old adage that luck was a matter of inches. Over Nantes, it had been a matter of micro millimeters. A fractional change in the gun settings of those batteries would have blown them out of the sky.

After Nantes, he began having nightmares. On nights before a mission, he would stay up reading until finally nodding off for an hour or two of ragged sleep. Maybe war was harder on pilots with vivid imaginations, he concluded.

Andy was born in Milwaukee, Wisconsin, in 1918; his mother had died in a flu epidemic three days after he was born. His father was a stoic man who had emigrated to the United States from Larvik, Norway. Later, he had become the captain of a Great Lakes ore ship, and was away from home for weeks at a time.

An introspective child, Andy became a voracious reader. Growing up, he imagined himself attempting great feats of daring like the young heroes he read about in books by Alexandre Dumas and Sir Walter Scott. When Charles Lindbergh came to Milwaukee to appear in a parade, Andy saw him pass by to the cheers of the adoring crowd. Afterward, he daydreamed that he would be the first eight-year-old boy to fly alone across the Atlantic.

After finishing high school, he devised a novel approach to broadening his education. Instead of going to college, he shipped out on a freighter to Europe. In Germany, he planned to study Goethe, Kant, and Schiller in their native language. Then he would head for France to apply the same approach to Racine and Molière. The last phase of his schooling would be in Italy, where he planned to study Dante and Petrarch, the father of Humanism.

In September 1939, his plans were interrupted by Hitler's invasion of Poland.

Returning home from Germany, he entered the Great Books of Western Civilization program at St. John's College in Annapolis, Maryland, where he developed a proficiency in ancient languages. For fun, he translated the New Testament into Greek.

With war raging in Europe, he decided to leave college. He was convinced that America would soon be in the war and joined the army air corps, winning his wings shortly before the attack on Pearl Harbor.

Blond, blue-eyed, and a rugged six feet tall, he hoped to become a fighter pilot, but at basic flying school in South Carolina, the colonel lined up the cadets by height. The shorter ones were sent into fighters, the tall ones into multiengine bombers. Andy was disgusted. To him, flying bombers was like driving a truck.

He turned out to be a superb truck driver. In addition to his flying prowess, he memorized the B-17 tech manuals, and learned everything he could about the plane's systems from the mechanics who worked on them. He became highly nuanced to the eccentricities of airplane engines. As a result, he was selected to become a flight instructor at the advanced flying school in Columbus, Mississippi.

There, he prided himself on being able to land a Flying Fortress so gently that his blindfolded students didn't know they had landed. He was particularly good at formation flying, and stressed to his students how important it was for them to maintain a tight formation, presenting the smallest possible target to German fighter pilots.

After six months as an instructor, he found himself frustrated. What would he tell his children someday, that with the whole world engulfed in war, he trained cadets in Columbus, Mississippi? He requested a transfer to a combat unit. The application was granted.

On Memorial Day in 1943, he and his crew took off from Bangor, Maine, to join the war in a brand-new B-17. As they started across the Atlantic, he looked back for a last time at the heavily forested coast of Maine and wondered if they would all get home safely. When they arrived in England, their shiny new B-17 was taken away from them. A week later, they were assigned to the 306th Bomb Group, and given a battered B-17 warhorse to fly.

Andy quickly ran afoul of his squadron commander, who informed him that the enlisted men in his crew would receive a one-grade demotion until they had flown five missions. He protested, telling him that it would be a hardship on their families back home. When Andy discovered that the other squadron commanders in the group didn't have the same policy, he appealed directly to the group commander, who reversed the edict.

The night before his first mission, Andy encountered one of his fellow flight instructors from back in Mississippi. He had come over months earlier, and was scheduled to fly his twenty-fifth mission the same day that Andy was flying his first. He invited Andy to attend the party at the officers' club the group commander was throwing for him when he got back.

Because losses in Europe were so steep, the air force had created a policy designed to provide at least some hope to a combat crew that they would make it through. All they had to do was complete twenty-five missions before being sent back to the States.

At that point in the war, one crew in three was getting that far. The party turned out to be a wake. Although the crew made it, Andy's friend had been killed by a 20-millimeter cannon round from a German fighter. It was the first time in his life Andy got drunk.

He soon discovered that aerial combat was a simple thing, but also quite profound. It wasn't until one met the enemy in the air that reality sunk in. The Luftwaffe pilots were brave and skillful. They were among the best in the world. And they were trying very hard to kill him.

A man earned a reputation quickly in an outfit, good or bad. After the air offensive against Germany began, it seemed like more pilots were finding reasons to abort a mission after takeoff in order to return to the base. Most had good reasons, like an engine breakdown or the failure of a supercharger. But one pilot had aborted five missions in a row. Another had turned back after discovering a problem with the fuel-air-ratio gauge, a minor instrument. Back at the base, he was berated by the group commander in front of everyone.

No one wanted to join the order of the white feather.

After ten missions, Andy's crewmen asked him why their B-17 didn't have flashy nose art painted on it like the scantily clad beauties that graced the noses of other Fortresses. He agreed and told them to come up with a name. In the meantime, he asked the crew chief to stencil five Latin words in small letters under his cockpit window.

Est Nulla Via Invia Virtuti . . . No Way Is Impassable to Courage.

In June, he bought an old bicycle so that he could explore the countryside around Thurleigh. One afternoon, he found himself lost on a country lane. Encountering a young woman, he asked her for directions, and she volunteered to walk along with him to show him the way. Andy thought she was the loveliest girl he had ever seen. When they reached the turnoff, he asked to meet her again, and she agreed. Her name was Mavis, and she was the nineteen-year-old daughter of a Bedfordshire landowner.

On their first date, they met outside the Baptist Chapel on High Street in Thurleigh. Although the landscape was almost entirely flat, the old church rested on the side of a hill. Andy had come to enjoy spending evenings sitting on the hillside, reading until dark and watching RAF bombers taking off from their nearby base for their nightly attacks on German cities.

He invited Mavis to join him there. On their first evening together, she warned him that the grass on the hillside was sprinkled with stinging nettles. The next night she brought a blanket.

Mavis had been raised and educated in London, and knew all the museums and historical places Andy hoped to visit when he got leave. She cherished poetry as much as he did, and one night they recited their favorite Shakespeare sonnets to one another.

She was also an excellent cook. After he brought her a bag of Washington State apples that the combat fliers had been given, she made delicious apple tarts out of them, which they shared the next night.

There was mystery in her, too. Andy always volunteered to walk her home, but she declined. Her father didn't like Yanks, she told him. She also wouldn't go with him to a restaurant or pub. Like a beautiful phantom, she would simply appear on the hillside when he arrived there on his bicycle.

He was sure there must be a line of suitors in her life. Why him? Whatever the reason, she made his life between missions special. After they had spent more than a dozen of the long English summer evenings together, she asked him to make love to her.

He might not be coming back, he told her. He also expressed

concern about her becoming pregnant. She said she would worry about that. After wrestling with the possible consequences, he decided to ignore the uncertainty of the future. They became first-time lovers. As the romance deepened, he hoped that she would eventually end the mystery in her background.

While he was falling in love with Mavis, Andy found another approach to curtail his nightmares. He had been reading Plato's *Phaedo*, about the death of Socrates, in an old pocket-book edition of poetry when he discovered the "Choric Song" of *The Lotos-Eaters*, Alfred, Lord Tennyson's musings on death during Ulysses's long voyage home from the Trojan War.

"All things have rest, and ripen toward the grave in silence; ripen, fall, and cease: Give us long rest or death, dark death, or dreamful ease. . . . Surely, surely, slumber is more sweet than toil, the shore than labour in the deep midocean, wind and wave and oar; Oh rest ye, brother mariners, we will not wander more."

Somehow, the words of the melancholy poem gave him peace of mind. It also led to a new ritual. As he sat in the cockpit waiting to take off on a mission, he would read a selection from the poem. After finishing it, he would place the pocket book in the breast pocket of his flight jacket over his heart.

He was prepared to die. He had lived to be twenty-four.

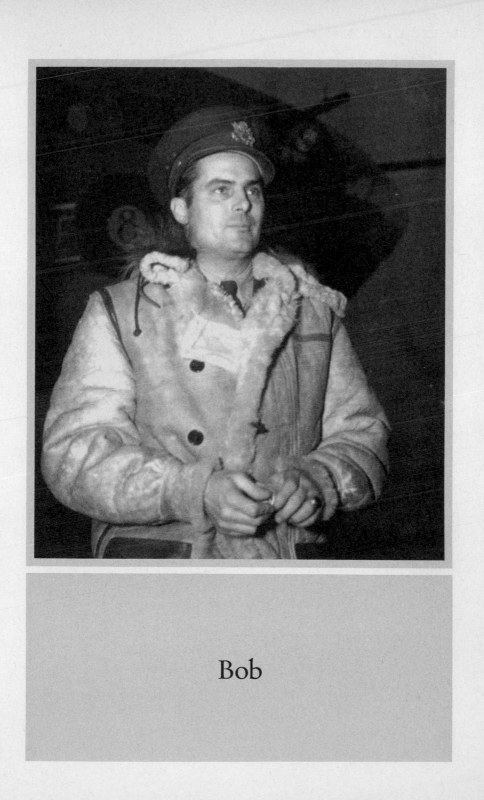

Bob

Monday, 6 September 1943
303rd Bomb Group
"Hell's Angels"
Molesworth, England
Brigadier General Robert F. Travis
0330

For the pilots of the 303rd, the predawn intelligence briefing for the attack on Stuttgart sounded eerily similar to the one they had received three weeks earlier for the Schweinfurt raid.

The intelligence officer even used some of the same words in describing it, talking about how their group could possibly change the course of history, and that if they were successful, the Luftwaffe would soon be grounded because the Germans would have no ball bearings left.

Before they took off for Schweinfurt on August 17, Lieutenant Colonel Kermit Stevens, the 303rd Bomb Group commander, had told them, "If every pilot in this group were to dive his ship, fully manned and loaded with bombs, into the center of the target area, the mission would still be considered a success."

His words hadn't raised morale.

When Colonel Stevens and his staff arrived for the Stuttgart briefing, they were accompanied by a tall young brigadier general. As soon as the intelligence officers finished their part of the briefing, Colonel Stevens came forward to introduce him as the new commander of the Forty-first Combat Wing of the Eighth Air Force, which included the 303rd, the 379th, and the 384th Bomb Groups.

His name was Robert Falligant Travis.

Colonel Stevens said that Brigadier General Travis would be leading the Stuttgart mission, and proudly noted that he would be flying aboard the 303rd's *Satan's Workshop*. It would be the lead plane of the entire First Bomb Wing, which was sending almost two hundred Fortresses to the target that day.

General Travis then delivered a brief talk to the combat crews. They had a job to do, he told them, his manner calm and self-assured. Their job was to destroy Germany's industrial muscle. It wasn't going to be easy. When it came to their military duties, he expected them to maintain the highest standard of performance, both in the air and on the ground. He would lead many of the missions to Germany personally, and from up front. He said he planned to complete the same twenty-five-mission tour they were required to fly. From his demeanor, there didn't appear to be the slightest doubt in his mind that he would make it through.

Although he had flown three missions as an observer since arriving in England less than two weeks earlier, he did not tell them that this would be the first combat mission he had ever led.

Sitting with the rest of the pilots at the briefing, Second Lieutenant Bud Klint, the twenty-four-year-old copilot of *Luscious Lady*, listened to the young general with rapt attention. To him, Travis looked like he had already been there and back, every inch a combat leader. At six feet five inches tall, he looked solid and manly, in the same mold as the movie star Gary Cooper.

Solid, manly, confident, brave, and determined were adjectives often used to describe Bob Travis throughout his military career. Some of his fellow officers, particularly those who had felt the sting of his sharp elbows as he climbed the promotion ladder, used other adjectives, such as ruthless and uncompromising. There was a seed of truth in each one. He was a complex man.

Robert Falligant Travis had been born in Savannah, Georgia, on the morning after Christmas in 1905. His father, Robert Jesse Travis, was a retired major general, and a descendant of Colonel William Travis, who was killed while commanding the Texas forces defending the Alamo in 1836.

Along with his younger brother and two sisters, Bob Travis had grown up in a loving and supportive family. Both parents believed strongly in the values of hard work, education, and personal discipline. Bob was both a good student and a model son. An all-around athlete, he was a superb squash player and expert skeet shooter.

After winning an appointment to West Point, he was commissioned a second lieutenant in the infantry in 1928 before winning his wings as a qualified army pilot. Once committed to aviation, he served in a variety of staff and operational positions until being permanently assigned to bombers in 1934.

To the men who served under him, he was a stickler for regulations and a man who displayed a fierce temper if his orders weren't carried out to his satisfaction. Although a smoker himself, he was noted for walking the entire flight line of his training command with a measuring tape; anyone found smoking within fifty feet of an airplane was busted in rank.

Like General Ira Eaker, he enjoyed playing high-stakes poker. Unlike Eaker, Bob Travis preferred to play with junior officers. At his Gowen Field training command, he would often appear at the officers' club when the games were in full swing, and politely ask the lieutenants around an open table if he could join them. He was never turned down. Whether he won or lost, he was always affable and polite.

To his friends, he was a model of Southern courtesy, especially around women. His wife, Frances Jane, was a superb helpmate, organizing the family moves to each new army post with efficiency and skill.

Bob Travis's affable demeanor masked a burning desire to succeed. Success in the army was measured by promotions and combat decorations. Unfortunately, he couldn't earn battle stars running a training command in Boise, Idaho.

Shortly after the Japanese attacked Pearl Harbor, he was promoted to group commander, and in September 1942, wing commander of a stateside training command. He put in for a combat assignment over and over again.

A year later, he finally received orders to take over the Forty-first Combat Wing of the Eighth Air Force. It was the plum job he had been yearning for. Bob Travis would be commanding three bomb groups in the air war over Germany. He planned to make the most of it.

More than almost anything, Bob Travis wanted to make his father proud.

Major General Robert Jesse Travis was an extraordinary man. Born in 1877, the elder Travis had received no formal education until the age of twelve, later attending Emory College in Georgia and graduating with first honors in 1897. While at Emory, Travis distinguished himself as a champion debater, and received scholastic medals in Greek and Latin. He then earned a law degree at the University of Georgia, before beginning his military career in 1899 with the First Georgia Infantry.

In World War I, Travis had commanded the 118th Field Artillery. After the war, he had returned to embark on what became a long and prestigious law career in Savannah, finding the time to also become an award-winning historian and the Grand Master of the Georgia Masons. He was one of the most respected men in the state, and maintained a friendship with many of the officers he had served with in the army, some of whom were now senior generals.

He was deeply proud of his son Bob as he assumed his first combat command.

After his arrival in England, Bob Travis began to take the measure of the other officers who shared his rank in the Eighth Air Force. Privately, he concluded that Brigadier General August "Aug" Kissner, who had become the chief of staff of the Fourth Bomb Wing, was "a cocktail hour playboy who attached himself to Curtis LeMay . . . and had no leadership abilities whatsoever. . . ." Brigadier General Herb Thatcher, who commanded a bomb wing, "had a good combat record, but is undeveloped, immature, and has poor leadership qualities."

In just that first week in England, he had come to the conclusion that the Forty-first Combat Wing was lax, inefficient, poorly led, and needed a tough hand at the helm. He would be that tough hand, molding it by personal example into the finest combat unit in the Eighth Air Force.

After flying as an observer on his first three combat missions, Bob

Travis wrote a letter to one of his former subordinates, Colonel "Pop" Arnold, who was serving in Travis's former training command at Gowen Field in Idaho.

September 2, 1943

Dear Pop,

Get Hank to show you his letter. I asked for you both. Have been too busy to see many of the boys yet, going on 3 missions my first 4 days here. Will slow down now that I have assumed command. You will like it here. We eat and sleep well. No time off but you are used to that. Don't even have time to spend any money. Bring silk stockings, bourbon whiskey, lip stick, 2 lighters, several sweaters, only woolen uniforms (greens preferred), raincoat, good overcoat. You are allowed 55. All you can carry (such as a case of 4 qts whiskey in it and overcoat over your arm) is not counted.

Pop, anything said about gunnery in the past was not enough. The air is full of Bosche sometimes 2 to 300 and they are shooting real bullets. We have to fight our way in and out. We are paying with lots of crews because our gunners can't shoot. I could have got one bastard with a skeet gun that my nose gunner missed yesterday. They come close but the boys won't lead and swing through. My best to you. Bob

Bob Travis was prepared and ready to become the finest combat leader in the Eighth Air Force, starting with the mission to Stuttgart, Germany, on the morning of September 6.

After the predawn briefing to the men of the 303rd at Molesworth, he rode out to the hardstand where *Satan's Workshop* was parked. There, he was introduced to the pilot who would be flying the lead plane of the 303rd Bomb Group.

Major Lewis Lyle was a seasoned veteran of the air war over Europe, and now commanded one of the 303rd's four bomb squadrons. He had already completed one twenty-five-mission tour as a pilot, and was five missions into his second tour. He was a tough, no-nonsense flight leader, with an intentionally gruff manner that kept his crew focused on their job in the air.

After meeting Major Lyle, the general shook hands with each member of crew, and then made a brief inspection of the plane. *Satan's Workshop* was a newer-model Fortress equipped with nine self-sealing Tokyo tanks that were mounted inside each wing and provided an additional thousand gallons of fuel.

The general pronounced himself pleased with the plane and the crew.

On a nearby hardstand, Lieutenant Bud Klint and his crew had just arrived to board their own Fortress, the *Luscious Lady*. Like *Satan's Workshop*, it was a new B-17 with Tokyo tanks. Over the past month, Bud had amassed a lot of confidence in the ship. It had brought them home from Schweinfurt peppered with bullet holes from nose to tail.

Judging from the length of yarn on the big map at the briefing, Stuttgart was even farther away from their base than Schweinfurt, which meant more time for the enemy fighters to maul them on their way into Germany, and on the long route back across France.

At the age of twenty-four, Bud Klint didn't know if they were going to change the course of history that day. What he did know was that a lot of fliers had paid the ultimate price over Schweinfurt. He hoped that Stuttgart would be a lot less costly. Maybe the dashing new brigadier general who was leading them that day would bring them some good luck.

When he and his pilot, Bob Hullar, attempted to start the engines, the inboard motor on *Luscious Lady*'s left wing wouldn't turn over. Repeated efforts failed to get it started. Finally, the crew was ordered to fly the spare plane in the group. It was an older-model B-17, with no supplemental gas tanks.

The ship was named *Old Squaw*. They had just started the engines when Bud saw the flare guns go off near the control tower, signaling the order to assemble for takeoff.

Ted

Sunday, 5 September 1943
388th Bomb Group
Knettishall, England
Second Lieutenant Ray Theodore "Ted" Wilken
2300

It had rained all that Sunday and well into the night, keeping the flight crews inside on ground duties, and cloaking the air base in swirling fog. A new movie, *The More the Merrier,* starring Joel McCrea and Jean Arthur, was shown at 1500 hours in the base theater.

In the evening, there had been a basketball game between two of the squadron teams. The incessant rain had put many of the men in a reflective mood. When the mission alert arrived from High Wycombe at 2240, Second Lieutenant Ted Wilken was finishing his nightly v-mail letter to Braxton.

Life in wartime England was definitely different for the married men, at least those who were faithful to their wives. For Ted, it was an easy choice. He had been blessed to find the young woman who made his life complete.

Ted hadn't expected to miss her so deeply. His longing was compounded by the news a month earlier that she had given birth to their first child, Katherine Ann. Whatever he was doing, wherever he was, particularly during the long combat missions, sudden images of Braxton would invade his mind, momentarily transporting him away from the war, giving him a brief sense of tranquility. He had tried to explain it in his nightly letters to her. Hopefully, she understood.

Ted was born to privilege and wealth in 1920; his forebears were Old

Dutch, the people who had founded New Amsterdam, later to become New York City. He had grown up in a fifty-room mansion in Bronxville, New York, and was driven by the family chauffeur each morning to Riverdale Country Day School.

An only child, he had enjoyed a golden youth, marked by triumph and accomplishment. A gifted horseman, he was equally adept at polo, dressage, and jumping, medaling at the age of twelve in the equestrian championships at Madison Square Garden.

After attending Riverdale, he was enrolled by his parents at Choate School in Wallingford, Connecticut. There, it seemed he did everything well, academics, tennis, football, baseball, debating, or bridge.

Elected captain of the football team, he led Choate to an undefeated season and earned the Prize Day Award as the finest athlete in the school. Of his contribution to the football team, his coach, John Maher, wrote, "Ted Wilken now takes his place in the hall of fame of the great Choate captains. He is one of the immortals—not only for the quality of his play, but also for the leadership and spirit he instilled into his team. There is about him a bond of sympathy, a spirit of camaraderie, and a determination for perfection." In his senior year, Ted was chosen All-American.

Ted had been accepted at Harvard, Princeton, and Yale, but chose instead to attend Dartmouth, where his two closest friends were going. There, he discovered that he preferred partying, dancing, and skiing to organic chemistry.

He had been raised to aim for perfection in every challenge he undertook, but in college he burned out. It was a great blow to his parents when he and a close friend left Dartmouth in his second year to join the crew of a sailing yacht owned by Otto Harbach, the famous lyricist of songs like "Smoke Gets in Your Eyes" and "Roberta."

One summer evening, the boat was tied up at the dock of the Larchmont Yacht Club. That was the night he met Braxton Nicholson. She was born in Edgefield, South Carolina; her mother, Nelle, was a classic Southern belle, and reveled in the culture and traditions of the Old South immortalized in Margaret Mitchell's *Gone With the Wind*. She named her daughter after Confederate General Braxton Bragg.

From an early age, Braxton was committed to breaking the mold. A free spirit, she grew up a Southern rebel, but it was in rebellion from the social dictates of the South, including its prevailing racial attitudes. She steadfastly refused to become the coquettish, simpering belle her mother had tried so hard to raise.

After leaving South Carolina as a teenager to attend the Bennett School for Girls in Millbrook, New York, she dropped out two years later to become an instructor at the Arthur Murray Dance Studio in hopes of pursuing a career as a professional dancer. Along the way, she dropped the name Braxton in favor of Betsy, or "Battling Betsy," as she was quickly nicknamed within the family.

One evening in July 1941, she had gone with several girlfriends to hear the new orchestra appearing at the Larchmont Yacht Club, and was watching the couples spinning across the floor when her eyes were drawn to a tall young man dancing with a blond girl.

At first, she thought he might be a professional. As a dance instructor, she could appreciate the gift, and silently wished he would ask her to dance with him. When the orchestra took a break, he and his dance partner were joined by two other couples. As Braxton watched them chatting, another member of the club stopped by her table to say hello. She found herself asking him who the young man was on the dance floor.

He immediately went over to the group and said in a booming voice, "Say, Ted . . . there's a girl over there who wants to dance with you."

Red-faced with embarrassment, she watched as he came over and politely asked her to dance. The orchestra began again with a rumba, the complex and energetic dance that required a solid dose of natural grace. They ended up dancing together the rest of the night. When she was about to leave, Ted asked to see her again.

In the months that followed, Ted came to see her as a "wonderful freak of nature."

The formal celebration of their engagement took place on a Sunday evening at the American Yacht Club in Rye, New York. She had bought a new dress for the occasion. Ted's mother had just picked her up to take her to the club.

"Have you heard the news, Braxton?" she said. "We've been attacked by the Japanese in Hawaii."

It was December 7, 1941.

The engagement party was only a few minutes old when their guests began leaving the celebration to cluster around the radio in the bar to hear the latest updates of the Pearl Harbor disaster.

On December 8, the same day President Roosevelt asked Congress for a declaration of war against the Japanese, Ted went down to the army recruiting office in Manhattan and enlisted in the army air corps.

Ted and Braxton were to be married the following summer in Scarsdale. Their mothers were already planning the celebration. The two women hoped it would be the society wedding of the year.

In February, Ted began air force training at Maxwell Field in Montgomery, Alabama. A few weeks later, he wrote to Braxton and asked her to visit him on Easter weekend. When she arrived, Ted said he wanted to get married right away. Braxton told him that their mothers would have a conniption. Ted said he didn't care. He didn't want to wait any longer to start their lives together.

After briefly returning to New York, Braxton crammed everything she needed into one suitcase, and rode by train down to Ocala, Florida, where Ted had begun primary flight training. She took a room near the base, staying with him until he moved on to basic flight training at Greenville, Mississippi.

There, an incident occurred that threatened his air force career.

After Ted allegedly allowed the cadet in the chair next to him to copy his work during an examination on radio procedure, both cadets were grounded from flying and suspended from the course, pending an investigation.

Almost insane with worry, Braxton decided she had to act. Scouring her meager wardrobe, she put on a gray dress and walked to the base home of the colonel in charge of the training command.

"I have to talk to you, sir," she said when he came to the door. "Ted Wilken is not a cheat. He is the most honorable man I've ever known, and you can't let his life be ruined."

The words were flooding out before she suddenly remembered that under air force regulations, they weren't even supposed to be married. It was too late now. At one point during her desperate plea, he had to turn away, and she saw that he was smiling.

"I'll think about it," he told her finally.

"That is all I can ask," she said, before adding, "If it ever gets back to Ted that you talked to me, you won't live to see another day."

He burst out laughing.

"This is between you and me," she pressed on. "Swear?"

He nodded.

Ted was required to take the course all over again. The cadet who had copied his work was expelled from the program.

They had moved on to Nashville for heavy bomber training when Braxton realized she was pregnant. Ted was overjoyed. He would probably be overseas when the baby arrived, but would be awaiting word.

Shortly before Christmas, the couple received a harsh note from Ted's mother expressing her disappointment at their lack of responsibility in saving money for the future. She had lavished a large cash wedding gift on them, and Ted was spending it in ways that she didn't support, including lending money to other young married couples who were in training with them, and living on a shoestring.

Braxton wrote back on behalf of both of them.

Dear Helen,

Teddy will probably be on combat in July. We have enough love and faith in each other to get through this. I utterly refuse to become a moaning war bride. It's going to be hard on all of us who adore and worship Teddy to have to sit and wait at home.

I haven't felt too badly—no early morning sickness (I just get sick in the morning and stay sick 'til evening). I know every inch of the bathroom quite intimately. Seems to me I can vaguely remember liking food. . . .

As for our financial discussion, I'm sorry if we appeared uppity when you advised us to save. I really believe that Teddy must take his own responsibilities now. We don't resent advice— please believe that. It's just that we feel <u>now</u> is the all important time in our lives. In the Air Corps you learn to live from day to day. To you that may seem a pointless philosophy. But to us who may never know a tomorrow, it is the only way to find peace and contentment. Money, now, is the most unimportant thing in our lives. You see, there is always the chance that this may be all the married life Ted and I will ever know—all there ever will be.

Don't you see, this is our rainy day. The wettest, stormiest, most hellish rainy day Teddy and I will ever know. I'm not writing this in a morbid or complaining way—I have thanked God every day for the privilege of being with him. I just wanted you to know how and why we reason like we do. It's just trying to live a lifetime in a little while. I guess war has made us a very hardened and practical lot. We saw that when Mil Stevens was killed at George Field. You learn to be thrifty with your emotions. Teddy has a dangerous job to do and it must not be cluttered with emotions. That's the hardest thing all of us Air Corps families have had to learn—to accept—not to question.

When Teddy goes on combat, I want him to remember how much we love him so he will have twice the incentive that anyone else has to be courageous and do his job uncomplainingly and with honor. It's an awful easy thing to die, but sometimes to live and do it gracefully is the seemingly impossible thing.

I tell you all this because I don't want you to think we are unfeeling or unthinking or extravagant for no reason. We have weighed the odds carefully and know just where we stand. Our morale is our wealth and happiness. We are trying the only way we know how. . . . We love and miss you terribly. Always, Betsy

In February 1943, Ted was on his way by train to Spokane, Washington, to be assigned his crew, when he got into trouble again. At one of the stops, he was taken into custody by military police after going to the Western Union office and sending Betsy a telegram telling her how much he missed her.

He had veiled the words in pig Latin, a jargon that was then the rage among the pilots, in which the beginning consonant of each word was transposed to the end. At the next stop, he was taken off the train and interrogated as a possible enemy spy. The telegraph operator had alerted the military police after reporting that he had used "a secret code." It took him several hours to convince the police it was harmless.

At Spokane, Ted was assigned a crew and they began training together. He began using the same principles he had employed as the captain of his championship teams to mold his flight crew into a solid fighting unit. Although air force regulations prohibited fraternization between officers and enlisted ranks, Ted quickly broke the boundaries.

Every Friday night, he would rent a hotel suite in Spokane for the crew to get together informally and play poker over drinks and dinner. If they were going to be fighting together, he told them, they might as well enjoy being together as friends whenever they had the opportunity. Once inside the suite, it was all on a first-name basis.

Ted also made sure every member of the crew had his personal affairs in order. He didn't want them to leave for England with any serious worries. Some of them needed money for their families. He lent it to them. Whatever the problem, he was there with advice and support. All for one. One for all.

Ted and Braxton spent his final fifteen-day embarkation leave together in Bronxville. The days went by in a blur, and then he was gone. She settled in for the long wait before he came back.

In England, Ted's crew was assigned a new Fortress. Together, they decided to name it *Battlin Betsy*. Ted wrote her that he thought he had the best-trained and most confident crew in the squadron. His copilot, Warren Laws, was very good in the air, calm and competent, and deserved his own ship. The rest of the men not only knew their jobs but could count on one another, no matter how tough things got. His training methods might have been unorthodox, but he thought they had worked out well.

On August 3, Braxton gave birth to their baby, Katherine Ann. They had already agreed on the name if it was a girl. Less than a week later, a letter was delivered to Ted at Knettishall. Included with it was a photograph of Braxton and their new daughter.

Dressing in the darkness of his Quonset hut for the Stuttgart mission, Ted put the photograph in the breast pocket of his flight suit over his heart. It would be his sixth mission.

Jimmy

"Lieutenant Armstrong?" came the disembodied voice behind the flashlight beam. "Briefing in half an hour."

The big man slowly hauled himself out of the narrow bunk. His copilot slept in the bed on one side of him, his navigator on the other. He made sure they were awake, too. Still groggy, he had to remind himself of which men remained from the original crew he had been assigned back at Gowen Field in Boise, Idaho.

His flight crew's confidence was at low ebb, and he wasn't sure what more he could do to bolster their spirits. Morale in the rest of the 384th Bomb Group wasn't much better.

Recent losses had cast a pall over the whole base. The group had lost ten Fortresses in June, and another twelve in July. Jimmy wasn't worried for himself. There was no doubt in his mind that he was going to make it through, but it was hard to maintain crew cohesion with so many men coming and going.

At times it seemed like his own constantly rotating crew was being sent by the League of Nations. Wilbert Yee, his new bombardier, was Chinese. James H. Redwing, the ball turret gunner, was a Hindu whose family came from India. He spoke English like some professor at Oxford.

Jimmy's former copilot, Luke Blanche, was a full-blooded Cherokee from Broken Toe, Oklahoma. The machine gunners included

Presciliano Herrera, a Mexican kid, and William Deibert, whose family was German. Sid Grinstein, his original flight engineer and top turret gunner, was Jewish.

After ten missions, Jimmy had reluctantly concluded that combat leaders in the air force were made, not born. He had come a long way in a short time from the athletic fields at Georgia Tech.

He was finishing the first semester of his sophomore year when he returned to his dorm room one Sunday afternoon and learned that the Japanese had attacked Pearl Harbor. Like his roommates, he was ready to fight. When he signed up for the air corps, the fun-loving giant was also looking for adventure. Ten months later, he was awarded his wings.

Jimmy was just nineteen years old. Someone told him that he was probably the youngest pilot in the whole air force. His next assignment as a newly minted B-17 pilot was at Hendricks Field in Sebring, Florida.

To celebrate winning his wings, he flew a Fortress to his hometown of Bradenton, Florida, where he dove down to an altitude of fifty feet before thundering over his parents' home at two hundred miles an hour, clipping the tops off the Australian pine trees that surrounded the property. The terrified officer flying with him in the copilot seat thought they had blown the roof off the house.

He came from a clan of warriors. The first Armstrongs in the colonies had arrived from Scotland in the mid-1700s. Two of his ancestors had fought against the British in the American Revolution. During the Civil War, both his great-grandfather and his grandfather rode with Custer's Michigan Cavalry Brigade. His father had battled German U-boats in the North Atlantic in the last war. After Pearl Harbor, his father had reenlisted to fight the Japanese.

In spite of his commanding physical presence, his tender age led to many awkward moments. As he tried to explain to his crew, all of whom were much older, he was not only big, but he was "rough cut."

The crew had begun flying combat missions in a B-17 named *Sad Sack II*. The figure of Sad Sack, a cartoon character in *Yank*, the army newspaper, had been painted on the plane's nose.

Things began to unravel for them on their fifth mission, which was the August 12 attack on Gelsenkirchen, Germany, in the Ruhr Valley.

In the preflight briefing, the flight crews had been told they would attack the target at an altitude of thirty-one thousand feet, which was far above the range of the German 88-millimeter cannons.

The briefer was wrong.

Of the seventeen planes in the 384th that reached the target, five were shot down by 88s. To complicate matters, the air temperature at thirty-one thousand feet was 55 degrees below zero Fahrenheit. Presciliano Herrera, the left waist gunner, had come back with frostbitten hands and was no longer able to fly.

On August 16, John Heald, Jimmy's original bombardier, and Sid Grinstein, his flight engineer, were ordered to join another crew as last-minute substitutes on a mission to Paris. The 384th Bomb Group lost only one plane that day, but Heald and Grinstein had gone down in it.

One day later, Jimmy had flown the Schweinfurt mission.

Sad Sack II was about a hundred miles into Belgium when the German fighters began coming up from the airfields along their route to intercept them. The attacks were the most intense he had ever encountered.

Another pilot in the 384th had once claimed to Jimmy that whenever he saw enemy fighters coming, he gave out with a Sioux war whoop on the intercom to inspire his crew. He had died with his crew over Germany back in July. Jimmy didn't believe in war cries. He just hoped his gunners shot well.

As *Sad Sack II* approached Schweinfurt, the bomber directly above them in the formation was hit by cannon fire, and its right wing burst into flames. Jimmy's waist gunners began screaming frantically on the intercom that the stricken Fortress was descending straight toward them. Jimmy managed to avoid the other plane, now engulfed in a ball of fire, as it plummeted past them in its death spiral.

After Wilbert Yee, his new bombardier, dropped their bombs through the flak cloud over Schweinfurt, the attacks intensified again. When a Focke-Wulf 190 suddenly came at them head-on, Jimmy lifted his right wing when he saw the first flashes of the fighter's guns. It didn't help. A moment later, machine-gun bullets began smashing into the cockpit. One of them sliced through his copilot's sheepskin-lined flight jacket and splintered the armor plate behind his seat. Amazingly, he was unhurt.

The fighters kept on coming, and his gunners kept firing back until they ran out of ammunition. In the next head-on attack, a 20-millimeter cannon shell set fire to his left inboard engine and sprayed the nose section with shrapnel, wounding Yee and Carlin, the navigator. When that engine caught fire, Jimmy feathered it to keep it from running out of control. As they finally approached the French coast, the attacks tailed off. Jimmy brought the Fortress home on three engines.

Once they were on the ground, Jimmy inspected the plane with James Flynn, his ground crew chief. Hundreds of brass shell casings covered the steel flooring of the fuselage. The metal skin was peppered with shell holes. The cartoon figure of Sad Sack had been almost obliterated by cannon shells. Flynn told him the Fortress was no longer flyable. It was a miracle they had made it back.

At the edge of the hardstand, Jimmy found Walter House, his radio operator, sitting on the ground and sobbing uncontrollably. At twenty-eight, House was the oldest and steadiest hand among the enlisted men in the original crew. Jimmy went over to talk to him.

"Sir," House began, his lips trembling, "I don't know what's wrong with me, but I can't take it anymore."

Jimmy didn't know what to say. According to regulations, a crewman was required to fly unless the plane commander thought he might endanger the rest of the men. If it had been one of the officers, Jimmy would have just told him to buck up and keep flying. But he knew that Walter House had a wife back in Kentucky waiting for him.

Putting his arm around the older man's shoulder, the twenty-year-old Jimmy said, "Walter, you need a change of scenery. I'll ask the squadron commander to give you a few days at a rest camp."

House thanked him through his tears.

The next morning, Sergeant Deibert, the machine gunner who had replaced the frostbitten Herrera, told Jimmy that he wouldn't fly anymore. He went to the hospital, where a doctor decided he was suffering from battle fatigue and could stand down.

Maybe it was something he was doing wrong, Jimmy thought. A few days later, he received a letter from the 384th's group leader, Colonel Budd Peaslee. It read:

Lieutenant Armstrong,

It is an honor and privilege to be able to commend you for your extraordinary achievement on the bombing mission over Germany, 17 August 1943. Your performance of duty on the most important penetration bombing mission yet conducted by this Wing over Germany was superior. In spite of the heaviest enemy fighter and flak opposition yet encountered by any formation, you coolly accomplished your duties as pilot. By your skillful airmanship and courage, you enabled our group and wing to deal a vital blow to the enemy inside his strongest defenses. I, as well as the entire 384th Bombardment Group, am proud of you. Budd J. Peaslee, Colonel, Air Corps, Commanding

The letter restored Jimmy's morale, if not the crew's. Stuttgart would be his tenth mission. At the predawn briefing, he looked up at the planned formation for the group that was chalked on the blackboard, and saw that they had made him an element leader of three Fortresses. Colonel Peaslee, the group commander, made a point of stressing the need for close defensive formations.

For the first time, it would be his responsibility to keep the element tucked into as tight a formation as possible to protect his two wingmen, Faulkner and Higdon, while providing enough distance from the higher elements to avoid getting hit by their falling bombs.

With *Sad Sack II* at a maintenance facility, he and what remained of his crew had been assigned to fly a B-17 named *Yankee Raider*. He wasn't familiar with the plane, but hoped it was one of the newer models equipped with Tokyo tanks to extend its range.

After the intelligence briefing ended, Father Nethod Billy, the Catholic chaplain of the 384th, invited those officers in the flight crews seeking general absolution to receive it on the stage of the briefing room. A small group of officers knelt together to receive his blessing.

As Jimmy left the briefing hut to drive out to the hardstand, he saw that Rocky Stoner, who was his third copilot, was still carrying his leather satchel. Rocky had begun bringing it aboard the plane before each mission and stowing it in the cockpit behind his seat. Jimmy finally asked him what was in it, and Rocky showed him the contents: socks, underwear, razor blades, candy, toothbrush, and cigarettes.

When they arrived at the hardstand, Jimmy was shocked at his first glimpse of *Yankee Raider*. The plane was a battle-scarred heap. Row after row of yellow bombs were painted on the nose of the fuselage, signifying that it had flown dozens of combat missions. The crew was already there, and he could tell they were angry and disheartened. The plane reminded Jimmy of the jalopies his teenaged friends patched together from junk cars.

His ground chief, James Flynn, gave him the maintenance reports. It was one of the B-17s that had come over in 1942 at the start of daylight bombing. The top turret had been replaced after being blown off on one of the raids. A week earlier, the *Yankee Raider* had returned to the base without completing its mission, the pilot reporting that its left outboard engine was running very rough, and the inboard engine on the right had suddenly lost forty pounds of oil pressure.

Since the plane had just come back from the repair shop, they had presumably given the aircraft a thorough inspection before declaring it ready for service again. He hoped so, since he didn't have any choice in the matter.

To bolster the crew's confidence, he decided to do a quick stem-to-stern inspection. As he went through the plane, Jimmy kept reassuring each man, telling them that it must be a lucky ship to have survived so long.

Up in the nose compartment where the bombardier, Wilbert Yee, would hunch over his Norden bombsight, a single .50-caliber machine gun should have been protruding through the Plexiglas nose. It wasn't there.

Behind the bombardier's station was the navigator's lair, with its desk, compass, drift meter, and instrument panel. Creighton Carlin, the navigator, was responsible for firing another machine gun that poked through an aperture on the left side of the fuselage. It wasn't armed.

A hatchway behind the navigator's desk led up to the cockpit, where Jimmy would be sitting in the left seat, Rocky Stoner in the right. Behind them would stand the crew's engineer, who was a new replacement named Bruno Edman. It was his job to monitor the instruments and engines in the cockpit, while also manning the top turret if they came under attack. The turret's twin .50-caliber machine guns spun in all directions except straight back along the fuselage to avoid shooting off the plane's tail. Jimmy introduced himself to Edman, and they shook hands. Edman reported that his heating unit didn't work. Jimmy asked Sergeant Flynn to look into it.

Behind the turret, a narrow steel catwalk led through the bomb bay, where ten five-hundred-pound bombs sat snug in their racks. As he moved through the fuselage, he could see that the plane had been hit many times. Metal patches, one of them as big as a manhole cover, covered the fuselage like scabs on a wound.

A door at the end of the catwalk led to the small radio compartment in the middle of the ship. His radio operator, Walter House, had returned from the rest camp, and had volunteered to fly again. He seemed all right, and thanked Jimmy for allowing him time off after the Schweinfurt mission.

Aft of the radio room was a floor hatch that led below the fuselage to the electrically powered ball turret, in which twin .50-caliber machine guns could spin and fire in any direction, principally at attackers from below. Sergeant Redwing, the little Hindu ball turret gunner, was waiting for the plane to take off before climbing inside.

Behind the radio room was the waist compartment, which housed the plane's waist gunners. Two more .50-caliber machine guns poked through large openings on both sides of the fuselage.

Jimmy had lost a number of waist gunners since the crew had first been formed. One new replacement had just come aboard. His name was Eldore Daudelin, and he was from New Hampshire. Jimmy welcomed him to the crew. The other new waist gunner still hadn't arrived.

In the tail compartment of the B-17's fuselage, which extended beyond the base of its vertical fin, another pair of .50-caliber machine guns protected the Fortress from any attacker coming at them from behind. Sergeant Cliff Hammock, the tail gunner, was an original member of the crew, and hailed from Arabi, Georgia.

He was very calm in battle.

"Fahhghter cummin in at six o'clock," he would report laconically on the intercom in his molasses-thick Southern accent.

The crew was standing around the *Yankee Raider* and waiting for the go signal when a military police jeep pulled up next to the hardstand. It had a single passenger. He was dressed from head to toe in cold-weather flying gear. As Jimmy went forward to meet him, he wondered what the man might have done to require a police escort.

"Sergeant Olen Grant reporting," said Reb as they shook hands.

The man smelled like a brewery, but there was no time to find out his situation.

"Get up in the nose and arm the bombardier's and navigator's guns," he told Reb.

It was stifling hot in the nose compartment. Reb was wearing a blue heat suit over his long johns, and the sheepskin-lined flying outfit over all that. By the time he was finished installing the guns, he was soaked with boozy sweat. The navigator glared at him as Reb squeezed by.

It wasn't a good beginning.

Outside, Jimmy pointed to a stack of crated ammunition on a tarp behind the plane. Put two more aboard, he said, telling Reb that they had run out of ammo on the Schweinfurt mission, and he didn't want it to happen again.

The wooden crates of belted .50-caliber ammo weighed almost two hundred pounds. Daudelin, the other replacement waist gunner, helped him carry the two crates into the compartment, where they stacked them in front of the door to the tail compartment.

Shooting flares erupted across the airfield, which signaled the pilots to begin taxiing out to the runway. Reb sat down next to his gun mount in the waist compartment as the *Yankee Raider* moved off the hardstand.

Just before takeoff, he always felt an unreasoning fear that the bomb-laden plane wouldn't lift off the runway into the sky. As the plane gathered speed, he couldn't help but think what a mess they would make if they blew a tire.

Then they were airborne.

Reb watched the little Indian guy climb into the ball turret. You had to be small to fit inside the plastic bubble under the ship. Even so, Redwing had to sit with his knees practically up to his chest.

Reb yelled over to Daudelin to ask where they were going.

"Stuttgart," Daudelin said.

Reb had no idea where it was, but he realized he was very hungry, and hoped it wouldn't be a long mission. He hadn't eaten anything since the fish and chips he had wolfed down the previous evening in Leicester before meeting Estella. He hadn't slept much, either.

Pulling out a plug of his favorite tobacco, he took a bite as the *Yankee Raider* circled the airfield with the rest of the formation. After chewing it thoughtfully, he spit a wad of tobacco juice onto the steel deck.

"What the hell is wrong with you?" demanded Daudelin. "You'll have to clean that mess up when we get back."

"Who says we're coming back?" said Reb.

THE MISSION

Juggernaut

Thurleigh, England
306th Bomb Group
Est Nulla Via Invia Virtuti
First Lieutenant Martin "Andy" Andrews
0420

The black sky over Thurleigh had bared its first hint of dawn when Andy Andrews emerged from the 306th's briefing hut with his copilot, Keith Rich, and got into one of the jeeps waiting to ferry the flight crews out to their planes.

The reek of exhaust fumes filled the air, along with the deafening racket of airplane and truck engines. It was pungent enough to sting the eyes. As on all mission mornings, the air base was a frenetic scene of activity, with headlight-dimmed vehicles crisscrossing the field in every direction.

Low-belly tankers were coming back from the hardstands after delivering aviation gas. Smaller trucks hauling trailers loaded with five-hundred-pound bombs crisscrossed in both directions, along with deuce and a halfs carrying ammunition, flanked on both sides of the concrete paths by flight-suited crewmen heading out to their Fortresses on bicycles.

Andy was approaching the hardstand where *Est Nulla Via Invia Virtuti* was parked when his driver suddenly stopped short. Ahead of them in the murky light, another jeep had overturned into a ditch, throwing its passengers out onto the concrete apron.

One man was lying on the pavement and screaming in pain as Andy ran toward the jeep. It was Sergeant Leo Liewer, Andy's top turret gunner and crew chief. Because Liewer was always steady in combat, Andy considered him the most important enlisted man in the crew. Another crewman, Corporal Kenneth Rood, the ball turret gunner, had been in the jeep, too, but appeared to be just shaken up.

Liewer had suffered a horrific fracture in his right leg. One of the bones was protruding through his pants. He had already lost a lot of blood, and Andy used his white silk scarf to fashion a tourniquet around Liewer's thigh before injecting his shattered leg with an emergency vial of morphine he carried in his flight suit.

He continued to cradle the injured man in his arms until an ambulance arrived. After Liewer was on his way to the base hospital, Kenneth Rood approached Andy and told him he couldn't fly the mission. Although the eighteen-year-old was physically uninjured, his hands were shaking. Andy told him it was all right, and that he would ask for replacements for both men as soon as he got to the plane.

The rest of the crew was visibly nervous when Andy arrived at the hardstand and they saw his bloody flight suit. After telling them what had happened, he began his regular check of the airplane with the ground chief. He had just finished when the two last-minute replacements, Ralph Biggs and Guido DiPietro, arrived.

After welcoming the new men, Andy climbed into the cockpit and tried to relax for a few minutes. Although he didn't consider himself religious, he knew that in a few hours they would be raining close to a thousand tons of bombs down on Stuttgart, Germany, and not all of the victims would be fire-breathing Nazis. Women, children, and elderly people would be killed, too. As he always did before a mission, he delivered a silent apology for the innocent lives that might be taken.

Far off to the left, he saw the flash of a flare gun above the Thurleigh control tower. It was the signal for the pilots to start their engines. There was no time to read a passage from the "Choric Song" of *The Lotos-Eaters.*

He pressed the starter button for the left outboard engine and heard the familiar whine as he injected a charge of fuel to prime it. The engine roared into life with an effusion of greasy smoke, and he began the same process with the inboard engine, closely monitoring the oil pressure and temperature gauges. He repeated the same steps with the third and fourth engines.

A second flare burst over the Thurleigh control tower. It was the signal for the Fortresses to taxi to the runway, forming into the takeoff line ordained at the premission briefing.

When the ground crew removed the wheel chocks from in front of the tires, *Est Nulla Via Invia Virtuti* began rolling slowly off the hardstand onto the perimeter apron. Beyond the left wing, Andy's ground chief was walking alongside the plane, gazing up at him like an apprehensive father worried about his son's first solo trip in the family car.

Andy gave him a reassuring wave, his fingers still sticky from Liewer's blood.

Buckinghamshire, England
High Wycombe Abbey
Eighth Air Force Bomber Command
0430

For the operational planners at High Wycombe, the task of organizing a maximum-effort mission against Germany was akin to assembling a gigantic jigsaw puzzle in the sky.

Zero hour for the Stuttgart mission had been set at 0720, the precise moment when all sixteen bomb groups participating in the attack on Stuttgart were expected to be in their respective positions in the twenty-mile train of bombers, each squadron in its assigned position within a group, each group in its designated place within a multigroup combat box formation, each combat box formation in its assigned position within the two bombardment wings, the entire armada of heavy bombers ready to depart for the enemy coast.

The combat box formations were critical to their chances for survival.

Colonel Curtis LeMay, who now commanded the Fourth Bombardment Wing, had created the concept of the combat box after flying a number of missions as commander of the 305th Bomb Group in 1942. It was as important to the development of the modern air war against Germany as the creation of the British square had once been in defending against a French cavalry charge.

LeMay's combat box formation began with an individual bomb group, which for a maximum effort consisted of twenty-one Fortresses divided into three squadrons, with the lead squadron out in front, the high squadron following closely behind and to the right at a slightly higher altitude, and the low squadron tucked in behind and beneath the lead squadron on the left.

LeMay's multigroup box formation utilized this same configuration on a larger scale. It typically consisted of three bomb groups, with the twenty-one planes in each group flying in the same staggered formation. The box was stacked by altitude, with the lead group in front, the low group below it, and the high group above it.

If the pilots were able to maintain a tight formation, the LeMay combat box created the maximum opportunity for massing the combined power of the Fortresses' .50-caliber machine guns in interlocking fields of fire.

The staggered formation in the combat box also contributed to better bombing accuracy. Once over the target, the groups were able to release each plane's bomb payloads in a concentrated pattern without endangering the Fortresses flying at lower altitude.

For the Stuttgart mission, which entailed the largest force to ever be sent against a target deep inside Germany, the assembly of the air armada in the skies over southern England was a mission in itself.

If all went well, it would take nearly two hours to put the train of bombers together. Since it would also be the longest mission ever undertaken, conserving fuel would be essential. It was vital that the assembly take place smoothly.

At the sixteen American air bases near medieval English villages like Bury St. Edmunds, Thorpe Abbotts, Molesworth, Grafton Underwood, Thurleigh, and Knettishall, the pilots of 338 Fortresses sat in their cockpits and watched the minute hands of their synchronized watches ticking down to the takeoff times that were set for them at the preflight briefings.

For the 388th Bomb Group in Knettishall, the first set of Frag (fragmentary) orders for the Stuttgart mission had arrived from High Wycombe on the group's Teletype machines at 2240 the previous night. After officially logging them in, the operations staff began preparing briefing notes for the flight crews, including an updated weather advisory, a group formation plan, and the final order of takeoff for the group's twenty-one bombers.

At exactly eighty-one minutes before zero hour, the 388th was to rendezvous with the 96th Bomb Group, which had been chosen to lead the air fleet. Their rendezvous would be at an altitude of forty-five hundred feet over the 96th's air base at Snetterton Heath.

To avoid possible confusion with one of the other fifteen bomb groups circling in the skies, the lead pilot of the 96th group would signal its presence by firing two yellow flares. The lead pilot of the 388th would respond by firing one yellow and one green flare to indicate his arrival before taking up position behind the 96th.

The two groups would then proceed to climb in slow circles to an altitude of six thousand feet, where, at seventy-two minutes before zero hour, the 96th and the 388th groups would rendezvous with the 94th and 385th Bomb Groups over Fakenham, the ancient Saxon parish in

Norfolk. Once those two groups were in tow, additional couplings of the bomber train would take place at seventy-five hundred feet, fourteen thousand feet, and seventeen thousand feet.

At 0720, the assembly of all sixteen bomb groups would hopefully be achieved as the lead Fortress in the 96th Bomb Group arrived over the coastal village of Dungeness, England.

Knettishall, England
388th Bomb Group
Second Lieutenant Ted Wilken
0515

In the gloom of breaking dawn, Ted Wilken and his copilot, Warren Laws, waited for the takeoff signal, still pondering everything that had already gone wrong that chaotic morning.

After the intelligence briefing, the two officers had arrived at their hardstand with the rest of the crew to learn that *Battlin Betsy* had been scratched from the Stuttgart mission due to radio communication problems. It created a brief stir of anger and disappointment.

Each B-17 had its own personality. There was something reassuring about a plane that was deemed to be lucky, and *Battlin Betsy*, which had been named for Ted's wife, had been deemed just that. They hated not being able to fly in her, particularly on what might prove to be a tough mission.

The spare plane they were assigned was named *Patricia*, and its fuselage was adorned with the garish painting of a nude woman. Warren Laws didn't appreciate the artwork. A serious young man, he was engaged to be married to his college sweetheart, Libby, and wasn't comfortable with the lurid symbolism.

As they were doing their preflight checks, the crew's regular bombardier, Gene Cordes, turned up ill, and Ted had to send for a last-minute replacement. When the new man arrived, it was too dark for Ted to even see his face as he disappeared into the nose compartment.

When Warren began checking over the equipment in the plane, he found that all their throat microphones were missing. Without them, there would be no way for the crew to communicate on the intercom. He dropped down through the forward belly hatch, jumped on his bicycle, and rode like the devil over to the squadron commander to report the problem. The commander proceeded to ream him out for failing to take care of his duties, and the flustered Warren never thought to tell him that they had just been assigned a spare plane.

He got back to *Patricia* with the throat mikes, only to discover that his parachute was missing from the pile of officers' chutes that the enlisted men had brought out to the hardstand. Shortly before their scheduled takeoff, one of the crewmen located an extra chute, and Warren stowed it under the copilot's seat.

With the preflight checks completed, Ted and Warren waited for the signal flare to start their engines. The two young officers had come a long way from the day they met back in Spokane when the crews were assigned. At first, they weren't sure what to make of one another.

Ted was a blue-blooded socialite with famous friends, had prepped at Choate and attended Dartmouth, was a superb athlete, larger than life, a born leader. He made everyone in the crew feel like they were the luckiest guys in the Eighth Air Force to have him as their plane commander.

Warren was guileless and introspective. He was a good listener. He made friends by listening to people talk about themselves. When the crew got together for poker games at Ted and Braxton's hotel suite, Warren would stand in the background with a big smile on his face sipping a soft drink. I play bridge, he said. Sometimes, he seemed to disappear within himself.

Although they hailed from different worlds, the two men had grown up close to one another, Ted in Bronxville, New York, and Warren in Stratford, Connecticut, a village founded by the Puritans in 1639 at the edge of Long Island Sound.

As a child, Warren suffered from asthma, and his mother became highly protective of him, not allowing the boy to enter grade school until he was seven. On Halloween, he was permitted to wear a costume, but not allowed to go outside. He would sit at the front window and watch the other children as they trick-or-treated down his block.

When he was nine years old, an event took place that changed his life.

It was the morning of May 20, 1927, and he was at home listening to the live radio coverage of Charles Lindbergh's attempt to become the first man to cross the Atlantic alone in the *Spirit of St. Louis*. Warren could hear Lindbergh gunning the plane's engine in the background before he took off down the runway at Roosevelt Field on Long Island.

When Warren heard the announcer say that Lindbergh planned to turn east over Long Island Sound, he rushed out of his house in the hopes of seeing him fly past. Looking up into the sky, Warren suddenly heard the sound of a distant plane engine. It was out over the water and he couldn't see the plane, but for a minute or two he could hear the distinctive whine of the Wright Whirlwind engine, all the time imagining the young Lindbergh in the cockpit as he flew alone into the unknown.

From that moment on, he wanted to fly.

The worldwide economic depression altered his career plans, as it did for so many others. In the 1930s, there was no demand for pilots, but there was always a need for teachers, and as the war approached, he was finishing his education at Danbury Teachers College. While there, he fell in love with a fellow student, Elizabeth "Libby" Minck, and they became engaged. The vivacious Libby was committed to helping Warren "have more fun" in life.

Then the Japanese attacked Pearl Harbor. It came as a shock to Warren's family when he went straight up to Hartford the following day and volunteered for the army air forces, just as Ted Wilken had done that same day in Manhattan.

They may have been different men, but in the course of training together, they learned they could count on one another. Warren never disappeared within himself while in the air. He was always focused on the tasks at hand, and ready to deal with the unforeseen problems that often cropped up in the heavy bombers. Unlike many copilots, he seemed born to the controls, and Ted felt comfortable turning the plane over to him.

At 0515, the two men watched an exploding flare shoot skyward near the control tower.

Major Ralph Jarrendt was leading the 388th that morning in *Gremlin Gus II*. At exactly 0530, Jarrendt thundered forward at full power between the twin rows of amber runway lights. He was followed at forty-second intervals by the rest of the lead squadron: *Iza Angel II*, commanded by George Branholm; Earl Melville in *Shedonwanna?*; Roy Mohr in *Shack Up*; and Bill Beecham in *Impatient Virgin*.

Demetrios "the Greek" Karnezis came next in *Slightly Dangerous II*.

After the eight bombers of the high squadron were up, it was the low squadron's turn. Al Kramer led the way in *Lone Wolf*. After Kramer's bomber clawed its way skyward to join the other two squadrons, Ted Wilken shoved the throttles forward in *Patricia*, and the B-17 began lumbering down the strip, followed by Dick Cunningham in *In God We Trust*, Lew Miller in an unnamed plane, James Roe in *Silver Dollar*, and Mike Bowen in *Sky Shy*.

It was 0540.

As soon as they were all in the air, the 388th began circling over Knettishall until each pilot found his respective slot in the group formation. When they were all in proper position, Ralph Jarrendt led them toward their first rendezvous point with the 96th group.

By then, the night mist had finally dissipated, giving way to a beautiful morning, with puffy cumulus clouds dotting the sky. Looking west, Joe Schwartzkopf, the big bear of a radio operator in Ted's plane, could see dozens of Fortresses climbing up from their fields across the English Midlands.

At five thousand feet, the bombers burst through the last bank of clouds into a bird's-egg blue sky. In every direction Joe looked, other bomb groups were banking gently in slow lazy turns as they spiraled ever upward into the crowded sky.

There was something comforting to him about the huge mass of bombers forming in the sky over England. Seeing them all come together, it was hard to believe that all the enemy fighters in Germany could challenge their impregnability.

When *Patricia* reached twelve thousand feet, Ted ordered the crew to put on their oxygen masks. Each mask was supplied by a rubber hose connected to metal oxygen canisters anchored along the plane's fuselage. At more than two miles above the earth's surface, it was impossible to breathe for long without one.

Once his face was encased in the mask, Warren felt cut off from the world below. From then on, his life was dependent on the continued expansion and contraction of the bladder beneath his chin. The crew would now be on oxygen all the way to the target, and most of the way back.

One by one, Warren asked the crew members to confirm that their oxygen masks were working.

At fifteen thousand feet, frost began to appear on the interior of the Plexiglas windows in the plane, and the men used scrapers to clear them. The air temperature was already far below zero degrees Fahrenheit. If a crew member removed his sheepskin-lined gloves for more than a minute or two, he would suffer severe frostbite.

As zero hour approached, several groups had failed to reach their rendezvous in the allotted times. It was 0734 when the lead plane of the 96th Bomb Group turned onto the compass heading that would lead the armada across the English Channel toward France.

Eight miles back in the bomber train, General Bob Travis sat in the copilot's seat of *Satan's Workshop*, the lead plane of the 303rd Bomb Group and the lead bomber of the First Bombardment Wing. Travis was now in direct command of all nine bomb groups following behind him. So far, his first combat mission was going smoothly.

Flying in the low group behind General Travis, Jimmy Armstrong was getting the feel of *Yankee Raider* as he flew for the first time as an element leader. Unlike *Sad Sack II*, the cockpit of *Yankee Raider* smelled rank, but so far it was handling well.

In the waist compartment of *Yankee Raider*, Reb Grant was enjoying a sight that never failed to give him delight as he gazed out at all the heavy bombers surrounding him. In the rarified atmosphere in which they were flying, each of the B-17s was trailing four beautiful white contrails, long cones of condensed water vapor produced by the exhaust gases from the airplane engines. To Reb, the fluffy plumes looked like silvery comets slashing across the blue heaven.

Once they were out over the English Channel, Jimmy Armstrong gave the order for the gunners to test fire the plane's eight machine guns. When Reb cut loose with his .50s, the vibration rattled his teeth and filled the compartment with the stink of cordite.

It was 0750.

The 96th Bomb Group was halfway across the English Channel when one of its Fortresses suddenly peeled away, banking into a 180-degree turn and heading back toward England. Its departure was quickly followed by another bomber in the high squadron of the 388th.

Under Eighth Air Force operational guidelines, if a pilot concluded that his plane could not complete the mission because of an unexpected problem, he was permitted to turn back.

Prior to the beginning of the air offensive against targets inside Germany, a few pilots aborted each mission. In the wake of the disastrous crew losses in July and August, the number of aborts had grown exponentially.

Now the migration became a steady stream.

As the twenty-mile-long bomber train continued east across the channel, a smaller train of bombers was already heading back, flying well below the attacking force, as if not wanting to be noticed.

Within the 100th Bomb Group, which had valiantly earned the sobriquet "Bloody 100th" due to its severe losses on previous missions, seven Fortresses out of the twenty-one planes flying in the group turned back. The remaining pilots in their combat box were forced to tighten up to fill the vacuum.

The exodus became contagious.

Five Fortresses aborted from the 390th group, four from the 95th, seven from the 94th, six from the 385th, and eight from the 305th based at Chelveston. More pilots continued to peel away as they neared the enemy coast.

The reasons for each pilot's decision extended to a wide range of problems. Low fuel pressure was reported in the left outboard engine of one Fortress, a ball turret gunner's hand had begun to swell at eight thousand feet due to past frostbite in another, an oxygen leak, a runaway propeller, high oil temperature in a right outboard engine, a sick tail gunner, a malfunction in the bomb bay doors, low oil pressure, a super-charger problem, a loose ball turret hatch, an intercom malfunction, a bomb bay switch failure, more oxygen leaks.

It was hard for some of the men still headed to Germany not to envy them.

As *Est Nulla Via Invia Virtuti* approached the coast of France, Andy Andrews tuned his radio compass to a program he had become familiar with on the BBC. It was called *Whistle While You Work*, and delivered only popular musical favorites. For one solid hour, there was nothing but music, music while you worked. Andy grinned as he imagined housewives all over England doing their ironing while he was on his way to bomb Germany.

The Golden Eagle

T he air base's Teletype machines had begun chattering well before dawn.

Using long-range receivers, Luftwaffe air controllers had monitored the testing of aircraft radios by American ground crews at more than a dozen bases in England, clearly indicating a major strike was under way.

At 0600, the Luftwaffe's radar platforms deployed along the "Atlantikwall" of France began monitoring several large masses of aircraft over southern England. In the next hour, it grew to the largest concentration of aircraft the radar controllers had ever recorded.

"It will be a good day for hunting," declared an eager pilot of Jagdgeschwader 2 "Richthofen" after the fighter unit was put on full alert. JG 2 "Richthofen" was one of the elite fighter wings in the Luftwaffe; it had been named in honor of Freiherr Manfred von Richthofen, the famed "Red Baron," who had scored eighty victories before his death in the First World War.

For Egon "Connie" Mayer, JG 2's commander, every day was good hunting. He was as naturally gifted as any combat pilot in the war. Since 1941, he had shot down seventy-seven Allied planes, including forty-eight English Spitfires.

In contrast to many of the other leading aces of the Luftwaffe, who had racked up their victories against the poorly trained and equipped Soviet air force, Connie Mayer had scored all his aerial victories on the western front.

A recipient of the Knight's Cross of the Iron Cross with Oak Leaves, he was one of the most decorated pilots in the Luftwaffe. Unlike some of his more flamboyant contemporaries, he never felt the need to exaggerate his accomplishments, and evidenced no desire to join in the spirited competition of those who sought to become Germany's highest-scoring ace. As a matter of personal honor, he never made a victory claim that couldn't be confirmed.

For Connie Mayer, fighting one's enemy wasn't a contest between medieval knights or modern gladiators. Germany was at war. He was a professional. His job was to help destroy the Allied planes attacking the Fatherland.

Born in 1917, he had grown up near Lake Constance in the alpine foothills close to the Swiss border. An exceptional skier, he had joined the Luftwaffe in 1937. Only twenty-six years old, he looked much older, the direct result of four years of arduous combat.

With the exception of his eyes, he looked more like an earnest peacetime lawyer than one of the most celebrated fighter pilots of the war. His eyes were hawk's eyes, intense and aware, which contributed to the deadliness of his aim and his tactical brilliance in the air.

He now had four fighter groups under his command, all of them based in the western quadrant of France. Their job was to defend the Paris region and the U-boat pens along the coast of France. Since the start of the war, the pilots of Jagdgeschwader 2 had achieved almost two thousand victories.

The once boundless confidence enjoyed by the Luftwaffe after the fall of France in 1940 was long gone. As the enemy grew ever stronger, it became clear to Connie Mayer and the other frontline commanders that Germany would eventually be defeated unless Hitler's claims of new secret weapons could change the balance. Mayer had become increasingly skeptical of the Führer's boasts.

He knew the personal odds. Most of his closest comrades were already dead. Two of them, Helmut Wick and Wilhelm Balthasar, had been killed while commanding Jagdgeschwader 2. Connie Mayer had now flown more than three hundred missions and been shot down four times, surviving against the odds. It was only a matter of time before his luck ran out.

Since the Americans had begun their daylight bombing campaign, JG 2's principal assignment was to intercept and destroy the Allied bombers attacking the Fatherland, and particularly the Flying Fortresses of the Eighth Air Force.

In November 1942, Connie Mayer became the architect of a bold and unorthodox strategy that was to alter the course of the air war. After his first few encounters with the Fortresses in their tight combat box formations, Mayer concluded that the approach then being employed by the Luftwaffe was ineffective and too costly in pilot losses.

Up to that point, German fighter pilots usually made their attacks on the B-17s from the "six o'clock low" position, coming in from behind with cannons and machine guns blazing, one plane at a time.

This left the fighters vulnerable to the .50-caliber machine-gun fire from the bomber's tail gunner, as well as to the massed firepower of the other Fortresses in the same combat box.

Mayer believed that attacking a Fortress from the front would provide the best chance of destroying its vital systems, including the cockpit controls, the engines, and the fuel tanks. He concluded that the Fortress's most vulnerable spot was its nose, which was equipped with only one .30-caliber machine gun manned by the crew's bombardier, not a trained machine gunner.

A frontal attack against a Fortress required extraordinary skill. The fighter pilot had to line up his target while the two were closing at a combined speed of 600 miles an hour. He had only a few seconds to open fire with his cannon and machine guns from a distance of about one hundred yards, and then dive away to avoid ramming the bomber.

Mayer added another difficult component to his tactical maneuver as well. He advocated rolling the fighter onto its back just before commencing the attack, because the belly of the Fw 190 was armor-plated, and largely impervious to the .30-caliber machine gun in the Fortress's nose.

Mayer also conceived the strategy in which attacks would be made by three or more fighters, flying wing tip to wing tip. This dangerous aerial ballet would concentrate more firepower on each target, and potentially force the unnerved bomber pilots to take evasive action, breaking up the combat box. If the formation's integrity could be compromised, the individual bombers would become more vulnerable.

His ideas were initially met with widespread skepticism and largely ignored.

On November 22, 1942, Connie Mayer was appointed commander of the III Group of Jagdgeschwader 2. One day later, he decided to put his new theories into practice. A mixed bomber force of B-17s and B-24s was attacking the German submarine pens at Saint-Nazaire when Mayer's staffel intercepted the lead bombers and attacked them head-on as they approached their bomb run.

He led the first of several waves of Fw 190 fighters, all flying three abreast. In their initial pass, the first wave of fighters shot down four bombers. Mayer himself accounted for two Fortresses and a B-24 Liberator before the action ended.

In the following weeks, Connie Mayer perfected his frontal pass techniques and trained the pilots in his group to master each maneuver. He quickly discovered that the ideal attacking path was from twelve o'clock high. Coming in on a slightly downward approach enabled him to better judge the distance between himself and his target as the planes closed at 600 miles an hour.

"Twelve o'clock high" quickly became the awestruck cry of B-17 pilots as they called out the compass heading of the attacking German fighters on the intercom.

As the victories in Mayer's group mounted, General Adolf Galland, commanding all Luftwaffe fighter forces, issued a memorandum to his groups. "The attack from the rear against a four-engine bomber formation promises little success and almost always brings losses. The attack from the front . . . is the most effective of all," he wrote.

In 1943, Connie Mayer became the premier Flying Fortress killer in the Luftwaffe, having shot down sixteen B-17s, along with four more Spitfires, an American P-47 fighter, a B-24, and three Hawker Typhoons. On June 26, he and his group destroyed five Fortresses in less than three minutes with the now patented head-on attacks.

He was promoted to command the Jagdgeschwader 2 a week later.

His skill in the air often astonished the American bomber crews who witnessed it.

On July 14, the 305th Bomb Group had been returning from a bombing run near Paris when two Fw 190s appeared ahead of them.

One of the B-17 navigators recalled what happened next. "Whoever it was gave a riveting display of aerobatics in front of our entire 102nd Combat Wing before slashing in to fatally damage the leading ship of the 422nd Squadron in the low slot."

The machine gunners in the other B-17s in the box then cut loose at the Fw 190. The American navigator reported that he had never seen such a tremendous volume of tracer go after one plane, but they hit nothing but air.

The Fw 190 pilot was Egon Mayer.

By the end of August, the Luftwaffe's fighter forces were delivering one brutal beating after another to the Eighth Air Force, which saw its losses rise on long-range missions to Hannover, Kassel, Gelsenkirchen, Schweinfurt, and Regensburg. The goal of the Luftwaffe was now simple: to force the Americans to suspend their air offensive against Germany.

To defend the Reich, twenty-nine staffeln, each consisting of about a dozen fighters, had been spread out at airfields across France and Germany along the corridor the bombers had to fly through to reach most of their targets. In the wake of the Schweinfurt-Regensburg raid, the Luftwaffe brought back two additional fighter groups from Russia to help meet the threat.

When an American bomber force was on its way, the fighter staffeln were scrambled from their fields as the formation approached. After completing their attacks, the fighters would return to their bases for more ammunition and fuel, and the next group of staffeln along the corridor would come up to take their place. After the B-17s bombed their target and finally turned for home, they would meet the same squadrons on the way back, now refueled and rearmed.

On September 6, dawn gave way to a sun-drenched sky over Normandy. At his headquarters in Tricqueville, Connie Mayer waited for orders to arrive from the Luftwaffe air defense command.

The day became confusing at the outset.

At 0710, Luftwaffe air controllers reported a large formation of bombers headed toward the Dutch coast, accompanied by an escort of twenty-four Spitfires. It was the American force of sixty-nine B-24 Liberators undertaking the first diversionary raid staged by the Eighth Air Force to divert German fighters away from the Stuttgart force.

Two staffeln from JG 2 were scrambled to intercept the B-24s, but by the time they located the formation, it had already turned back from the Dutch islands to return to England. The staffeln were then ordered to patrol over northern France.

At 0725, German air controllers reported that a separate force of B-26 Marauders with escorting Spitfires had crossed the French coast and was attacking the marshaling yards at Rouen, along the Seine River northwest of Paris. Four more staffeln in Mayer's group were sent up to intercept them.

Minutes later, another bomber force was monitored over Dungeness across the English Channel. The staffeln of JG 2 were ordered to divert from their positions near the Seine and fly north toward the Somme River, where they circled while waiting for further orders.

At 0745, yet another formation of light bombers was reported to be attacking Boulogne Harbor. It was the last of the diversionary raids planned by the Eighth Air Force, and it drew off another staffel of Mayer's Fw 190s.

His staffeln began running short of fuel.

At 0752, the German air controllers, now aware of the magnitude of the heavy bomber force heading for France from Dungeness, ordered Mayer's JG 2 to return for refueling and rearming.

Most of the fighters were about to land when several hundred Fortresses thundered across the sky above them. For those under their flight path, it sounded like the continuous rumble of a vast freight train.

The Luftwaffe air defense command had no idea where the bomber force was going, but the Americans would soon have to show their hand. Once the target region was determined, they would mobilize their fighter groups in Germany to destroy it.

For Connie Mayer and the pilots of Jagdgeschwader 2, one thing was certain. The Americans would have to come back through western France to reach England. He would be waiting for them.

Into the Valley

As *Est Nulla Via Invia Virtuti* crossed the French coast, Andy Andrews was leading an element of the 306th's high squadron. He was part of the sixty-two-plane combat box that included the 92nd and 305th groups, and flying at seventeen thousand feet. The formation was maintaining a cruising speed of 180 miles an hour.

Once past the French coast, the group turned onto the predesignated compass heading that would take them on a southeasterly path toward the city of Saint-Quentin, eighty miles inside the French border.

Within moments of entering French airspace, the Luftwaffe's 88-millimeter flak batteries along the bombers' flight path began opening up, pumping hundreds of the twenty-pound cannon shells into the crowded sky. Compared to the intense umbrella barrages Andy Andrews had endured over Germany, these salvos seemed meager and uncoordinated.

As the first black puffs of greasy smoke reached up toward him, Andy again noted the fact that there was no sound to the explosions when the shells detonated in and around a formation. With his helmet and earphones on, it was impossible to hear them over the deafening roar of the plane's four supercharged engines.

Unless it was a direct hit.

Even if he couldn't hear the shells explode, he could definitely feel their impact when one came close. The burst would concuss the air so violently that *Est Nulla Via Invia Virtuti* would leap upward like a bucking stallion.

At 0815, one of the Fortresses in the 92nd group received a direct hit, and dropped away from the formation. Five men were able to bail out of the stricken bomber before its wing sheared off at sixteen thousand feet. One parachute failed to open. Another was on fire.

Two minutes later, another B-17 in the 306th's combat box absorbed a direct hit. A large red burst suddenly lit up the center of the plane's fuselage. On fire and out of control, it disintegrated while falling earthward.

Death was purely a matter of fate in a flak barrage. The fickle finger. Andy took comfort in the fact that *Est Nulla Via Invia Virtuti* had come back with plenty of flak holes, and no one in his crew had been badly wounded. A pilot could only steel his nerves and keep going. Andy took his mind off the carnage by keeping his plane in formation and retreating into his imagination.

From seventeen thousand feet, the beautiful landscape below them looked like a lot of places back home, blue-green fingers of rivers coursing through a fertile landscape of farmland and forest, interspersed with towns and cities, all lying placid in the sun.

He knew the placid landscape was deceiving. They were flying over ancient Gaul. In 58 BC, Julius Caesar had invaded the places they were now flying over, and had conquered nearly all of them. It struck Andy that there were probably more horses in the four Wright Cyclone engines of his single B-17 Flying Fortress than all the mounts in ten Roman legions.

It was 0825.

Eight miles ahead of the 306th in the lead combat box of the sixteen-group bomber stream, Ted Wilken glanced out of the pilot's window in *Patricia* at the left edge of the 388th's formation and saw several dozen fighters approaching from the northwest.

He was relieved to see that they were P-47 Thunderbolts from the 56th Fighter Group, rendezvousing with the lead combat box to provide air cover across part of France. A few minutes later, forty P-47 Thunderbolts from the 355th Fighter Group arrived from the southwest and took up positions along the formation's right flank.

A few staffeln of Fw 190s and ME-109s came up to intercept the striking force near Cambrai, but so far the attacks weren't mounted with the ferocity that characterized the Schweinfurt-Regensburg mission. After dueling briefly with the P-47s, they disappeared. At that point, all fighter attacks abruptly ceased.

It was 0844.

Where were they? Had the Germans changed their tactics after Schweinfurt? It was an ominous sign, and seemed to indicate that the Germans were marshaling their forces for an all-out attack after the formation reached Germany.

This fear was strengthened when the bomber train thundered past the fortified city of Metz, the headquarters of the Luftwaffe's Jagdivision 3, which controlled the movement of all enemy fighter units in that sector. No fighters came up to contest them.

When the 388th reached Le Châtelet, the flight leaders of the P-47 fighter groups signaled that their fuel supply had reached the critical point and they were turning back. The groups would fly back along the length of the bomber train, providing air cover for the trailing groups.

From now on, the Fortresses were on their own.

In conformance to the operations order, Major Ralph Jarrendt, the lead pilot of the 388th, slowly climbed to twenty-three thousand feet. The rest of the bombers followed suit. Air temperature inside the planes quickly dropped to 25 degrees below zero Fahrenheit. As the 388th neared German airspace, the cloud layer beneath them began to grow progressively thicker.

In *Patricia*, Warren Laws was making routine oxygen checks every fifteen minutes, asking each crew member to confirm over the intercom that he was okay. A few minutes later, Ted's replacement navigator, Vic Sandes, reported that they were over German airspace. He estimated they would reach the initial point of the bomb run near Stuttgart at about 0930.

Glancing down, Ted saw that the weather was continuing to deteriorate. In France, the big puffy stratocumulus clouds had left plenty of ground visibility around them. This was a large front of stratus clouds, which were layered horizontally with a uniform base. Ted could only hope that the front didn't extend farther south along their designated flight path.

Flying 150 feet above *Patricia* in the second element of the lead squadron, the Greek glanced down at the same pristine white landscape and wondered how the lead bombardier in their group was going to find the target.

A few moments later, the white landscape was no longer pristine. As he watched, dozens of Luftwaffe fighters burst through the top of the dense cloud layer like winged swords.

The planes bore so many different unit markings and war paint that the Greek knew they had to have come from all over Germany. Some had yellow checkered noses, others red and white noses. Although most of the ME-109s were black and silver, one was silver with a red cross instead of a swastika, and another had orange stripes with black borders. Many of the Fw 190s were painted light green and equipped with belly tanks for additional range.

Every type of fighter in the Luftwaffe arsenal had apparently been summoned into the battle, at least two hundred aircraft or more. In addition to the Fw 190s and ME-109s, there were twin-engine Bf 110s and ME-210s, along with Ju 88 heavy fighters and Ju 87 Stuka dive-bombers.

The sky around the combat boxes was soon so crowded with enemy machines that there were too many for the gunners to count. Still outside machine-gun range, about forty Fw 190s formed up in a circular formation before peeling off in elements of four. Flying at nearly 400 miles an hour, they were quickly reduced to black specks in the distance.

Ted braced himself for what he knew was coming, warning all the gunners in *Patricia* to be ready. Their squadron of six Fortresses was in coffin corner, the low squadron of the low group in the first combat box in the formation. Al Kramer, who was leading the low squadron in *Lone Wolf,* ordered them all to tighten up.

As even more fighter groups continued to arrive, German air

controllers began to divide their forces among the bomber groups following behind the lead formation. Eight miles back in the bomber stream, Bf 110s with air-to-air rockets mounted under their wings appeared on the flanks of the 306th group and began launching rockets at the bombers on the outer flanks of the combat box.

After the rockets were fired, a staffel of ME-109s made an attack on the 306th's high squadron from out of the sun. Andy Andrews saw them coming and called out their position on the intercom.

Three of the fighters headed straight for *Est Nulla Via Invia Virtuti*. Rolling onto their backs, they flashed past in a blur of tracer bullets and cannon fire. Andy felt a shudder in the controls. Checking his instruments, he saw that the oil pressure in the left inboard engine was dropping fast. One of the cannon rounds had severed the engine's oil line.

When the oil pressure dropped to zero, he was forced to cut power to the engine and feather the propeller to prevent it from spinning out of control. Without lubrication, the spinning propeller would have built up enough heat to melt its metal housing.

He had a critical decision to make. With only three engines, it wasn't possible for *Est Nulla Via Invia Virtuti* to keep up with the rest of the 306th. Andy asked Keith Rich, his copilot, for their fuel situation. It would be tight, Rich told him, but Stuttgart still lay within their range. They were less than thirty minutes from the target.

Andy could also turn the plane around and head straight back for England, but that seemed like quitting. There was another factor, too. He had faced a similar crisis three weeks earlier on their mission to Gelsenkirchen. On that one, they had just crossed the German border when the superchargers had frozen up on both of the right-side engines.

To stay in the air, it had been necessary for him to keep the wing with the two good engines canted down low to prevent the plane from going into a flat spin. As they headed back across France, he was flying lopsided.

A formation of several dozen fighters approached them, and he saw that they had inline engines. Spitfires and ME-109s had inline engines. He hoped they were Spitfires.

They weren't. The planes were ME-109s flying to intercept the rest of the bomber stream. A dozen of them made passes at *Est Nulla Via Invia Virtuti* as they flew past. Three came back to play with them, and it soon seemed as if everything was going to pieces in the plane. All the guns on the bomber were blasting away while Andy tried to keep the plane straight up so they would have a good field of fire. Almost miraculously, the cavalry had come to the rescue in the form of a squadron of P-47s, but the memory of the ordeal was fresh in his mind.

He knew there was a measure of safety inside the massive bomber stream. Within it, their Fortress was just one more schooling fish. Alone as a cripple in broad daylight, they would offer German fighter pilots a tempting opportunity to rack up a four-engine bomber kill. Since *Est Nulla Via Invia Virtuti* was in the high squadron of the lead group, he could afford to slowly drop back inside the stream without ending up easy prey.

Andy made his decision. He told Keith Rich that as soon as they dropped their bombs on the factories at Stuttgart, he would dive for the deck and head back at treetop level across Germany, France, and finally the English Channel to their base at Thurleigh.

As *Est Nulla Via Invia Virtuti* began slowly falling back in the formation, one of the pilots in the element behind them moved up to take over his position as the element leader.

He gave Andy an encouraging thumbs-up as the Fortress surged past.

The Blind Leading the Blind

One moment they were tiny black smudges in the distance, maybe dirt specks on the cockpit windshield. A few seconds later, they were four Fw 190s coming toward them at 400 miles an hour.

For Ted Wilken, the hardest thing about being a B-17 pilot was not being able to personally shoot back. He could only fly stolidly along in the bomber train, keeping *Patricia* slotted into its position in the combat box, while trying to provide his machine gunners with good fields of fire.

The first wave of German fighters headed straight for the low squadron.

In an astonishing acrobatic display, the Fw 190s simultaneously rolled over onto their backs and opened fire at a hundred yards. If the beautifully calibrated maneuver hadn't been so lethal, the sheer artistry of it would have been breathtaking.

The top turret gunner opened fire on one of them with his twin .50s, and Carl Johnson, the bombardier in the nose compartment, cut loose with his single .30-caliber peashooter.

In the cockpit, it began to smell like the Fourth of July. The muzzles of the top turret guns were less than three feet above Ted's head, and he could feel their reassuring vibration through his gloved hands on the steering column.

Seconds later the fighters were gone, diving beneath the bombers before peeling off to the right and left in preparation for another attack. Out ahead of the formation, another wave of fighters materialized behind the first one.

The attacks on the low squadron quickly struck home. Lieutenant James Roe, the pilot of *Silver Dollar,* was flying directly behind and beneath Ted in the second element as the fighters continued diving at them. A 20-millimeter cannon round slammed into the nose of *Silver Dollar,* killing the bombardier, Manley Frankenberg, and wrecking many of the cockpit controls.

Before the plane tipped over into a flat spin, Roe ordered the rest of his crew to bail out. Parachutes blossomed around the fuselage as it fell away. One of the enemy fighters continued to follow the Fortress down, firing short bursts into it as if to hurry it along. The pilots in the combat box behind the 388th watched it go.

Sky Shy, piloted by Lieutenant Myron "Mike" Bowen, was flying alongside *Silver Dollar* in the second element of the low squadron when a fighter attacking from the left side raked it from fore to aft, wounding both waist gunners and blowing the head off the top turret gunner. In a simultaneous frontal attack, a second fighter knocked out one of Bowen's engines. Determined to keep going, Bowen increased the manifold pressure in the three remaining ones to try to keep up.

While the initial attacks were concentrated on the low squadron, the lead and high squadrons of the 388th faced their share, too, with the fighters coming in frontally and from both sides. Lou Krueger was piloting *Passionate Witch II* in the first element of the high squadron when a cannon round shattered the cockpit, instantly killing him and seriously wounding his copilot, Johnny Mayfield, who fought to retain consciousness as the attacks continued.

A few of the German fighter pilots were recklessly brave, waiting until they were no more than fifty yards from the bombers before opening fire. This daring maneuver gave them a better chance of delivering a mortal blow, but a deadly collision was no more than a heartbeat away.

Watching them come in, the Greek was reminded of how the

fighters' tracer rounds always looked to him like landing lights. But these pilots weren't landing. They were trying to kill him. As one of them rolled and fired at *Slightly Dangerous II*, Sergeant Arthur Gay, the Greek's top turret gunner, unleashed a short burst from his twin .50s.

The ME-109 disintegrated in front of their eyes. A fraction of a second later, bits and pieces of the plane's fuselage, engine, and pilot sped past the side windows of their cockpit.

For another five minutes, the fighters darted through the 388th's formation with almost maniacal ferocity. Major Ralph Jarrendt, the lead pilot of the 388th in *Gremlin Gus II*, estimated that the group absorbed at least twenty separate attacks in the first minutes of the battle.

And just as suddenly, it was over.

The reason for the fighters' abrupt departure quickly became obvious when the first barrage of black greasy explosions materialized above the solid cloud layer and erupted around them. Even if the Americans couldn't see Stuttgart, the hundreds of antiaircraft batteries surrounding the city obviously knew they were there.

Stuttgart, Germany
388th Bomb Group
Gremlin Gus II
First Lieutenant Henry W. Dick
0942

From his small cushioned chair bolted to the deck of the nose compartment in *Gremlin Gus II*, Henry Dick, the lead bombardier of the 388th, pressed his right eye to the hard rubber eyepiece on his Norden bombsight and tried to find the ball-bearing factories they had come to destroy.

The superbly engineered bombsight had three primary components, including an analog computer, a small telescope, and the electric motor that adjusted the gyros after it had locked onto the target. Once the target was acquired, the bombsight would engage, and then automatically adjust itself as the aircraft headed toward the bomb release point.

Before the Norden bombsight could generate a good target solution, however, it was necessary for Henry Dick to visually locate the target using the bombsight's telescope. He then needed to input the approximate distance to the target as well as the plane's ground speed and altitude into the computer.

He had already made an estimate of ground speed based on a combination of wind drift and the plane's airspeed. Now he had to visually find the target in order to estimate the distance they were from it.

The difficulty of the current problem was compounded by the intensity of the flak barrage they were now flying through. It was as heavy as he had ever seen, and the plane was being buffeted wildly in the turbulent air as cannon shells exploded above, below, and around them.

When *Gremlin Gus II* reached the initial point of the bomb run, Major Jarrendt turned over control of the plane to Lieutenant Dick. Theoretically, the bombsight should now have been flying the airplane, automatically correcting its course until the target was reached, when it would automatically toggle the Fortress's payload of ten five-hundred-pound bombs.

The rest of the bombardiers in the group were watching and waiting for Lieutenant Dick to open his bomb bay doors and release his payload. That would be the signal for them to drop their share of high explosives on the ball-bearing factories.

Henry Dick was very good at his job, but his current predicament was unprecedented, at least in his experience. As hard as he tried, he was unable to make out any of the identifying features he had been briefed to look for. The stratus clouds were impenetrable. If Stuttgart was down there, he had no way to confirm it.

Up ahead of them, the 96th Bomb Group suddenly turned left off the formation's original flight path. Unable to make his own independent observation, Henry Dick assumed the lead bombardier of the 96th had a good target solution, and swung *Gremlin Gus II* to the left to follow them. The rest of the 388th trailed behind.

As he continued to stare through the eyepiece of the bombsight, the cloud cover briefly thinned out, and Henry Dick thought he could make out one of the checkpoints he was looking for. Through the thick, creamy haze, there was no way to be sure, but he believed they were now on the right course.

A few moments later, the lead planes of the 96th made a turn to the right. Confident that he was now headed in the right direction to reach the target, Henry Dick continued to steer the lead plane of the 388th on their original course.

The five bomb groups coming behind them, the 94th, the 385th, the 95th, the 100th, and the 390th, all fell into line behind the 388th. As the formations began to diverge, the umbrella barrage intensified, and 88-millimeter cannon rounds began to find their mark.

Wolf Pack, flown by Lieutenant Eddy Wick, had already lost one engine, and he was trying to keep up on the remaining three when a flak burst exploded beneath them, knocking out a second engine. Out of control, the plane began flying straight up in the air for several agonizing moments before falling away.

Eddy Wick was trying to regain control of the Fortress when its right wing was blown off by another shell burst. Ralph Jarrendt's crew saw five chutes open before it disappeared through the clouds.

As *Gremlin Gus II* neared what Henry Dick hoped was the bomb release point, the cloud cover again thinned long enough for him to see that they were already past the target area. It was too late to release the bombs.

Now that he was sure he knew where they were, he requested that he be allowed to make another run on the target. Ralph Jarrendt passed the request along to the 388th group leader, Major Satterwhite, who was riding in the copilot's seat. By then, the 96th and the 388th were widely separated. Satterwhite rejected the request for a second bomb run and ordered Jarrendt to rejoin the 96th.

Flying behind Jarrendt in *Slightly Dangerous II*, the Greek was getting increasingly frustrated. When were they going to drop? Why were they circling so long over the flak belt? Who was running this show?

As the 388th turned right to rejoin the 96th group, its low squadron lost yet another bomber. *Sky Shy* was alone in the second element after

Silver Dollar went down. Mike Bowen had already lost one engine in the first fighter attacks, and was desperately trying to keep up with the rest of the planes.

With his top turret gunner dead and both waist gunners wounded, he planned to drop his bombs and then head for Switzerland. A flak shell suddenly exploded directly under their fuselage and knocked out his elevator controls. He ordered his crew to bail out.

A Ride in the Whirlwind

Stuttgart, Germany
303rd Bomb Group
Satan's Workshop
Brigadier General Robert Travis
0949

I t might have been his first combat command, but from General Travis's steadiness in the cockpit, he might as easily have been taking his wife and children out in the family car for a Sunday drive.

Sitting in the copilot's seat next to Major Lew Lyle in *Satan's Workshop*, he had spent most of the mission making notes on the large clipboard that rested in his lap. As they approached Stuttgart, the thirty-seven-year-old general was poised to unleash the biggest bombing strike mounted by the First Bombardment Wing so far in the war.

Close behind *Satan's Workshop* was the rest of the 303rd, packed snugly into the first combat box, along with the 384th in the low position and the 379th in the high. Behind them were six more bomb groups. Even with all the mission aborts, General Travis still had nearly 160 Fortresses to destroy the Bosch Works in Stuttgart. Eighty thousand pounds of high explosives dropped in the right place would level them.

So far, the mission had gone according to plan. After reaching German airspace, Major Lyle had briefly led the First Wing off its predesignated course to avoid a concentrated flak barrage, but the 303rd was still on schedule when it arrived at the initial point of the bomb run over Stuttgart.

From the copilot's seat of *Old Squaw* in the second element of the

303rd's high squadron, Lieutenant Bud Klint gazed out at the vista ahead of them. It was an unbroken carpet of white vapor, almost like newly fallen snow, stretching as far as he could see.

Tucked into the same lead combat box, Jimmy Armstrong glanced around at the other elements of the 384th, three, six, nine, all of them in good, tight formations. Being an element leader was proving to be tough on the twenty-one-year-old's nerves, but so far he was holding his own.

When First Lieutenant Norman Jacobsen, the navigator of *Satan's Workshop*, reported on the intercom that they had reached the initial point of the bomb run, Major Lyle handed over control of the plane to the group's lead bombardier, First Lieutenant Jack Fawcett.

Moments later, the bomb bay doors of *Satan's Workshop* slid open. It was the signal for the other fifty-three Fortresses in the first combat box to open theirs as well. Ordinarily, it took no more than a minute or two before the first payload was released from the lead plane once they were on the bomb run.

Lieutenant Fawcett would release his bombs first. After the lead plane dropped its bombs, the rest of the bombardiers would drop theirs as each element of the staggered formations passed over the drop point. Once all the bombs were away, the train of Fortresses would turn together in the same tight formation and head for home.

Crouched over his Norden bombsight in the nose compartment of *Satan's Workshop*, Jack Fawcett immediately confronted the same obstacle faced by Lieutenant Henry Dick.

Straining his eyes through the eyepiece at the stratus cloud cover below them, Fawcett was unable to acquire a fix on the Bosch Works. Finally, he reported on the intercom that Stuttgart was totally obscured.

General Travis pondered the problem. It was the most important command decision he had ever made. Should he continue trying to find the primary target or move on to hit one of the secondary targets?

This was his first chance to prove himself in the air. He knew that Hap Arnold was back in London waiting for the results of the mission. The First Wing had been ordered to attack the Bosch Works because of its strategic importance, and they had come a long way to do it.

According to intelligence estimates, the factories down there were producing 90 percent of Germany's magnetos and fuel injection nozzles.

Cloud fronts often broke up pretty quickly. If they circled over the target and made another bomb run, his bombardier would hopefully be able to make a visual observation of Stuttgart's prominent topographical features in order to lock onto the primary target.

"We're going around again," he told Major Lyle.

Flak bursts began erupting around the formation as Major Lyle put *Satan's Workshop* into a big sweeping turn to the left. It was a simple maneuver for him to swing the Fortress around in a full circle. It was no easy task, however, for the long train of bombers in their tightly constructed combat boxes to stay in formation behind him.

Satan's Workshop quickly became the hub of a gigantic wheel.

The pilots of the Fortresses on the outer rim of the wheel faced the biggest challenge. They had to dramatically increase speed in order to keep up in the tightly packed formation. For the pilots on the inner rim of the wheel, it meant slowing down to almost stall speed in order to stay in place.

As the long bomber stream began circling over the Stuttgart flak batteries, the bomb bay doors of *Satan's Workshop* remained open. To the rest of the bombardiers, this indicated that a bomb release might be imminent. They waited with their fingers on the toggle switches to drop their own payloads right after the lead bombardier.

If a pilot on the outer rim of the wheel wanted to save fuel by attempting to swing in closer to the hub, it meant coming under the open bomb bay doors of General Travis and the rest of the 303rd, and no one knew when Lieutenant Fawcett would drop his payload. They all stayed out on the rim.

It reminded Jimmy Armstrong of the child's game he had once played called crack the whip, in which the kids would hold hands and the leader would tear around in a circle, forcing the children at the end of the tail to run faster and faster until they fell away.

Yankee Raider was on the outer rim of the combat box and Jimmy had shoved the throttles forward to almost takeoff speed in order to stay in his element leader position. It was not only putting a big strain on the engines but draining gas at the fastest rate possible.

In the waist compartment of *Yankee Raider*, Reb Grant stared out at the little patch of sky he could see through the fuselage as he searched for enemy fighters. To Reb, it was obvious that the German 88s were beginning to find their range.

The flak explosions were getting thicker all the time, and the plane was bucking wildly. At least there weren't any enemy fighters around. He assumed they were waiting out there beyond the flak belt like a pack of coyotes to wade in on the stragglers when the barrage ended.

Bob Travis remained calm and unruffled as *Satan's Workshop* was repeatedly rocked upward by the concussion of the flak bursts. He had been monitoring the fuel situation. With its new Tokyo tanks, their plane could fly another thousand miles if necessary.

After finally completing his 360-degree turn, Major Lyle came in for their second run on the target. Once more, he turned over control of the plane to Lieutenant Fawcett, who again stared through the telescope of his bombsight, desperately looking for the identifying features he had memorized from the photographs at the predawn briefing back in Molesworth.

It was unbelievably maddening. Aside from a few tantalizing hints of ground objects, the swirling cloud cover made it impossible to get his bearings. He stayed on the bombsight until he realized they must have passed over the target again, and then reported the bad news to Major Lyle and General Travis.

Bob Travis thought over his next decision. If anything, his determination to succeed had only grown stronger. He had been ordered to destroy the Bosch Magneto Works. That was what he planned to do.

"We'll go around again," he told Major Lyle.

Bud Klint watched *Satan's Workshop* bank into another broad sweeping turn to the left. In all his combat missions, he had never seen anything like this before. They were going around again with all their bomb bay doors open. It made absolutely no sense to him.

Bud continued to glance at *Old Squaw*'s fuel gauges. They were below the halfway mark, and at the bomber's accelerated rate of speed, he could almost visualize the fuel draining down the tanks. He wondered if General Travis knew how bad the gas situation was for the older-model B-17s.

Jimmy Armstrong had never met General Travis, and he had no idea what was going on. All he could do was try to keep the *Yankee Raider* locked into the increasingly ragged formation within the first combat box. As they banked around to the left a second time, Jimmy Armstrong turned to Rocky Stoner and growled, "When are we going to quit flying these cloverleafs?"

How long can this old crate take the strain? Jimmy wondered, keeping his eyes glued on the squadron leader's plane ahead and above him in the formation. How long can I take the strain?

Flying on only three engines in *Est Nulla Via Invia Virtuti*, Andy Andrews had fallen farther and farther back in the bomber train. After dropping out of the 306th group, he had temporarily joined the next one, and then the next, while Keith Rich, his copilot, continued to give him ominous reports on their fuel situation.

Something had definitely gone wrong up ahead. He repeatedly checked their compass while they completed the three-sixty. No one was talking about it on the radio. It was like they had been sucked into a giant maelstrom, aimlessly circling in this huge mass of orbiting planes over southern Germany.

Andy had been running the three remaining engines on full manifold pressure and maximum rpms to try to keep up with their full payload of two and a half tons of bombs, burning fuel by the minute.

Flak bursts were erupting all around them as *Est Nulla Via Invia Virtuti* drifted back toward the last group in the long train. Off to the left, a bomber suddenly burst into flames. Fire quickly engulfed the cockpit. He could see the copilot open the side window, as if he was planning to crawl out of the blazing mass. A moment later, he was hidden by the flames.

Andy thought of his favorite passage from the "Choric Song" of *The Lotos-Eaters: "All things have rest, and ripen toward the grave . . . ripen,*

fall, and cease. Give us long rest or death, dark death, or dreamful ease."
It wasn't much comfort.

He wondered which general was commanding this mission. Whoever it was, he was an idiot. Andy wasn't thrilled with generals anyway. On a previous mission, he had been informed that an infantry general wanted to go along as a passenger on one of the bombers to find out what it was like. The group commander had chosen Andy to give him the ride.

Fortunately, it was one of the uneventful missions, with light flak and few enemy fighters. After they landed back at Thurleigh, the infantry general had congratulated Andy on a successful mission. Later, the general had been awarded the Silver Star for flying it with them.

Screw the generals.

From the waist compartment of *Yankee Raider*, Reb Grant continued to scan the small patch of sky outside his port for enemy fighters. The flak seemed thicker than ever, and he noticed that what had once been a tight formation of bombers was now spread out across the sky.

The carefully constructed combat box formations were rapidly dissolving all along the length of the train as the elements, squadrons, and groups struggled to stay together.

Flak explosions continued to rock *Satan's Workshop* as Major Lyle concluded his second 360-degree turn. In the copilot's seat, General Travis seemed imperturbable. When they again reached the beginning of the bomb run, Major Lyle turned over control of the bomber to Lieutenant Fawcett for the third time.

Staring into his eyepiece, Jack Fawcett couldn't believe it. If anything, the cloud cover was thicker than before. He continued to try to acquire the target until he was sure they had again passed over the Bosch Works, and then reported the news.

This time there was little hesitation on General Travis's part. No one would ever accuse him of lack of determination.

"All right," he said. "Let's do it again."

Major Lyle swung *Satan's Workshop* into another banking turn to the left. The planes coming behind turned to follow him, all of them with their bomb bay doors still open.

Now that the flak batteries around Stuttgart appeared to be zoned in on the formation, Major Lyle began to take some evasive action. He put the bomber into a steep dive.

Bud Klint watched in amazement as *Satan's Workshop* headed down. All the planes in the combat box attempted to follow it as the lead Fortress dropped several hundred feet before leveling off.

Close behind *Old Squaw* in the last position of the high squadron, Lieutenant David Shelhamer was piloting *S for Sugar*. On the Schweinfurt mission, he had led an element of coffin corner. This fiasco was even more horrendous, he thought. They had circled three times with their bomb bay doors open, and were now being forced to do acrobatics over the target.

After making a turn to the left, *Satan's Workshop* banked into an extreme turn to the right. Shelhamer couldn't see into the lead cockpit, but he was certain that General Travis had to be flying the plane. Major Lyle had never done anything like this before. How the hell could they all follow him through extreme evasion tactics and still stay in the combat box?

Shelhamer had seen enough. They had now been over the target nearly thirty minutes. He ordered his bombardier to make certain there were no B-17s below them and to then salvo their payload of ten five-hundred-pound bombs. The bombs went out a few moments later, and the plane was suddenly much easier to handle. No one knew where the bombs had gone.

When *Satan's Workshop* began its fourth bomb run, Lieutenant Fawcett again took control of the plane and crouched over his bombsight. Through the dense mist, he thought he could see several oil tanks. He was turning the bomber onto a heading that would take them over the tanks when for some reason Major Lyle retook control of the plane.

Lieutenant Fawcett immediately turned on his cushioned bombardier's stool to flip off the rack switches that would prevent an accidental release of their bomb load. Unfortunately, he had left the bombsight switch on. Before he could reach the rack switches, the bombsight toggled the bomb release, and his bombs began to fall.

It was the signal that the rest of the bombardiers had been waiting for after flying thirty minutes with their bomb bay doors open. Most of the planes following *Satan's Workshop* dropped at the same point.

Lieutenant Fawcett was disconsolate. Sergeant Nordyke, the radio operator, had been looking through the open bomb bay after the release, and Fawcett asked him if he had seen where they went. Sergeant Nordyke couldn't be sure, but he said it looked like a town of some kind.

In *Old Squaw*, Bud Klint was watching a straggler trying to keep up on the outer edge of the circling formation. They had gone around so many times that many of the groups were now mixed up together. There was a sudden yellow burst of fire underneath the straggler as an 88 exploded. It began spiraling downward.

"Fortress going," someone called out on the intercom.

In one of his mission briefings, Bud and the other flight officers had been assured that just one flak burst in a thousand ever hit a Fortress, and that with the odds so greatly in their favor, it made no sense to take evasive action. It also made no sense that they would be required to circle so many times over a concentrated flak belt.

Bud found himself silently reciting the Lord's Prayer: *"Our father, who art in heaven, hallowed be thy name, thy kingdom come, thy will be done . . ."*

Then it was *Old Squaw*'s turn. Bud never heard the burst that hit them, but shrapnel ripped through the right wing and severed a fuel line to the right inboard engine. From the copilot's window, he could see precious gas seeping out along the lower edge of the wing.

In *Yankee Raider*, Jimmy Armstrong watched the planes ahead of him dropping their bombs, and ordered Wilbert Yee to get rid of theirs. He no longer cared if the bombs landed on the Bosch Works. At least they would fall on enemy territory, and then they could head for home.

What remained of the 384th's formation turned onto a northwesterly bearing toward France. They still had six hundred miles to go to reach their base at Grafton Underwood.

A few minutes later, the right inboard engine on *Yankee Raider* began to falter. Jimmy knew right away what had happened. With all the strain on it, the engine's supercharger had frozen up. He had no alternative but to throttle back. Down to three engines, he began losing ground to the rest of the group. His first opportunity to fly as an element leader had come to an end.

Jimmy's wingman, Lieutenant Russ Faulkner in *Lucky Thirteen*, slowly moved past him to join the next echelon of the formation. *Lucky Thirteen* was peppered with flak holes, but all four engines were still operating. Jimmy hoped Faulkner knew that he had tried his best in leading the element.

From his position in the left waist, Reb Grant had no idea they had been flying in circles, but he knew they had been over the target a long time. Although the flak was no longer as intense, occasional bursts were still exploding in the sky around them.

He had watched as one of the Fortresses in the formation above them exploded in a sudden bright orange cloud, just like a clay pigeon on a skeet range. Parts of the shattered bomber, hatch covers, guns, and bodies had fallen past *Yankee Raider*.

Suddenly, Reb heard a sharp crack, as if someone had hurled a rock against the side of the ship next to his gun port. A moment later, he felt a stinging pain in his upper left arm. Numbness began to spread down past his elbow.

Jimmy Armstrong came on the intercom to say that a flak burst had hit the plane, and that it had ruptured one of the fuel tanks. Reb found that he could still move his fingers. With all the other problems, it didn't seem important to report he had been hit, too.

At that moment, Lieutenant Carlin, the navigator, checked in on the intercom.

"Let's go to Switzerland," he said. "I can see the Alps from here."

Jimmy had no intention of going to Switzerland. There was plenty of life left in the old crate, he thought. He remembered the fuel transfer valves that were mounted on the front bulkhead of the bomb bay.

"Go back to those transfer valves and see if you can salvage the rest of the gas from the punctured tank," he told Rocky.

Silence resumed on the intercom as *Yankee Raider* slowly headed west in company with several other stragglers, all with different group markings, and all with feathered propellers or obvious flak damage that was slowing them down.

They were no longer part of the air armada. They were in the band of cripples.

Andy Andrews had also fallen farther and farther back in the bomber stream. Like most of the other bombers, *Est Nulla Via Invia Virtuti* had been hit by flak numerous times, but the damage hadn't been serious, and no one was wounded.

The plane was still carrying a full bomb load. Andy asked his bombardier, Bob Huisinga, if he could see anything through the clouds. Huisinga reported that he thought they were over a forest. Andy ordered him to jettison the bombs.

By then, he knew they weren't going to get back to England. He wasn't sure there was enough gasoline left in the plane to get back to the French coast. He discarded the idea of flying back at treetop level. The crew wouldn't be able to parachute out that close to the ground.

There were two options left. One was to fly as far as possible into France and bail out with at least some hope of escaping. The second was to head for Switzerland, which was less than a hundred miles to the south. But that still seemed to him like quitting. He decided they would head for France and get as far as they could before bailing out.

His decision was punctuated by an urgent cry on the intercom. It was his tail gunner, Henry Hucker.

"Number-four engine is on fire," he called out.

And the Sky Rained Heroes

Strasburg, Germany
388th Bomb Group
Gremlin Gus II
First Lieutenant Henry Dick
1010

L ead bombardier Henry Dick sat hunched over his bombsight and
wondered what could go wrong next. After being unable to find
the primary target at Stuttgart, he had turned control of *Gremlin
Gus II* back to Major Jarrendt, and the 388th had reconnected with the
96th Bomb Group southeast of Stuttgart.

Upon leaving the primary target, the 96th had swung around on a
westerly heading that led to the secondary target, a complex of armament factories near Strasburg, Germany. The 388th and the five bomb
groups behind it followed in staggered formation at twenty-three thousand feet.

The stratus clouds appeared to cover most of southern Germany,
but Henry Dick continued using his bombsight's telescope to try to
identify ground features that would give him a clue to where they were.

Captain Thomas Hines, who was the lead bombardier of the 96th,
was attempting to accomplish the same purpose. When his navigator
indicated that he thought they were approaching Strasburg, Captain
Hines fired a flare. The rest of the planes in the group opened their
bomb bay doors.

The flak batteries at Strasburg began throwing up flak as they came
over the area. Through a small break in the clouds, Hines spotted a topographical feature that looked familiar enough for him to set a course

for the initial point of the bomb run. He hoped it would lead to the backup industrial target they had come to destroy.

In *Gremlin Gus II*, Henry Dick still couldn't see anything through the clouds. The 388th was beneath and to the right of the 96th as they headed in. He assumed that Captain Hines had been lucky enough to have found a break in the clouds and was now locked on to the target.

Henry Dick looked up through the Plexiglas nose window and saw the lead plane of the 96th make a hard turn to the right. This was unusual. Once a formation was in the last seconds of a bomb run, it usually went straight down the alley with no evasive turns. Henry Dick wasn't sure if they were still on the bomb run as the 96th group suddenly moved into a position directly above the 388th.

Major Jarrendt, seeing what was happening, made a sharp right turn to avoid a possible catastrophe. The 388th and all the groups following behind it turned with him, breaking up the formation.

As the lead pilots maneuvered to get back onto the bomb run, Henry Dick attempted to discern what Captain Hines was aiming at. Through a fleeting break in the clouds, he caught a glimpse of open terrain. He couldn't see anything that approximated an industrial target.

Captain Hines released his bombs a few moments later, followed by the rest of his group. Henry Dick then dropped his bombs in the center of the 96th's pattern. The groups coming behind them followed suit.

It was only as they were leaving the target area that the cloud cover broke long enough for Captain Hines to see what they had bombed. They hadn't hit Strasburg. It was someplace surrounded by a forest. As he scribbled his mission notes, he wondered what town it might be.

* * *

Strasburg, Germany
388th Bomb Group
Slightly Dangerous II
Second Lieutenant Demetrios Karnezis
1020

The 388th had barely finished jettisoning their bombs when the Greek glanced down and saw a staffel of ME-109s coming up through the haze. As always, their rate of climb seemed astonishing.

Like a school of darting fish, the fighters swept past the slower-moving bombers, all of them keeping out of machine-gun range. They were ME-109s. He knew what would happen next. The fighters would make their base leg turn a few miles ahead, and turn back to hit them head-on.

The frontal attacks resumed with deadly ferocity.

In one of the first waves, three ME-109s came in together at the lead squadron, cannons blasting. The Greek's bombardier, Dick Loveless, fired a solid burst at one of them, and it blew up.

As they waited for the next pass, the Greek looked up at the plane ahead of him in the first element of the formation. It was *Shedonwanna?*, flown by Earl Melville. He saw a spurt of yellow flame blossom on the outer edge of its right wing. One of the fighters had done some damage.

"Mel . . . your number four's on fire," the Greek called out to him on the radio.

Earl was one of his good friends in the squadron. There wasn't time to get to know too many of the pilots. They came and went quickly, but Earl Melville had made it through the toughest raids, including Hannover, Kassel, and Regensburg.

He had that kind of "aw shucks" Jimmy Stewart personality, and it was real. He was always trying to help some other guy, particularly if he was having a hard time with combat. When the 388th had landed in Algeria at the end of the Regensburg mission, Earl had even befriended two Arab boys who begged him to take them back to England.

So far, *Shedonwanna?* was keeping up with the rest of the formation in spite of the engine fire. The Greek radioed him again, but Earl didn't respond. Inside his stricken Fortress, it was chaos.

Cannon rounds from the enemy fighter had not only set his out-board engine on fire but had shattered the nose compartment, setting off a second fire there. The nose gun was still functional, but the bombardier had bailed out without waiting for orders.

Earl Melville asked the radio operator, Sergeant Frank Aldenhoevel, to come up to help put out the fire and to man the nose gun. Aldenhoevel was in the midst of extinguishing the fire when the next wave of fighters came through, blowing off his foot and wrecking many of the ship's cockpit instruments. Trailing flame and smoke, Earl banked away from the rest of the squadron, and headed down.

Shedonwanna? quickly absorbed two more attacks. In one pass, the tail section was destroyed by a cannon round, killing Walter Creamer, the tail gunner. Knowing his plane was doomed, Earl ordered everyone to bail out, remaining at the controls long enough to give them a chance before the plane went into a spin.

The navigator tied a tourniquet around the thigh of Sergeant Aldenhoevel, pulled the rip cord of his parachute, and pushed him out the forward escape hatch. As he dropped through the sky, his body was rammed by one of the enemy fighters.

Earl Melville had waited too long. When the plane went into an uncontrollable spin, centrifugal force kept him pinned in the cockpit. He rode down in the burning Fortress.

The fighter attacks kept coming in regular waves of three or four as the Luftwaffe pilots vigorously attempted to break up the 388th's formation.

"Beecham's gone," said the Greek's copilot, Jack George, over the deafening racket of the machine guns. Bill Beecham had been flying alongside them on the right in *Impatient Virgin*.

Beecham was another good friend, and he had already seen enough combat action to last a lifetime. Over Hannover, he had been wounded when a 20-millimeter cannon round slammed into his cockpit. While his copilot was attempting to aid him, their plane had collided with the Fortress above them, shearing off the vertical fin of *Impatient Virgin's* tail section. Beecham couldn't bail out because his parachute had been shredded by the cannon shell. It was a miracle that they made it back.

Now he was gone, too. The Greek moved up into Beecham's number-two slot behind Roy Mohr, Jr., in *Shack Up* as the German fighters continued their all-out assault on the formation.

The gunners in *Slightly Dangerous II* were almost out of ammunition. One by one they reported in as their belts ran out, the top turret gunner, the bombardier, and the navigator. How were they going to make it across France? the Greek wondered.

Up ahead, a cannon round suddenly exploded on *Shack Up*'s right wing, opening up an eleven-foot hole and setting the inboard engine on fire. Another round from a fighter attacking from the side killed the ball turret gunner and wounded both waist gunners. As the plane lost power and began to fall away, Roy Mohr ordered everyone to bail out. Like Earl Melville, he and his copilot were trapped in the cockpit as the plane plunged to earth.

The Greek moved up to take Roy Mohr's position behind Ralph Jarrendt in the group's lead plane. Between attacks, he glanced down through the side window. The 388th's low squadron wasn't there anymore.

The Luftwaffe pilots had succeeded in breaking up the lead combat box.

The low squadron, or what was left of it, was now on its own. After the destruction of *Silver Dollar* and *Sky Shy*, only four bombers remained in the ragged formation. With each loss, one-sixth of the original firepower from the bombers' massed machine guns went with it.

Lew Miller, who had been leading the second element of the low squadron, was shot down next. He was halfway through his twenty-five-mission combat tour. Lew was from Colorado Springs and loved the high country.

The plane had absorbed several direct hits in the frontal attacks. Everyone up front, including the copilot, navigator, and bombardier, were dead or dying. Four chutes emerged from the back of the plane as it went into a steep dive. Lew would never see the high country again.

The last three Fortresses in the low squadron, *Lone Wolf, Patricia,* and *In God We Trust*, were still holding together when *In God We Trust* began falling away. After losing an engine, Dick Cunningham's bomber became easy prey for the swarming fighters.

In the top turret of *Patricia*, Joe Schwartzkopf was firing at a fighter coming in from one o'clock high. After it passed below them, he swung the turret around and saw that Cunningham's plane was missing. He reported the news to Ted Wilken.

Al Kramer, the lanky, easygoing pilot from Kew Gardens, New York, had led the low squadron all the way across France and Germany. Since leaving Strasburg, *Lone Wolf* had sustained heavy damage from both machine-gun and cannon rounds.

They had just crossed into French airspace when one of the enemy fighters delivered the coup de grâce, shooting out his cockpit instruments and setting the nose compartment on fire. While desperately trying to keep the Fortress from going into a flat spin, Kramer ordered his crew to bail out.

Warren Laws saw *Lone Wolf* plunge over into a steep dive. Several men emerged from the hatches of the plane and immediately pulled the rip cords of their parachutes. As the crew members slowly descended earthward, one of the ME-109 pilots flew toward the parachutes, firing his machine guns at the descending men.

Patricia was the last plane left in the squadron.

Est Nulla Via Invia Virtuti

"Number-four engine is on fire," tail gunner Henry Hucker had shouted out on the intercom, and Andy looked past his co-pilot, Keith Rich, to gauge the extent of the new damage.

Billowing clouds of black smoke were pouring out of the cowl flaps. The engine had probably been hit by flak at some point. Whatever the cause, it was now overheating and he had no alternative but to throttle back on it.

The last Fortresses in the long bomber train had already disappeared in the distance. *Est Nulla Via Invia Virtuti* was alone in the sky over Germany, a two-engine cripple.

His original plan had been to get as far into France as possible, but after circling Stuttgart three times at full manifold pressure and maximum rpms, Rich was no longer sure they had enough fuel to make it to France. Andy didn't want to go down over Germany.

He made his decision, telling the crew on the intercom that he was heading for Switzerland while they still had a chance to get there. He asked the navigator, Gordon Bowers, to give him his best compass bearing, and turned *Est Nulla Via Invia Virtuti* south.

"Fighters . . . twelve o'clock high!" called out Bob Huisinga from the nose compartment.

There were four of them, all Fw 190s, heading northwest to intercept the retreating bomber train. They reminded Andy of feral birds, as impersonal as eagles searching for prey. He knew how tempting a target *Est Nulla Via Invia Virtuti* must be with one propeller feathered and another engine trailing thick clouds of black smoke.

They came in one by one, rolling over with their bellies up to fire at the stricken bomber. Andy could see the tracers from the first Fw 190's guns arcing toward them. One round hit the propeller of the left outboard engine, but the engine continued running true as the fighter disappeared below them.

Andy remembered a poster that someone had once put up in the 306th's officers' club back at Thurleigh. It was designed to improve the morale of the pilots after several missions with heavy losses. The poster showed a ruggedly handsome actor uniformed as a B-17 pilot smiling into the camera. Below him were the words "Who's afraid of the new Focke-Wulf?"

One of the pilots in the 306th had taped a piece of paper to the bottom of the poster with the words "Sign here." Every flight officer in the group at the time had signed, including the group commander.

The second Fw 190 came at them using the same frontal approach. Again there was a burst of machine-gun fire and 20-millimeter cannon rounds, but this one failed to score a hit. The third and fourth fighters followed him in. Their aim was better. Several rounds hit home in the guts of the instrument panel, shattering several of the gauges.

If the fighters came back to play with them again, Andy knew it was the end of the line. Another hit to one of the remaining engines, and they were going down. But as the seconds turned into minutes, none of the four came back.

Maybe they were inexperienced pilots, Andy thought. Or possibly saving their ammunition for the bomber train up ahead. Whatever the reason, he was grateful for the reprieve.

To save gasoline, he put the plane into a power glide, and they began shedding altitude. When they arrived over the German city of Friedrichshafen at an altitude of ten thousand feet, its Luftwaffe antiaircraft batteries began hurling up a new barrage of shells.

This time, the welcome was focused solely on *Est Nulla Via Invia*

Virtuti. Again and again, the deadly black puffs exploded around them and the plane was buffeted upward.

Once more they made it through a concentrated flak storm.

As they passed over Friedrichshafen, Andy saw a deep blue lake stretching out to the west and south of it. He thought it might be Lake Constance. If so, part of it had to lie in Switzerland. But which part? From grade school geography, he seemed to recall that the most level part of Switzerland was in the northwestern part of the country.

He could see the gleaming snow-covered Alps looming up in the distance to their south, and called Gordon Bowers over the intercom to tell him that he thought they should turn right on a westerly heading.

Although there were no maps of Switzerland aboard the plane, Bowers was carrying an escape kit in the pocket of his flight suit. Along with a small pocketknife, a compass, and a bar of concentrated chocolate, it included a folded handkerchief that had a map of Europe printed on it.

Switzerland made up only a tiny section of the map, but as Bowers studied it, he became convinced that if they turned right over Lake Constance, they would end up over Germany again. After listening to his conclusions, Andy continued flying south.

As *Est Nulla Via Invia Virtuti* approached the foothills of the alpine range, he saw that they were going to have very little clearance over the tops of the peaks. Andy ordered the two waist gunners to lighten the plane by jettisoning all the machine guns and remaining ammunition into one of the snow-choked canyons. He told Bob Huisinga to destroy their Norden bombsight.

With a torrent of black smoke still streaming from the right outboard engine, the crew became nervous that they wouldn't make it over the high peaks. Vernon Scott, the radio operator, called Andy to ask if it would be all right for the crew to bail out.

"You guys could get killed doing that," he told them, immediately realizing the absurdity of his words after everything they had already come through. "Don't worry. We'll make it."

After clearing the alpine divide, they emerged over a broad grassy plain. In the distance, Andy could see a control tower and the intersecting runways of an air base. Soon, he could see planes parked on the aprons. From the nose compartment, Bob Huisinga scanned the base through his binoculars.

"There are swastikas all over the place," he called out excitedly on the intercom.

Andy was now sure they were in northern Italy. Banking quickly to the right, he asked Gordon Bowers to come up to the cockpit with the handkerchief map. While he waited, Keith Rich informed him that the gas gauges had all reached empty. *Est Nulla Via Invia Virtuti*'s engines would run out of fuel at any moment.

When Bowers arrived with the map, Andy spread it across one knee and examined it closely. From their position just south of the alpine range, it looked like there ought to be another large lake off to their right. The northern end of it appeared to be inside the Swiss border. He turned the plane onto a northwesterly course to find it.

"Fighter at six o'clock low," called out Henry Hucker from the tail.

With a sinking heart, Andy concluded that it must have been scrambled from the base in northern Italy. He berated himself for having ordered the machine guns thrown out to lighten the plane. Now they had no way to defend themselves.

As he watched, the fighter flew up alongside them on the left. Instead of a swastika on the fuselage, he saw a white cross on a red field. Swiss markings. The pilot gestured at Andy with his finger, repeatedly pointing down.

Ahead of them was the lake he had seen on the map. At the northern end of it was a small grass-covered field. Andy had never landed a Fortress on grass before, but with nearly all their fuel expended, and with their bombs and weapons already jettisoned, the plane was very light. He could come in low over the lake and use every bit of the field. With their tanks on empty, he had no choice.

In one of Andy's first briefings back in England, the pilots had been instructed that if they were ever to land in a neutral country, it was incumbent on the pilot to destroy the plane.

They had four thermite bombs aboard to do the job, each one

the size of a fruit can. The bombs had been manufactured for use by the Royal Air Force, and were simple to detonate. One struck the cap against a hard object, and within a few minutes the contents would burn white hot.

On the intercom, Andy told the navigator to set one off in the nose compartment and the radio operator to set off the second one behind the bomb bay. Keith Rich was to detonate the third one in the cockpit. Andy planned to climb out onto the left wing to ignite the last one over the gas tanks.

Coming in at lake-top level toward the grass-covered field, he saw that the place was ringed with troops, all carrying rifles. For a moment, he worried that the whole thing might be a German ruse, and that the Luftwaffe was looking to capture an intact B-17.

He was relieved when he saw they weren't wearing German uniforms. He got on the intercom for the last time to say, "I see soldiers everywhere and they all have guns. Go out with your hands in the air!"

With the dexterity of a former flight instructor, he brought the big Fortress's front two wheels down within a few feet of the lake's edge and brought it to a stop before running into the cordon of soldiers. Two more trucks filled with soldiers raced up to the plane.

The first three incendiaries had already been ignited and Andy was crawling out the side window of the cockpit to deploy the fourth one when one of the soldiers began screaming at him from the ground. Swiss German was a dialect Andy found incomprehensible, and he had no idea what the man was yelling.

Seeing so many rifles pointed at him from point-blank range, he thought better of igniting the bomb on the wing. Instead, he clambered back into the cockpit and set off his bomb next to the one set by Keith Rich. He used the forward belly hatch to reach the ground.

As Andy and his crew advanced toward the soldiers with their hands in the air, the scene was being witnessed through binoculars by a man standing on the balcony of a nearby lakeside hotel. Andy had brought *Est Nulla Via Invia Virtuti* down at Locarno on the edge of Lake (Lago) Maggiore.

The man on the balcony was portly and gray-haired, with a

well-trimmed mustache. His name was Allen Dulles, and he was the station chief of the United States Office of Strategic Services (OSS), the American spy network.

Dulles told an aide to arrange a meeting with the pilot of the Flying Fortress.

Theirs Not to Reason Why

Champigny, France
388th Bomb Group
Slightly Dangerous II
Second Lieutenant Demetrios Karnezis
1055

T hey were alone in the sky.

The Greek had no idea what had happened to the rest of the lead squadron, much less the rest of the 388th, or the other fifteen bomb groups in the once massive bomber stream.

It was every plane for itself.

The Greek felt played out. He had been piloting the plane more than five hours, first through the tedious process of assembling the bomber train, then the effort to find the primary target, followed by the meandering route to the secondary target, all the while trying to stay in close formation. Of course, it was no different for all the other pilots of the 388th, at least the ones who had survived so far.

He knew that the German fighters must have eaten their way straight up the food chain, starting with the low squadron, just as they usually did. He thought of Earl Melville, Beecham, Mohr, and the others who had gone down under the enemy fighter attacks. He could only hope that *Slightly Dangerous II* wasn't going to be one of the "Did Not Returns" in the postmission missing crew reports.

"Fighter . . . two o'clock high," his copilot, Jack George, called out on the intercom.

A fresh burst of adrenaline kicked in as the Greek saw the first

Fw 190 coming at them. It opened fire with its cannons, but passed beneath them without inflicting any obvious damage.

When the next one began its attack from the same quadrant, Jack George grabbed the hand grip of the copilot's window and slid it back. Pulling his Colt .45 semiautomatic out of his hip holster, he stuck it through the opening, aimed at the oncoming fighter, and began firing.

Against the noise of the wind and engines, the shots sounded like firecrackers, and the Greek burst out laughing at the sheer idiocy of it. By the time the fighter had rolled over and disappeared, the .45's magazine clip was empty. Jack turned and saw the incredulous look on the Greek's face.

"What? I had to do something!" he said.

If they made it home, the Greek looked forward to repeating the crazy story to the rest of the pilots back at the officers' club in Knettishall. If they made it home. At least six fighters were stalking *Slightly Dangerous II* as it continued its escape across France.

The Greek never saw the enemy pilot who put the next wounds into them.

Attacking from below, he fired directly into the Fortress's belly, raking it fore to aft with a full volley of cannon rounds. Over the engine roar, the Greek heard a loud hammering crash in the accessory section behind the cockpit, and the flight deck immediately filled with the sulfurous stench of an exploding shell.

A moment later, the steering yoke went dead in his hands. One of the rounds had severed the cable from the steering column to the hinged ailerons on the trailing edges of the two wings. The Greek could now only fly the plane using the elevator trim tabs and power controls. He put the Fortress into a steep dive as choking smoke began to fill the flight deck.

The top turret gunner had been standing behind the cockpit, his ammunition long gone. Seeing the steering column flop over, he grabbed Jack George's parachute, which was tied with a slipknot to the back of the copilot's seat. Dropping behind the flight deck, he crawled to the forward escape hatch, released the lever, and bailed out.

"We're going down to the deck," the Greek called out to the crew on the intercom. "Navigator, give me a heading."

"Two hundred seventy degrees," Lieutenant Frazier came back from the nose compartment.

Glancing across the cockpit, the Greek saw that Jack George's steering column was still upright and realized that his aileron controls must still be intact. He motioned to Jack to change seats. From the copilot's seat, he pulled the ship out of its dive and banked to the left to throw off his pursuers.

The next two attacks came in from the side and tail. Within a few moments, the machine guns in the waist and rear went ominously silent. With the forward machine guns already out of ammunition, the plane was defenseless.

Lieutenant Dick Loveless, the bombardier who had already shot down at least one enemy fighter with his .30-caliber machine gun, crawled up behind them in the cockpit. With his ammunition expended, it was safer on the flight deck than in the exposed nose compartment.

They were down to sixteen thousand feet when *Slightly Dangerous II* was nailed again by a fighter attacking from below. A cannon round ruptured the plane's hydraulic lines and pierced the oxygen tank behind the pilot's seat.

The combustible mixture exploded, and the Greek was suddenly breathing fire through his oxygen mask. Feeling his skin burning, he ripped the mask off, along with the rest of his head gear. As the fire began to spread through the accessory compartment, he knew it was time to go.

Without his earphones and throat mike, he was unable to verbally give the order to bail out. He ordered Loveless to find the navigator and for them to bail out together. He told Jack George to get out, too.

The Greek flipped the spring-loaded switch that set off continuous alarm bells throughout the aircraft, the signal for anyone still alive in the plane to bail out. Standing up in the smoke-filled cockpit, he turned to reach for his parachute. Like Jack George's, it was tied with a slipknot to the back of his seat.

The chute pack was smoldering, apparently hit by one of the shell bursts. He saw that there were three shrapnel slits across the front of the pack. He had never used a parachute before, and hadn't received any training in how to jump or when to pull the rip cord.

None of that would matter if the silk chute was fatally compromised. He forced the horrible image of free-falling three miles to earth out of his mind, and clipped the slashed chest pack onto the d-rings of his parachute harness.

He was about to leave when Jack George appeared through the smoke, returning to the flight deck after a frantic and unsuccessful search for his parachute.

"We've got to get out," shouted the Greek.

Jack George began yelling back at him as the Greek headed toward the forward escape hatch. With all the noise and smoke, the Greek thought he was telling him he was afraid to jump.

"Just follow me," shouted the Greek, heading for the open hatch.

Left behind on the flight deck, Jack George continued his desperate search for his missing chute. Surmising that the top turret gunner might have taken it, he began sifting through the large mound of spent brass shells and ammunition belts beneath the top turret. He found the gunner's chute buried under the litter.

Clipping it to his chest harness, he dropped through the belly hatch and immediately pulled the rip cord. The parachute billowed out above him, and he began gently floating downward. Below him, he saw four other parachutes, which meant that at least some crew members in the rear section of the bomber had also gotten out.

One of the enemy fighters was still circling. It suddenly dived toward the parachutes below him and the pilot began firing. With mounting horror, Jack George saw two of the crew hit by machine-gun fire, going limp in their harnesses. After a single strafing attack, the fighter disappeared.

Far below them all, the Greek was still in free fall, dropping at a speed of more than a hundred miles an hour. With each passing second, he wondered what would happen when he finally pulled the rip cord. Was the silk torn by shrapnel? Would it open cleanly?

He decided to postpone pulling the rip cord until the last possible moment. If he waited until he was closer to the ground, the rig would hopefully hold together long enough to give him a safe landing. If it didn't open, he would have but a few seconds before meeting eternity.

The Greek had studied enough physics to know that he had reached terminal velocity when the air began making a kind of cushion beneath him. By then, he was on his back with both legs above his head. The unzipped sheepskin-lined "bunny boots" he was wearing over his GI brogans were flapping wildly in the wind.

With less than a mile to go, the Greek decided it was time for his moment of truth. With the painted icon of his namesake and patron saint, St. Demetrios, snug in the breast pocket of his flight suit, he pulled the rip cord.

The white silk bundle burst out of the canvas chest pack and its shroud lines twisted upward. As the panels of the parachute filled with air, he could see that one of them was badly slashed, and several of the shroud lines were severed. Instead of the expected sudden jerk, he felt a mild jolt when the parachute opened, and he began slowing down.

Hearing the sound of airplane engines, he looked up to see the approaching bulk of *Slightly Dangerous II*. As it descended earthward, the derelict ship was still turning in a broad circle. At one point, it appeared to be heading straight for him, as if not wanting to be left behind.

The plane's bomb bay doors were still open. A cloud of black smoke was trailing out of the gun openings. The twin .50s in the ball turret were pointed downward. There was no sign of life in the waist area, and he wondered if the rest of the crew had made it out. Over the noise of the engines, he could hear the continuous sound of the alarm bells as the plane swept by him in its final death dive.

When *Slightly Dangerous II* hit the ground, there was an initial flash of light followed by an orange ball of flame. He slowly counted the seconds until the sound of the explosion reached him. Five seconds, which meant he was about a mile from the crash site. He reasoned that the Germans would probably head there first unless they had seen the parachutes and were following them instead.

In the distance, he could see a paved road, a winding blue river, and a small town lying beyond it. To his right, the gently sloping terrain ended in what appeared to be dense forest.

As the green earth loomed up below him, he knew he was traveling faster than he should be. He wished there was a shallow pond to welcome him, but it looked like a rock-strewn pasture.

He hit the ground so hard that he bounced, immediately knocking the air out of his lungs. For a minute or two, he lay on his back gasping for breath. When he could finally breathe again, he realized his back was throbbing with acute pain and he thought he might have cracked his spine.

In spite of the pain, there was no time to waste. Using his hands to gain support, he slowly got to his feet. After removing the parachute harness, he rolled the silk into a big bundle with his bunny boots and stuffed it all under some shrubbery.

Glancing around, he saw an old man standing at the edge of a country lane about fifty yards away. The man had a small child with him. They were both staring at him. Neither one made a move. It took the Greek a minute or two to hobble over to them. "Bosche . . . Bosche here?" he asked.

The Greek didn't speak French, but he knew that "Bosche" was a French slang word for Germans. In response, the old man shrugged and shook his head, no. The boy just stared up at him with wonder in his eyes.

He decided to head for the forest that he had seen from the air. With his coccyx bruised or possibly fractured, it took him several minutes to cover the distance with a slow shambling gait. Reaching the tree line, he turned to look back. The man and the boy had disappeared, but a German light weapons carrier was coming fast up the lane a couple hundred yards away.

He knew they had seen him as he struggled through the undergrowth of the woods, angling off to the left as he went. He heard the truck grind to a halt and stopped to look back through the foliage. Two German soldiers were walking toward the tree line, their rifles at the ready.

When he felt he was deep enough into the woods to avoid immediate capture, he used his hands to carefully lower himself to the ground. Fortunately, there was a dense thicket to mask him from view. He could hear the soldiers shouting to one another, but they weren't close. Ten minutes later, he heard the truck moving off.

The Greek knew he needed to make a decision before the soldiers in the weapons carrier returned with enough men to make an organized search of the woods. He spent a few minutes taking stock.

He was wearing his leather A-2 jacket over flight coveralls, and he emptied all the pockets on the ground. It wasn't much of a haul. Along with the St. Demetrios icon, he had a book of matches, a fingernail file, and two passport-sized photographs of himself in civilian clothing that were supplied by G-2 so identification papers could be more easily forged if he was lucky enough to connect with the underground.

The only other thing he found in the coveralls was a single stick of Beechnut gum. He removed the wrapper and began to chew. Wouldn't this make a good *Life* magazine ad? he thought. The simple pleasure of chewing the sweet stick of gum actually began to calm his nerves.

He checked his wristwatch. It was close to noon, and he imagined the 388th was probably nearing the French coast on their way home to Knettishall. There, they would go through a quick debriefing with the intelligence team, take a hot shower, and maybe get an evening pass to London. From past experience, he knew that his own bunk would be stripped, and his personal possessions boxed up by the headquarters staff before they got back.

It was time to move out. From a mile high in the air, the forest had looked pretty sizeable. Using the sun as a guide, he decided to head all the way across it and see where he came out.

After finding a stout wooden stick to help ease his back pain, he began walking west. The forest was overgrown with vines and creepers and grew increasingly dense as he made his way through. It would be hard for the Germans to find him unless they had dogs, he thought.

Hobbling along, the Greek began replaying the Stuttgart mission in his mind. It was definitely one for the history books, he decided, remembering the famous words from "The Charge of the Light Brigade":

> *Someone had blundered: Theirs not to make reply,*
> *Theirs not to reason why, theirs but to do and die.*

To the Last Beat of the Heart

The prospect was astonishing.

In almost a full year of combat against the American heavy bombers, Connie Mayer had never seen anything like it. Three hours earlier, he had watched the massive bomber train passing over on its way to Germany, a seemingly indestructible, twenty-mile-long formation of tightly knit combat boxes.

Now, as the Americans made their way back across France, the air controllers of the Luftwaffe air defense command vectored Jagdgeschwader 2 into an excellent position to intercept the returning Fortresses.

It was no longer a bomber train.

To the pilots of JG 2, it looked more like an African elephant stampede, with ragged formations of bombers strung out across the sky. Even during the Schweinfurt battle, the American bomb groups had maintained formation integrity while enduring the worst beating the Luftwaffe had ever dealt them.

Whatever had caused this force to disintegrate, it gave the fighter pilots an opportunity to inflict maximum damage on the strays and stragglers. Given another hundred fighters, they would have had a feast.

Three days earlier, Connie Mayer had enjoyed one of his best days in the air, single-handedly shooting down two Fortresses in less than an hour. Those two engagements had brought his victory total of American multiengine bombers to seventeen, but the stoic Mayer wasn't counting.

No matter how many B-17s he and his fellow pilots shot down, increasing numbers of them were attacking the Fatherland every month, and it was only a matter of time until the Americans had long-range fighters with belly tanks to escort them all the way to Germany and back. Mayer would do his best as long as he lasted.

At 1110, he was leading a staffel of Jagdgeschwader 2's Fw 190s ten miles northeast of Troyes in the Champagne-Ardenne when he waded into a cluster of bombers approaching from the southeast.

Attacking from twelve o'clock high, he rolled over and headed down toward his first quarry. Opening fire at a distance of thirty meters, he watched the tracer rounds from his drum-fed 20-millimeter cannons disappear into the bomber's cockpit before he passed beneath it.

By the time he had turned for a second attack, the stricken bomber had already nosed over in a dive, blowing up when it hit the ground near the village of Mailly-le-Camp.

He had posted his eighteenth bomber kill. He went looking for more.

Troyes, France
388th Bomb Group
Patricia
Ted Wilken
1117

Ted and Warren could see them coming.

It was a big swarm of fighters, twenty at least. They had inline engines. Warren hoped they were Spitfires, the ones promised in the premission briefing that would meet the returning bombers over France to escort them home.

They weren't.

The first waves of fighters were ME-109s. Several of them peeled off from the pack to attack *Patricia*. They each made only one pass before moving on to attack the formations coming behind. None of the cannon fire struck home.

The ME-109s were quickly followed by a staffel of Fw 190s. Warren counted at least fifteen of them, some with silver and black crosses on the fuselage, others with yellow and black checker markings.

Connie Mayer led the first element.

He closed on *Patricia* at 400 miles an hour and opened fire with a short burst from his cannons, passing beneath the bomber a few moments later. An immediate explosion rocked *Patricia*'s nose as one of the shells demolished the bombardier's plexiglass screen. Another shell ignited a fire in the compartment.

When Ted used his throat mike to ask for a damage report in the nose, Swede Johnson, the young navigator, said that the new bombardier was dead and that he was badly wounded.

Lyle Merrill, the top turret gunner, started down to the nose compartment to help Swede, but Warren told him to get back in the top turret and keep firing until the attacks ended. Desperate for more speed, Ted told Warren to take over the flight controls while he adjusted the mercury levels of the four superchargers to maximize their engine power.

Connie Mayer made his next attack on *Patricia* from below and behind.

With practiced dexterity, he raked the bomber's fuselage from the waist section to the nose. One of the 20-millimeter shells exploded behind the armor-plated seat backs in the cockpit.

A piece of shrapnel hit the ship's compass, spattering flammable fluid around the cockpit. One metal shard sliced into Warren's left arm. Another took off a small section off his finger.

"I'm hit . . . I'm hit," cried out Johnny Eichholz, *Patricia*'s eighteen-year-old ball turret gunner, on the intercom.

Ted called down to ask him if he could continue to man the gun, but no answer came back. In the radio compartment, Joe Schwartzkopf noted that the waist guns had also gone idle. Looking back along the interior of the fuselage, he saw that the two machine gunners were both down.

As acrid smoke began filling the flight deck from the fire in the nose compartment, Connie Mayer drove into them again with another frontal attack. One of the shells blew out a large section of the cockpit windshield in front of Ted, severely wounding him in the hands and face.

Behind him in the top turret, Lyle Merrill was hit in the chest by another round, killing him instantly. Warren turned to see his body collapse onto the floor of the flight deck behind the cockpit.

Ted's face was covered with blood. Icy wind flooded the cockpit through the shattered windshield, sending a foggy red mist through the air. The already wounded Warren found himself wondering how much of it was his and how much was Ted's.

Along with the blaze raging in the nose compartment, something ignited the fluid that had spattered the instrument panel, and the cockpit began filling with smoke. Mingled with the smell of melting rubber was the odor of burning flesh.

When the fire began to burn the back of his feet, Warren reached down for his parachute. He kept it under the copilot's seat so that he could occasionally kick it during the course of the missions to make sure it was there.

The fourth and final pass by Connie Mayer had severely damaged *Patricia*'s control levers and rudder cables. Fire was now all around them, burning Ted's hands as he clutched the steering column to try to keep the plane under control. *Patricia* began sliding over into a flat spin.

"Get out, she's going," Ted called to the crew over the intercom.

In the radio compartment, Joe Schwartzkopf grabbed his parachute from the deck and clipped it to his chest harness as *Patricia* slid over. The overhead escape hatch was directly above him, and he pulled the emergency lever.

The hatch dropped away, and with the strength of desperation he climbed through the narrow opening. The force of the wind slammed him into the vertical radio antenna. He held on to it for dear life.

For Joe, the stricken plane still seemed more solid and reassuring than the idea of falling through three miles of space by himself. The two-hundred-pound giant also had a distrust of parachutes, and had heard numerous stories of them failing to open. He decided to stay with the plane as long as he could.

Flames and smoke were belching out of the top turret when he lost his grip on the antenna rod and fell away, careening into the right wing before skidding off and falling into space.

After plummeting several hundred feet, he pulled the rip cord on the chute pack.

Nothing happened. He looked down to make sure that he had pulled it all the way out. The cord was no longer connected to the chute, but the canvas pack remained tightly sealed as he continued to drop through the sky.

The ground was rapidly getting closer when he used his hands to rip the canvas cover open, and its white silk innards escaped into the sky. He felt a surge of relief when the parachute blossomed above him.

Ted remained at the controls of *Patricia*, trying to keep it in the air long enough for the others to all get out. When Warren started down toward the forward emergency hatch, the catwalk between the flight deck and the nose compartment was a mass of flames.

No one could be alive in the compartment now. Groping across the deck in the smoky haze, he found the emergency lever and pulled it. The hatch dropped away from the plane.

Joe Schwartzkopf was staring up at *Patricia* as he slowly fell earthward. The ship was now in the grip of a flat spin, and he wondered if anyone else had made it out. Suddenly, he saw the forward escape hatch door come sailing past him. A few moments later, a man came out of the forward belly hatch headfirst.

Warren pulled the rip cord as soon as he was out of the plane. There was a tremendous jolt as it filled with air, and he immediately slowed down. For the first time, he realized how badly injured he was. Along with the burns to his face, long shreds of skin hung loose from his fingers and hands.

Still inside the cockpit, Ted knew he had only moments to get out. The heat was excruciating. Like Warren, he had already suffered burns to his face and hands. Fighting centrifugal force, it took all his athleticism and endurance to reach the open belly hatch from the cockpit in the spinning plane.

Olivier Mauchamp, a young French farmworker, was plowing a field at the edge of the Grange-l'Évêque near Montgueux when his horse suddenly took fright. He looked up to see an American bomber falling out of the sky. The plane was trailing fire and black smoke.

As he watched, an aviator dropped through an opening in the forward part of the plane. A few seconds later, the aviator's white silk parachute opened like a gigantic umbrella, and he began to drift earthward.

Above the man in the parachute, the flaming bomber was skewing crazily as it came down, slowly closing the distance to the man who had just escaped it. Olivier watched as the bomber caught up with the parachutist, narrowly passing over him.

One of the plane's propellers appeared to hook the shrouds of the parachute. A moment later, the air was gone out of it. Olivier could only watch with mounting horror as the bomber slammed into the ground, towing the aviator behind.

He grabbed his bicycle and rode straight to the scene of the crash. The plane was on fire when he reached it, and unexpended bullets were still going off. Ted Wilken was lying dead on the ground near the plane, his parachute still attached to the propeller root.

A mile away, Warren landed in an open field of hard-packed dirt. He was attempting to remove his parachute harness with his burnt fingers when he heard the roar of an approaching fighter plane, and looked up to see an Fw 190 diving toward him.

Pulling up at the last moment, Connie Mayer roared past him at a height of twenty-five feet. Warren could see his face before he disappeared into the distance a few moments later.

At first, he thought the pilot had been planning to machine-gun him and had run out of ammunition. Then, Warren wondered if he might have been performing some kind of chivalrous act after shooting them down.

After shredding the loose skin from his fingers, he was finally able to remove the parachute harness. Leaving the chute on the ground, he began running toward a wooded area that might hopefully provide temporary cover.

He had reached the edge of the thick undergrowth when he saw a man in a green uniform lumbering toward him. If it was a German soldier, Warren knew there was no point in trying to hide. He stood and waited.

When the man came closer, he saw that it was Joe Schwartzkopf.

With Joe leading the way for the wounded Warren, the two of them crept through a thicket of bramble bushes on their knees. Behind them, two trucks full of German soldiers arrived. The two men continued crawling deeper into the undergrowth until it completely closed in around them.

There were more than a dozen German soldiers, enough for them to fan out in a long line and begin to search methodically through the wooded area where the Americans had hidden themselves. At one point, a soldier came within a few feet of their hiding place, but the bushes were so thick he didn't see them.

When the Germans had finally suspended their search and driven away, the two men sat up in their rabbit lair. Joe helped Warren remove his Mae West life jacket and his throat mike.

When Joe asked him about the fate of the rest of the crew, Warren said that he didn't think anyone else had gotten out, telling him that Ted had remained at the controls in order to give the rest of the crew a chance to bail out.

It was hard for them to believe that Ted was gone. He had seemed so indestructible. Unashamed, Warren began to cry. When he looked up, the big man was crying, too.

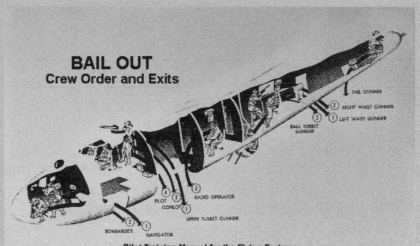

BAIL OUT
Crew Order and Exits

Pilot Training Manual for the Flying Fortress
**Published for Headquarters, AAF, Office of Assistant Chief of Air Staff Training
by Headquarters, AAF, Office of Flying Safety (circa 1943-44)**

<u>**How to Ditch the B-17**</u>

When an emergency develops and it becomes necessary to abandon the airplane in flight, there is no time for confusion or second guessing. Procedure of the entire crew in bailing out of the airplane must be almost automatic. Each crew member must know (1) his duties, (2) through what hatch he is supposed to exit, and (3) how to bail out, open his parachute, and land.

As airplane commander, your first responsibility is to be sure that your crew is thoroughly trained, by regular ground drill, in the proper procedure for bailing out of the B-17.

Before taking off on any flight make absolutely sure that:

- An assigned parachute, properly fitted to the individual, is aboard the airplane for each person making the flight.
- The assigned parachute is convenient to the normal position in the airplane occupied by the person to whom it is assigned.
- Each person aboard (particularly if he is a passenger or a new crew member who has not taken part in your regular ground drill) is familiar with bailout signals, bailout procedure, and use of the parachute.

Hard Landings

B ud knew they weren't going to make it.

Their fate had been ordained by the flak burst that ripped through the right wing of *Old Squaw* while they were making their third sightseeing trip around Stuttgart. The shrapnel holes in the right inboard feeder tank now meant there was no chance to reach England.

Heading away from Stuttgart at twenty-five thousand feet, they had been attacked by Fw 190s and ME-109s. Bob Hullar, *Old Squaw*'s pilot, took aggressive evasive action during the attacks. His superb flying probably prevented more serious damage to the plane, but the maneuvers ate up fuel at an even higher rate.

When their right inboard engine ran out of gas, the Fortress began lagging farther behind the bombers still left in the 303rd's original formation. The navigator estimated they were nearly halfway across France.

Bob Hullar told the crew to begin jettisoning any superfluous equipment to lighten the plane. The machine gunners retained enough ammunition to defend the plane in the event of more fighter attacks. The rest of it went over along with clothing, spare radio parts, and other gear.

North of Paris, the left inboard engine suddenly lost power. With two engines out, they could only drone along while the machine gunners scanned every quadrant of the sky for enemy planes. The minutes passed with agonizing slowness. Bud found himself reliving everything that had happened over Stuttgart. There was no excuse for it. The new general had run them out of gas.

He was staring west into the sky ahead of them when a squadron of fighters materialized out of the distant haze. The planes all had inline engines. His fear that they were ME-109s turned to elation when he saw they were Spitfires.

Two of them moved into formation alongside *Old Squaw* and radioed their willingness to mother the damaged bomber home. The offer was gratefully accepted.

When the French coast appeared ahead of them in the distance, it gave some of the crew members hope that they might make it to Molesworth.

Bud knew better. They had been rapidly losing altitude and were now down to a few thousand feet. Bob Hullar ordered the crew to jettison the remainder of the ammunition, along with the machine guns.

Out over the channel, the gas gauges reached empty.

There was an important decision to make. Should they bail out while there was still time or attempt to ditch the plane in the sea? If they did ditch, the plane might break up in the crash. If they ditched too close to France, they might get picked up by a German patrol boat and spend the rest of the war in a prisoner-of-war camp.

The plane's radio suddenly came alive with SOS messages from other B-17s.

"Mayday . . . Mayday . . . Mayday."

A lot of the B-17s on the Stuttgart mission were obviously facing the same critical fuel situation, and they were now jamming the assigned radio frequency with distress calls. The crews reported their positions and compass headings so that the English rescue boats would be able to locate them after they went down.

The decision of whether to ditch or bail out was settled in *Old Squaw* when the radio operator discovered that his parachute had been mistakenly jettisoned by one of the waist gunners, along with some spare radio gear.

A few minutes later, their third engine ran out of gas.

Neither Bud Klint nor Bob Hullar had ever ditched in the sea before, much less landed on one engine. As they dropped below five hundred feet, Bud remembered being told that if the plane hit a wave broadside, it was like flying into a concrete wall. He looked down at the sea. It looked anything but calm. The water was gray and rough, with long angry swells.

The crew carried out the prescribed ditching procedures, and then assembled in the radio compartment. The top escape hatch had been removed and stowed in the tail compartment. From the copilot's seat, Bud kept them informed on how soon they would be hitting the sea.

They were down to two hundred feet when the last engine died.

After more than six hours of continuous, ear-splitting noise, the plane fell eerily silent. Only the keening moan of the wind accompanied them as Bud feathered the last propeller and they glided down to the sea.

The Fortress was still making 80 miles an hour when it plowed into the top of a wave, shattering the Plexiglas nose and bringing *Old Squaw* to an abrupt stop. Seawater gushed into the open nose, surging straight through the forward compartment and up toward the flight deck.

With its gas tanks empty, the plane remained buoyant for a minute or two before it began to sink. The crew members crawled out of the top hatch of the radio compartment and out onto the fuselage. By the time the last man was through the opening, the water in the radio compartment was waist-deep.

Bud had climbed out onto the right wing to retrieve one of the plane's two rubber life rafts. Each one held five men. After inflating his life jacket, he opened the small bay where the starboard raft was stored and pulled it out. The raft was supposed to automatically inflate, but its CO_2 cartridge malfunctioned, and the raft was only partially full when he launched it in the water.

The sea was rough. Five-foot-high waves were breaking over the raft. When it got away from him, he had to jump into the sea to go after it. One of the crewmen, Pete Fullem, had fallen in the water and was rapidly tiring as he fought to keep seawater out of his lungs.

Bud was fighting the same swells, rising over the crest of each wave and then sliding fast down the trough behind it. When he saw Fullem drifting away, he swam after him, finally catching up and then slowly dragging him back to the raft. Norman Sampson, the ball turret gunner, thought it was one of the bravest things he had ever seen.

The men were in the rafts when *Old Squaw*'s tail section rose vertically up from the sea. Moments later, the ship slid down nose-first and disappeared under the roiling waves.

Unlike the many other Fortress crews that were ditching in the channel up and down the English coast, they were lucky. A rescue launch from Newhaven was patrolling the Beachy Head area where *Old Squaw* went down, and it arrived less than fifteen minutes later.

The entire crew was safely aboard by 1245. The captain of the rescue boat had orders to continue patrolling the same area for several more hours. While waiting for the rocking boat to head in to shore, Bud wondered how many planes in the 303rd group had made it home.

Molesworth, England
303rd Bomb Group
Satan's Workshop
Brigadier General Robert Travis
1320

The ground crews were all at their concrete hardstands, nervously awaiting the familiar roar of the approaching Wright Cyclone engines that would signal the return of the group. According to the projected return time in the operational orders, the planes were already late.

The 303rd's ground crews had sent off nineteen bombers in the maximum effort. Two of them had been forced to abort before reaching the French coast. Seventeen had gone on to the target.

They first appeared as tiny specks on the eastern horizon. When the specks in the traffic controllers' binoculars slowly grew into Flying

Fortresses, a siren began wailing, and ground personnel in crash trucks and ambulances rapidly took up stations along the perimeter tracks near the runways.

As the bombers approached the field, seventeen ground crews anxiously scanned the sky looking for their planes. The ground chiefs would only breathe a sigh of relief after their birds were back in their nests.

There were five Fortresses in the gangly formation. At first, they thought it might be a squadron, the first one to return. The bombers circled over the field and began to come in. Major Lew Lyle landed first, followed by two of the four squadron leaders, Captain George Stallings and Lieutenant Don Gamble.

It was the entire group.

Fears of a catastrophe were dispelled when Captain Stallings arrived at the briefing hut. Most of the group had survived, he assured the group commander. With many of the pilots running low on gas, they had been forced to land elsewhere.

"There were quite a few stragglers before we reached the French coast," Captain Stallings reported. "On the route home, everyone seemed to spread out and head for England."

Stallings's B-17 had only sixty gallons of gas in the tanks when he touched down.

In his own report, Lieutenant Gamble focused on the fuel situation as well, stating that he had eighty gallons left when he landed. "Everyone took off on his own making for the nearest airdromes," he said.

A number of news correspondents had come to Molesworth to interview General Travis after he led his first combat mission to Germany. Although he had been in the air for seven hours and twenty-five minutes, the young wing commander appeared to one of the newsmen as calm and relaxed, as if he had just finished a solid round of golf. In his spontaneous remarks, General Travis was highly complimentary of the mission and the men who flew it.

"If the weather had been better," he said, "it would have been a perfect mission. Despite that, we had to circle the target several times. Major Lyle did a wonderful job of flying that plane. I can't commend him enough for it. He was constantly talking to all crew members, pepping them up and reporting enemy fighters that were coming within range of our plane. He kept them on their toes all the time.

"It could have been a lot worse but those gunners of ours just raised hell with those fighters. Two of them just disintegrated in the air in front of us. The fighters were attacking us all the way to the target and back out, but our boys kept them out there pretty well. The flak was quite intense over the target, but Major Lyle took evasive action when it was necessary, and it didn't bother us much."

Major Lyle was asked about his own view of the mission.

"It was not really as rough as I thought it would be," he responded.

As to the bombing results, he said, "We dropped the bombs where they will do some good . . . I am sure of that. We had to take three passes at the target to do it."

The Last One Left

After more than seven hours in the air, they were on the final leg home.

They had been flying on three engines since the turbocharger on their right inboard engine had frozen up. According to the navigator, Creighton Carlin, they had already crossed a good chunk of Normandy and were definitely in range of the Allied fighter escort that had been promised in the premission briefing.

The French coast was less than fifty miles off to the northwest. If they could avoid enemy fighters the rest of the way, there should be enough gas to make it to the channel.

Jimmy had seen plenty of enemy fighters since leaving Stuttgart. He had watched two Fortresses go down under their cannon and machine-gun fire. Several fighters had made passes on *Yankee Raider*, and had scored hits, but none had been mortal. So far the venerable *Yankee Raider* had led a charmed existence.

After crossing into France, Jimmy had begun cloud-hopping along their northwesterly route to England. Clusters of big cumulus clouds were all over the sky, and they provided perfect cover as he hopscotched between them.

In the nose compartment, Wilbert Yee, the Chinese bombardier from Hawaii, gazed through the Plexiglas dome at them. Aside from being good cover, they were gorgeous, creamy white, and sculpted like marble. Each time the plane was enveloped inside one, he couldn't see anything but white mist.

Jimmy felt bone weary after the frustration of running at full throttle around and around the target with the bomb bay doors open, never knowing when the lead plane would drop its bombs, while he tried to maintain a tight formation with Higdon and Faulkner behind him on each wing, followed by the ferocious attacks from the German fighters.

The twenty-one-year-old knew it wasn't a good idea to dwell on the gloomy side, but it was hard not to on this mission. Jimmy's grandfather had been with General Custer's Michigan cavalry. On the Schweinfurt mission a few weeks earlier, he had wondered if the men who followed Custer to the Little Big Horn had felt as clueless as he did about the strategy for winning the aerial war against Germany.

He moved on to the next cloud.

Standing at his left waist gun, Reb Grant gazed out at the vista and wondered how long it would be until they got back to Grafton Underwood. He was hungry. The last thing he had eaten was the fish and chips meal he had wolfed down in Leicester before meeting Estella the previous afternoon.

His left arm was still numb from the flak wound over Stuttgart. Blood continued to trickle out of the blue heat suit he was wearing underneath his sheepskin-lined leather flight jacket. He hoped he would still be able to handle the kick of his machine gun if there was another fighter attack.

"Fahhghters at six o'clock high," drawled Clifford Hammock, the tail gunner from Arabi, Georgia, on the intercom.

The next round in their battle for survival had begun.

There were only two of them this time, both Fw 190s. Jimmy was almost relieved. Around Stuttgart, the fighters had been flying in packs of a dozen and more. As tired as he was, he felt confident they were going to make it. They had come a long way.

He put *Yankee Raider* into a dive toward the nearest cloud cluster as the fighters split up to make separate attacks. At least they weren't going to run out of ammunition, as had happened on the Schweinfurt mission.

Jimmy had made sure of that before takeoff. Extra crates of .50-caliber belts were stacked both forward and aft.

At the nose gun, Wilbert Yee tried to remember the things they had taught him in gunnery training, angle of deflection, trajectory, and all the rest. He could see the enemy tracer rounds lighting up the wings of the first fighter as it came in. He tried to lead it with the barrel of his machine gun, but it was only in his field of fire for a few seconds before it disappeared.

Jimmy was barely inside the first cloud cluster when the second fighter made its attack, weaving and turning as it raked *Yankee Raider* from the tail to the nose. This Luftwaffe pilot was good.

One of the cannon rounds exploded in the nose compartment, wounding Wilbert Yee. He felt the shards of hot metal slashing into his thighs and buttocks, narrowly missing his most important appendage. Blood began seeping through his pants as he waited for another chance to fire back.

Another 20-millimeter shell slammed into the left wing. Through the side window, Jimmy saw an eight-foot-long section of metal sheeting on top of the wing begin flapping up and down like a gigantic flag.

He tried to burrow deeper into the cloud cover, but the first enemy pilot seemed to divine exactly where he was going as the next attack came in from the other side of the plane.

In the top turret, Bruno Edman was blasting away at the twisting enemy machine with his twin .50s. The muzzles of his guns were just a few feet above Jimmy's head and the din was incredible. He kicked the rudder and put the plane into another dive in an attempt to throw off the enemy pilot's aim.

Reb Grant and Eldore Daudelin, the right waist gunner, were standing back to back in the waist compartment, firing at the fighters as they darted in and out of the clouds. Both men had fought in close quarters before, and had learned to move in synch like tango dancers, swinging their machine guns up and down, back and forth trying to make a kill.

The second Fw 190 again raked *Yankee Raider*'s fuselage with 20-millimeter cannon rounds. One of them exploded in the accessory compartment behind the cockpit, setting off a fire in a fuel line that crossed the fuselage in front of the bomb bay. A sheet of flame quickly spread from the bomb bay toward the flight deck.

Glancing out the window, Jimmy was startled to see one of the fighters coming up alongside them off the left wing, almost as if he was flying escort. Normally, fighters stayed far out of range, but this pilot must have been cocky. He was too far forward for the left waist gun to reach him, but perfect for the navigator's gun on the left side of the nose compartment.

"Carlin . . . open fire," he demanded on the intercom.

There was a pause before he heard Yee's voice.

"He's gone," said Yee. "He bailed out."

Jimmy felt a quick surge of anger. He had given no orders to bail out. How could Carlin have abandoned the crew? There was little time to dwell on it. The fighter was swinging around to make another attack.

Bruno Edman had left the top turret to try to quell the flames with a fire extinguisher. It was rapidly spreading toward the cockpit. There was no way to control it.

Jimmy could feel the heat of the flames searing the air behind his seat. It was time to get out. He called Redwing on the intercom and told him to come up out of the ball turret.

"Bail out," he ordered the rest of the crew on the intercom. "Bail out."

In the waist compartment, Reb waited for another chance to fire at the Fw 190s. He gripped the handle of the machine gun as tightly as he could with his numb left hand and fired another burst as one of the fighters hurtled past.

He felt someone poking him in the back. When he turned, Daudelin was pointing at his headphones and saying something to him. Reb couldn't hear anything. His earphones were dead. Daudelin then pointed at his chest harness, and began heading back to the rear of the compartment, where he had stowed their parachute packs.

Reb could hear the roar of a fighter coming in again from the other side, and waited for his opening to fire as it passed above or beneath the plane. A moment later, there was a sudden, blinding flash, as if someone had exploded a bomb in his right ear.

He found himself sitting on the deck, his back slumped against the curvature of the fuselage, his legs splayed out in front of him, surrounded by brass shell casings. Everything was suddenly quiet. He could see out of his left eye, but he couldn't feel anything. There was no pain. He wondered if he might be dead.

Walter House, the radio operator, glanced back from the radio compartment and saw him go down. He didn't know Reb's name, but called Jimmy on the intercom to tell him the new left waist gunner had been hit by a cannon round. It looked like half his head had been blown off.

In the copilot's seat, Rocky Stoner clipped on his chest pack and picked up his survival satchel from under the copilot's seat. The flames were right behind them. Jimmy told Stoner he would keep the plane steady until they were all out.

Stoner dropped down to the tunnel of the nose compartment. The belly hatch was already open. Bruno Edman had bailed out. Wilbert Yee was putting his chute on. Stoner went out next. Yee followed him.

In the tail section, Cliff Hammock had heard the order to bail out and was trying to get back into the waist compartment, but the compartment door was blocked by the two crates of .50-caliber ammunition Reb had stacked there. Hammock finally gave up and squeezed out of the emergency hatch in the tail.

Daudelin had clipped on his parachute and was returning with Reb's when he saw him sitting slumped on the deck, motionless. Looking down at his face, he was horror-stricken.

The cannon round had hit him in the right temple and come out through the front of his face, blowing out his right eye and most of his cheekbone. The eye was hanging out of its socket and resting on what was left of his cheek. Blood from the gaping wound had flowed down his chest and was coursing along the deck to the ball turret.

He began trying to clip on Reb's parachute, but his fingers kept slipping on the bloody chest harness. A few moments later, Walter House pressed past them from the radio compartment. His chute was strapped on, and he didn't linger. Right after he bailed out the side door of the waist compartment, the plane nosed over into a shallow dive.

"Get out," Reb grunted. "I'm done."

It was clear to Daudelin that Reb wasn't going to make it. Nodding, he left Reb's parachute pack next to him and followed Walter House out the side door, pulling the rip cord as soon as he exited the plane.

In the cockpit, Jimmy trimmed the plane one last time to keep it from going into a flat spin before he bailed out. He could feel his face and hands burning as he dropped down behind the cockpit and headed to the forward escape hatch.

He had done everything he could, he thought, dropping through the hatch feetfirst. When he looked up again, *Yankee Raider* was headed away from him, hurtling toward the ground trailing fire and smoke.

In the waist compartment, Reb was conscious, but too weak to move. He was sitting opposite the ball turret when it suddenly began to move through its retrieval rotation. The turret stopped and he watched the ball turret gunner climb out.

It was the little Hindu guy with the Lord Haw Haw accent. Like Reb, he had apparently never heard the order to bail out. When Redwing tried to stand, he slipped on the bloody catwalk and fell forward on his hands.

Taking in Reb's gruesome wound, Redwing's eyes registered the same shock as Daudelin's. It didn't last more than a few moments. Seeing the parachute pack lying next to Reb, Redwing clipped it to his chest harness, and pulled the rip cord on it. The parachute would open on its own as soon as he dropped Reb out of the plane.

After putting on his own chute, Redwing began dragging him across the compartment to the open doorway. Reb tried to tell him to get out, to save himself, but his voice was gone. He knew Redwing was trying to give him a chance to survive. He deserved a medal.

Redwing had reached the doorway when one of the Fw 190s came back for another pass, spraying the fuselage with machine-gun fire. Redwing jerked upward, hit in the chest. Letting Reb go, he collapsed to the deck. The bomber was pitching and rolling as it continued its final plunge to earth. As Reb watched, Redwing rolled out into space.

Reb was now closer to the doorway, but it was still too far to make it.

There were only seconds left before the plane went down. He felt himself going. I'm going to die, he thought. He discovered he wasn't afraid. He would go down with the plane. That would be the end.

Still floating in his parachute, Jimmy watched *Yankee Raider* plow heavily into an open field outside a small French village. As soon as it hit, the bomber was enveloped in a huge cloud of smoke and dust. He waited for the wreck to explode, but it didn't. There was no gas left to ignite.

A minute later, Jimmy hit the ground. He felt a brutal jolt of pain in his right ankle and tumbled backward. While lying on his back, he unclipped his parachute harness and rolled free.

When he tried to stand up, his right leg gave way and he fell down again.

SLIPSTREAMS

Generals Arnold and Eaker (far left) inspecting an air base, September 1943.

A clearly angry Ira Eaker lets it be known, 1943.

General Robert Travis (left) with General and Mrs. Maurice Preston, England, 1943.

Olen Grant relaxes with fellow sergeants, 1943.

False identity photograph taken of
Jimmy Armstrong by the French
underground, 1943.

Warren Laws, 1942.

Braxton Wilken, 1942.

Ted and Braxton Wilken, 1942.

COURTESY OF BRAXTON WILKEN ROBINSON

COURTESY OF BRAXTON WILKEN ROBINSON

Braxton and her daughter, Kathy, 1943.

COURTESY OF BRAXTON WILKEN ROBINSON

Warren Laws's false identity papers prepared by
the French underground, 1943.

Joseph Schwartzkopf's false identity papers prepared by
the French underground, 1943.

COURTESY OF MARTIN ANDREWS

Martin Andrews while interned in Switzerland, 1944.

Demetrios Karnezis and Marie Therese Andre,
France, 1943.

Robert Travis and William Calhoun shake hands after
the Oschersleben mission, January 11, 1944.

James Armstrong receives the Purple Heart, 1944.

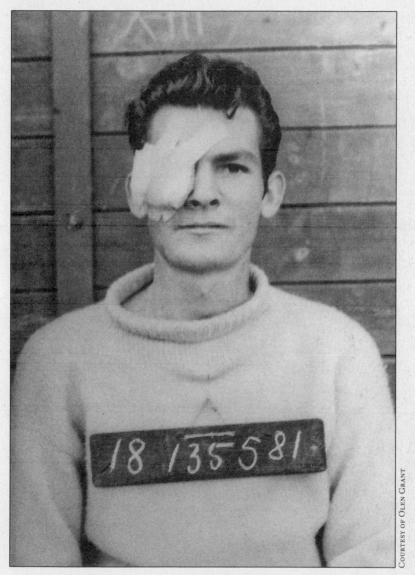

Olen Grant's prison photograph, Stalag 17, Krems, Austria, 1944.

Remains of the Day

Monday, 6 September 1943
Grafton Underwood, England
384th Bomb Group
Colonel Budd Peaslee, Commanding
1330

All their eyes were on the eastern sky as the scheduled time approached for the 384th's return. Colonel Budd Peaslee stood on the railed widow's walk at the top of the control tower and anxiously scanned the horizon through his binoculars. The scheduled arrival time came and went with no sign of the group's eighteen Fortresses.

Budd Peaslee had commanded the 384th since its arrival in England back in June, and he had led many of the group's toughest missions himself. He had agonized over the calamitous loss of half his original crews in July and August. He had watched good pilots crack up under the strain and tension of what they had gone through, and he privately wondered how long they could go on.

He considered the Stuttgart mission to be an important milestone. For the first time in the war, more than four hundred bombers had participated in a maximum-effort raid deep into Germany. Major Ray Ketelsen had led the mission, and he was an experienced combat leader. He would bring them back.

As the minutes passed with no sign of the group, Colonel Peaslee's level of apprehension began to mount. The fuel factor had been calculated very carefully prior to the mission, and there was little margin for error.

A voice suddenly called out. Two planes were approaching the base. They were Fortresses. With growing shock, Colonel Peaslee realized they were the entire remnants of the 384th that were able to return to the base. Two out of eighteen. He watched the two B-17s land and rumble across the field to their hardstands.

Eighth Air Force Bomber Command
High Wycombe Abbey
Brigadier General Frederick Anderson, Jr., Commanding
1400

Fred Anderson was anxiously awaiting the first reports on the Stuttgart mission.

It was Hap Arnold's last full day in England before flying back to Washington, and Anderson's direct superior, Ira Eaker, was eager to deliver good news about the strike to General Arnold before his departure.

Across southern England, intelligence officers in each of the sixteen bomb groups were conducting postmission interrogations of the bomber crews. After each Fortress landed, the crews were sent straight from their hardstands to the briefing huts.

The intelligence officers were responsible for compiling an accurate account of each group's performance, including how many tons of bombs were dropped on the intended targets, how many enemy fighters had been engaged and possibly destroyed, how intense the enemy flak had been along their flight path, and how many Fortresses and crews were lost or missing.

Fresh recollections were critical to gleaning the truth. Among other things, crew members often witnessed the last moments of other B-17s, which helped the intelligence branch determine where they had gone down, and if any parachutes had been seen.

Once the debriefings were completed, the information would be collated into a preliminary group summary, a "Flash Report," and sent by Teletype to Eighth Air Force Bomber Command at High Wycombe, where it would be incorporated into a preliminary report being compiled for the entire attacking force.

Under the meticulously planned operational orders, all the bomb groups had been projected to return to their bases by 1330. Flash Reports were to be forwarded to High Wycombe by midafternoon.

For this mission, the information-gathering process was taking longer than expected, because scores of fuel-starved bombers had landed at other airfields after reaching England. They had to be refueled before the flight crews could return to their own installations and be debriefed.

This pushed back the timetable for General Anderson to complete his comprehensive report. He wouldn't be able to provide General Eaker with a mission summary until late that afternoon or evening.

Entrépagny, France
384th Bomb Group
Yankee Raider
1400

A truckload of German troops arrived at the crash site of *Yankee Raider* within fifteen minutes of it slamming into the ground. The sugar beet field where it crashed was very close to a small French airfield now occupied by the Luftwaffe.

Accompanying the first German soldiers to the site was Robert Artaud, a fifteen-year-old French youth who was employed at the local hospital and drove its ancient ambulance. Along with many other villagers, he had seen the bomber circling overhead while under attack from the German fighters.

After watching it fall, he drove straight to the scene. Smoke was still billowing out of the front cabin, but the rear section of the aircraft, including the waist and tail, looked relatively undamaged.

The Germans had already found one dead crew member lying on the ground near the plane. He was wearing a parachute, but its rip cord had not been pulled. The man wore a wedding ring and his dog tags identified him as James H. Redwing. There was a bullet wound in his chest.

One of the soldiers climbed onto the wing and opened the storage bay in the fuselage where its life rafts were stored. He quickly retrieved the cartons of American cigarettes from their waterproof containers, while other soldiers looked through the cockpit windows for the pilot who had crash-landed the B-17.

Robert Artaud approached the right side of the aircraft with great trepidation, wondering if it might still explode. Through the open hatch, he saw a man in a leather flying suit lying inside.

When the aviator suddenly moved, Robert shouted to one of the soldiers. Together, they brought the man out and laid him on the ground. His head and face were terribly mutilated, and he had obviously lost a great deal of blood, but he was still alive.

The officer in charge of the party ordered two of the soldiers to escort the wounded American to the local hospital. Robert ran to the ambulance and brought back a stretcher. He assumed the man had to be the pilot since they had found no one else inside. The plane couldn't have landed itself.

The two Germans carried the American to the ambulance. As Robert was leaving the crash site, the rest of the soldiers were already stripping the aircraft of its machine guns and other valuable equipment.

The boy hoped that the brave American pilot wouldn't die.

London, England
Claridge's Hotel
General Henry H. Arnold
1630

Hap Arnold was worn out.

Since arriving in England, he had maintained an arduous schedule of fifteen-hour workdays, during which he met with dozens of the

Allied commanders, visited training and maintenance facilities, and inspected many of the bomber and fighter groups.

Earlier that day, Arnold had flown up to Burtonwood, where nearly ten thousand American mechanics and support personnel repaired and maintained the aircraft engines so vital to the fighter and bomber arms.

Afterward, he enjoyed a working lunch at the Savoy Hotel in London, where he was briefed by British commanders on the aerial battle against German U-boats in the North Atlantic as well as the latest intelligence on the Russian front.

He spent the remainder of the afternoon in a leisurely shopping excursion with Ira Eaker, who escorted him to several exclusive shops where he could find special gifts for his family and close friends.

By the time the two generals returned to Claridge's, it was 1630. General Arnold went up to his suite to rest before dinner. A nervous General Eaker still waited for word from Fred Anderson on the results of the Stuttgart mission. The inordinate delay seemed ominous.

For General Arnold's last night in England, Eaker had planned a sumptuous supper party at Claridge's. In attendance would be thirty-six senior Allied army commanders and diplomats in the European theater, including Air Chief Marshal Sir Charles Portal; Marshal of the RAF: the Viscount Hugh Trenchard; Air Chief Marshal Sir Arthur "Bomber" Harris; Lord Louis Mountbatten; Air Marshal Sir Trafford Leigh-Mallory; Roosevelt's emissary W. Averell Harriman; the American ambassador, John G. Winant; the diplomat Anthony Drexel Biddle, Jr.; and Lieutenant General Jacob Devers, the overall commander of U.S. Army forces in Europe.

General Eaker had made sure his staff pulled out all the stops to make the evening memorable. His dog robbers had done an extraordinary job acquiring the aged beef, fresh seafood, fruit and vegetables that would make it a memorable occasion.

In addition to a substantial array of fine wines, Kentucky bourbon, and other spirits, each guest would celebrate General Arnold's visit with after-dinner toasts and Eaker's favorite hand-rolled cigars.

* * *

Entrèpagny, France
Sergeant Olen "Reb" Grant
1700

He regained consciousness in what appeared to be a cellar, with low whitewashed stone walls. It was very cold. He realized he was naked and wondered what had happened to his blue heat suit and warm leather flight jacket.

He was lying on a white metal table, and there were people standing around him. They were talking to one another in loud voices, but he didn't understand what they were saying. He faded out again.

Champigny, France
Second Lieutenant Demetrios Karnezis
1500

The Greek had hobbled through dense forest for more than an hour, his coccyx in continuous pain as he meandered slowly westward. When he came to the far edge of the forest, he paused to observe the landscape ahead of him.

It was open farmland. The crop had already been harvested. There was a single farmhouse in the distance, maybe five hundred yards away. Its roof was shining in the late afternoon sun. Next to the house was a barn and several other outbuildings, all connected by low stone walls.

He waited in the silence of the trees and watched, but no one went in or out. He saw no farm animals or vehicles. There was no activity of any sort, which finally gave him the confidence to approach the house.

It was very quiet in the packed-earth courtyard behind the stone walls. No faces appeared in the windows. He slowly walked to the nearest door. Without knocking, he turned the handle and pushed it open.

He was looking into a stone-floored kitchen. A woman of about forty was standing by the sink under the window. A girl, maybe seventeen, was sitting at the kitchen table. Apparently, they had just finished a meal. There was bread and a bowl of fruit on the table.

They both stared at him, seemingly awestruck. Finally, the woman motioned him to come inside. As soon as he closed the door, both of them began speaking to him in French. He couldn't understand what they were saying.

The girl offered him the bowl of fruit and he took a piece and ate it. The woman poured him a glass of red wine. He shook his head and pointed at the sink. Then he saw there was no running water.

He haltingly tried to explain that he was an American pilot, but they already seemed to have figured that out. Seeing him hobble across the stone floor, the woman realized he had injured his back and found cushions for one of the kitchen chairs. After he sat down, she brought over a hand mirror.

When he looked at himself, the Greek was forced to laugh out loud. Most of his face was flash-burned and looked like it was covered with charcoal. When he rubbed his upper lip, his carefully nurtured Errol Flynn mustache fell away in flakes of black dust.

He began to wonder if she would turn him over to the Germans as soon as she had the chance. Then the woman removed a jar of ointment from one of the kitchen cupboards and began applying it to his burned hands. There was kindness and sympathy in her eyes. He decided to trust her.

A few miles away from the farmhouse, the Greek's copilot, Jack George, was walking along a macadam country road, still dressed in his flight suit and Mae West. He was distraught at the murder of the crew's two waist gunners by the strafing fighter, and no longer cared what happened to him. A car came up behind him, slowed down, and stopped. Two men were inside. One of them motioned him over.

Eventide

Eighth Air Force Bomber Command
High Wycombe Abbey
Brigadier General Frederick Anderson, Jr., Commanding
1830

What was he supposed to do now?

The thirty-eight-year-old Fred Anderson was career army, a graduate of West Point, and mindful of the potential missteps that could break a man's career on the path to high command.

His immediate superior was Ira Eaker, and Anderson owed him plenty. He had been a staff colonel when Eaker asked him to join the Eighth. Anderson hadn't even served as a group commander before being given command of an entire wing.

Now he had overall command of the Eighth's bombers, receiving the promotion two months earlier when Arnold demanded that Eaker fire Anderson's predecessor for failing to be aggressive enough in the bombing campaign.

Anderson had witnessed all the vitriolic cables passing back and forth between Eaker and Arnold during the period when they seemed to spend more time fighting one another than the Germans.

He had helped Ira Eaker plan the new campaign against strategic targets inside Germany. After Schweinfurt, Eaker had been reluctant to continue it without long-range fighters. Anderson agreed with him. Now they had more evidence of the rightness of their position.

But Hap Arnold ran the corporation.

In about an hour, Anderson would be joining both generals at

Claridge's for the dinner in Arnold's honor. At some point, he knew that General Arnold would ask him for the results of the Stuttgart mission. As head of bomber command, it would be his job to provide the details.

He had already sent the preliminary summary of the results to Ira Eaker at his headquarters at Bushy Park, about fifteen miles southwest of London. After reading the report, Ira would hopefully give him some guidance on what to tell Hap Arnold.

There was no way to sugarcoat this one.

Of the ninety-one operations undertaken by the Eighth Air Force since the commencement of daylight precision bombing in 1942, Stuttgart was the worst failure of the war.

Based on the interrogation reports from all sixteen groups, not one of the bombers that attacked Stuttgart had claimed to hit one of the intended targets specified in the operational orders, principally the Robert Bosch factory complex and the SKF instrument-bearing plants.

Of the 338 Fortresses that had taken off from the sixteen air bases that morning, 44 of them, nearly 15 percent of the entire force, had aborted the mission before reaching the French coast due to reported mechanical and instrument failures. Another 32 bombers had crossed the enemy coast but failed to reach the target due to other causes, including reported bad weather or navigation error.

Of the 262 Fortresses that had reached Stuttgart, nearly 50 were still unaccounted for. Although a handful of them had landed at airfields where they were still unable to make contact, at least 45 had been confirmed as shot down or otherwise lost.

Forty-five bombers out of 262 meant a loss of more than 17 percent, the highest of any mission yet undertaken in the war, even worse than Schweinfurt.

But they had hit the target at Schweinfurt.

Eleven B-17s had been destroyed in the 388th Bomb Group alone. Its entire low squadron of six Fortresses had been wiped out. The 92nd group had lost seven bombers, the 305th and the 384th, five each.

A dozen Fortresses had been forced to ditch in the English Channel when they ran out of gas. Fourteen had landed at small RAF fighter strips along the coast, the first fields they had found after crossing the coast. Two were wrecked in crash-landings when the pilots ran out of gas in search of an airfield. Another five Fortresses had apparently attempted landings in Switzerland.

By any description, it was a disaster.

If even a few of the Fortresses in the two bomb wings had managed to hit the principal targets, he could at least make a case that the heavy losses were worth it. In truth, the majority of the B-17s had bombed "targets of opportunity," which in many instances were identified as "a forest" or "a farm community." Most of the bomber crews had no idea where their bombs went.

The one positive element of the report was that the crews claimed to have destroyed ninety-eight enemy fighters along with twenty probable kills. It was a good result, although fighter claims had to be discounted because more than one machine gunner would usually be firing at the same fighter at the time it was destroyed, and they would both naturally claim to have shot it down.

Before the dinner at Claridge's, Anderson needed guidance on how to characterize the mission results to General Arnold. It was no exaggeration to conclude that his future might be on the line.

Entrépagny, France
384th Bomb Group
Second Lieutenant James Armstrong
1830

It was damp and cold in the briar patch.

While lying there, he considered a number of different strategies for making his escape from occupied France. The problem was that all of them required an ability to walk.

That didn't seem to be a likely possibility anytime soon. Since making his hard parachute landing, Jimmy's right ankle had swollen to twice its normal size. He could only hope it wasn't broken. When he had tried to stand up after hitting the ground, he fell over on his face.

Yankee Raider had gone down only a mile or two away from where he had landed. He knew that after the Germans searched the plane, they would immediately start looking for the missing crew members. He needed a place to hide until the pain in his ankle receded enough for him to walk on it.

Next to the field where he had landed was a small copse of woods. He had crawled to it on his hands and knees. Near the edge of the tree line, he had spied a massive thicket of briars, intertwining vines and stems that rose almost five feet high and extended a hundred feet into the woods. He doubted that the Germans would be thrilled about going in there to search for him. He could only hope they didn't have blood-hounds. The dogs wouldn't care.

As he began to wriggle and burrow into the briar patch, he remembered that this was Labor Day, the first Monday in September. Back in his hometown of Bradenton, Florida, they celebrated the holiday with picnics and an air show.

Well, he had participated in an air show all right, but this was no picnic. He didn't have any food, and he kept being stuck with painful pricks from the nettles and thorns inside the patch.

It took a long time for the six-foot, two-hundred-pound pilot to penetrate halfway in. He finally stopped to take stock of his situation. He was bareheaded, wearing a leather A-2 jacket over woolen trousers, khaki uniform blouse, and high-top shoes. He hadn't bothered to bring his army-issue Colt .45.

Among the few things he found of possible use in his pockets were the little compass he carried on each mission and a small escape hand-kerchief on which was printed a map of France. He knew he was north-west of Paris. If he walked far enough southeast he would hit the Seine River and could follow it straight into Paris. Paris was supposed to be full of resistance fighters.

Even if the pain in his ankle subsided, he was worried about drawing unwanted attention after starting the journey. He knew his face was badly swollen from the burning cockpit. That would be sure to attract notice, along with his badly burned hands. He would need help from somebody.

Above all, Jimmy didn't want to be captured and spend the rest of the war in a German prisoner-of-war camp. The way things were going, the war was bound to go on for a long time.

Through the rest of the afternoon, he lay quietly in his lair and waited. Aside from birdsong, he couldn't hear a thing. No German search parties, no bloodhounds, no vehicles, no human voices.

As night fell, he became hungry and thirsty. He hadn't had anything to eat or drink since around five that morning back at the officers' mess in Grafton Underwood. He wished he was back there now, sinking his teeth into a ham sandwich and enjoying a glass of beer. He thought about leaving the lair to try to find water, but then became worried he might not find his way back.

The moon came up, allowing him to see the dense assemblage of vines and stems surrounding him in the thicket. His ankle was hurting worse than ever, and the damp cold made his burns ache. He seemed to be a magnet for spiders, ants, and other tiny creatures, but they didn't bother him.

In the morning he knew he had to find water. He hoped he would be able to walk far enough on his bad ankle to reach it. There was nothing else he could do for now but rest. He fell into a fitful sleep.

London, England
Claridge's Hotel
General Henry Arnold
2200

The mahogany table was fifty feet long. Its starched, white damask linen tablecloth was covered with an array of Claridge's best china and flatware. Sterling silver candelabras threw off warm cones of candlelight every five feet along the spine of the table.

The elegant supper had been absolutely splendid, with each course prepared by Claridge's superb chefs with the provisions supplied by the dog robbers on Eaker's headquarters staff.

The guest of honor appeared to be enjoying himself immensely.

In the spirit of Allied cooperation, the thirty-six British and American guests were intermingled. No French commanders had been invited. Air Chief Marshal Sir Charles Portal sat on Arnold's right, with Ira Eaker on Arnold's left. Marshal of the RAF: the Viscount Hugh Trenchard and Air Chief Marshal Sir Arthur "Bomber" Harris were also close by. He had easy access to his closest intimates, both English and American.

Air Marshal Sir Trafford Leigh-Mallory was sitting at the end of the opposite side of the table next to Brigadier General Fred Anderson. Leigh-Mallory had just been chosen to become commander of the Allied Expeditionary Air Force, which included both RAF units and the U.S. Ninth Air Force. He was immensely proud to be commanding American medium bombers.

Leigh-Mallory found himself increasingly charmed with Arnold, whose self-deprecating personal style was in stark contrast to some of Leigh-Mallory's English colleagues. He thought Arnold was a "grand" raconteur and storyteller.

Sitting next to him, Fred Anderson was nervously waiting for Hap Arnold to ask him about the Stuttgart mission. When the question came his way, he was ready with his answer, but there was at least some hope that the subject wouldn't even come up. Arnold and the senior commanders were covering far more important strategic issues. Maybe the Stuttgart mission would be forgotten under their weight.

Arnold was having a particularly frank discussion with Lord Trenchard, who had been just as instrumental in establishing the Royal Air Force in its infancy as Arnold had been in creating the modern U.S. Army Air Forces.

They were both known as the "fathers" of their respective air forces, and Arnold admired him greatly. Trenchard had been an early advocate of strategic bombing, and his words at the dinner were sweet music to Arnold's ears. At seventy, the old man hadn't seemed to have lost his edge.

During a lull in the general conversation, Arnold turned and asked Fred Anderson how the day's mission had gone.

Anderson smiled and said, "The bombing results were excellent, sir."

He had decided not to provide specifics. Thankfully, Arnold didn't ask for any.

General Anderson added that the excellent results had come at high cost.

"We lost over thirty planes," he said.

Strictly speaking, he was telling the truth. Eighth Air Force Bomber Command had lost more than thirty Fortresses that day. The actual number was forty-five, which Anderson well knew.

Arnold did not press him on the point. Losses were inevitable, especially now that they were going after Germany's industrial base. To Arnold, excellent results meant the Eighth Air Force had pasted the ball-bearing factories in Stuttgart, and were that much closer to destroying Germany's capacity to wage war.

Later, over Ira Eaker's excellent cigars, there were toasts to General Arnold, to Prime Minister Churchill, and to President Roosevelt. At 2230, General Arnold excused himself from the gathering and headed upstairs to his suite.

All in all, he had found the inspection trip a profitable use of his time. Most important, he had lit a fire under Eaker and his staff. Back in Washington, he could never rely on the information and reports that came up through regular channels. He needed to be there to get the full story.

After retiring to bed, he was briefly awakened by something he hadn't heard in London since his visit in April 1941 at the height of the blitz. It was pitch dark in the suite, but through the thick blackout curtains he could hear the mournful wail of air raid sirens. Unlike 1941, they were not followed by the roar of exploding bombs and the bark of antiaircraft fire.

They didn't disturb his dreams.

The Day After

Andy Andrews found himself tormented with guilt at what had ensued after he had landed *Est Nulla Via Invia Virtuti* in the grass airfield at the edge of Lago Maggiore. For one thing, none of the four British thermite bombs he and his crew had ignited to destroy the plane had worked. They were all duds. A serviceable B-17 was now in another country's hands.

He had failed.

He felt even greater guilt at having taken the plane out of combat. His copilot, Keith Rich, attempted to reassure him that he had made the right decision. With two engines out along with most of their fuel, they would probably have gone down over Germany. The crew was grateful, Rich told him. He had heard them cheering after *Est Nulla Via Invia Virtuti* touched down alongside the lake.

None of it relieved Andy's gloom.

After they were arrested by the Swiss troops, the crew had been brought to a Swiss military installation. In response to a question from a Swiss intelligence officer about the details of their combat mission, Andy told him that he had no idea what the man was talking about.

"Then what are you doing in our country?" demanded the Swiss officer.

"We're tourists," said Andy.

This appeared to amuse the Swiss, but they continued to demand answers.

"I can tell you nothing until I've spoken to a U.S. military attaché," he said finally.

That evening they were transported under guard to an empty school in the nearby town of Bellinzona. They were each given blankets, and they spent the night sleeping on the floor.

The following morning they were put on a train to Zurich. Andy was told by a Swiss officer that they would be questioned further at Dübendorf Air Base, the headquarters of the Swiss Air Force.

He was sharing a compartment with the other three officers in his crew. The train had just left the station when the interior door of the compartment slid open, and a portly, middle-aged man stepped inside. Gray-haired with a trim mustache, he was wearing an expensive European-style suit.

"May I speak to the pilot of the U.S. plane that landed yesterday in Magadino?" he asked.

The Swiss had evidently agreed to allow the man to have access to them. Why? He appeared to have a refined American accent. Andy suspected that the man might be a spy.

When Andy said that he was the pilot, the man introduced himself as Allen Dulles, a fellow American, and shook his hand. He asked Andy to join him in his compartment for a private conversation. Intrigued, Andy went with him.

When they were alone, Dulles told Andy that he was the station chief of the United States Office of Strategic Services (OSS), the American spy network in Europe. He was using neutral Switzerland as his base of operations for intelligence gathering on the Continent. His operatives ranged across Germany, France, and Italy, seeking the latest data on Axis military operations.

A cautious Andy responded by saying, "Look, Mr. Dulles, I'm sure you're for real and I've heard of your brother John Foster Dulles, but until I meet the military attaché here in Switzerland, I can't tell you anything about what I was doing yesterday. I'm perfectly willing to talk about my boyhood in Wisconsin or about my days in college, but not about what I did yesterday."

He could tell from Dulles's smile that the old man liked that. Andy didn't know that Dulles was already considering using him as an undercover agent for a secret mission that would be as important as any Andy had flown with the Eighth Air Force.

Dulles wanted to know more about his personal background, and Andy spoke about his classical education at St. John's College. Dulles seemed impressed with Andy's facility with languages, and his ability to recall the long passages in Latin and Greek that Dulles asked him to recite.

For his part, Dulles began talking about his childhood in Auburn, New York, and his own student days at Princeton. He confided to Andy that he was returning to Bern after a clandestine meeting with Allied agents in Locarno.

In Zurich, the two men shook hands. Dulles wished him luck.

Tuesday, 7 September 1943
Entrepagny, France
384th Bomb Group
Jimmy Armstrong
0600

Jimmy awoke desperately thirsty.

It had been twenty-four hours since he had a cup of coffee in the officers' mess at Grafton Underwood shortly before the mission briefing. Almost a lifetime ago, as it turned out.

With the first hint of dawn, he began wriggling out of the briar patch. Reaching the end of the thicket of vines and thorns, he attempted to stand up again. The pain in his right ankle was searing, but he found he could make forward progress by taking one step at a time with his left foot, while keeping as little weight as possible on the right.

He searched the landscape for a stream or a farmer's well. There was nothing promising as far as he could see. He began crossing the wide field. There was no one about. He wondered how a Frenchman would react to seeing him dressed in his flight suit with burned face and hands, and hobbling along like a crippled old man. Would he help or turn him over to the Germans?

A building slowly emerged from the haze at the far end of the field. It was an imposing-looking château, and he decided not to approach it. Jimmy had attended escape training classes at Grafton Underwood, and he remembered one of the instructors telling them to stay away from rich landowners, because they had more to lose and were more likely to turn him in.

His ankle was breaking down again, and he decided to head back to the protection of the briar patch while he could still make it. The sky was much lighter now. While recrossing the field, he spotted what appeared to be a shallow drainage ditch. Coming closer, he saw there was water in it. The flow was less than two inches deep, but it was welcome just the same.

Jimmy followed the ditch back to the protection of the tree line and sat down to drink. He was greedily swallowing the brackish water when he heard someone coming through the woods. His immediate thought was that it might be a German soldier who had seen him crossing the field.

When the figure emerged through the trees, Jimmy saw it was an old white-haired man wearing a black beret and knickers. He appeared to be just as startled as Jimmy.

The man took in his flight jacket and burned face.

"*Allez*," he said loudly, pointing deeper into the woods. Jimmy sensed that "*allez*" meant go. He stood up again and hobbled deeper into the woods. With the pain in his ankle, he didn't make it far before stopping.

Turning around, he saw that the man had disappeared. He sat down with his back to a tree and waited. If the man had gone to turn him in, there was no way he could escape anyway.

Less than an hour later, the old man was back. He was carrying a pan of beef stew in brown sauce with carrots and potatoes. It was accompanied by a chunk of bread and a jug of red wine. Nothing had ever tasted better to him.

Through a combination of sign language and a few common words, Jimmy understood that the Germans were still looking for him, and had searched all the houses in the area. Taking the empty pan, the man indicated he would bring more food the next day.

Jimmy nodded and said, "Mersey bo-coop." The man went away again.

He spent the rest of the day making a crude bed of leaves and branches. His pillow was a tree root covered by his A-2 jacket. He had another night of fitful sleep. The next morning, the man came back with more food.

His name was Gaston Viguier, and he was a French army veteran from World War I who had fought at Verdun. He detested the German occupiers. He made it clear that he would continue to bring food as long as he could.

Although Jimmy was anxious to get moving, he decided that the respite in the woods was a good thing. He would probably need to walk a long distance, and he developed a daily regimen to slowly strengthen it by walking short distances in the woods. Each day his ankle would feel a little stronger.

On the second night, he awoke to the slow, steady patter of raindrops. Soon, it became a downpour, washing away the little umbrella of branches and leaves he had erected over his sleeping place. He could only pull the collar of his leather A-2 jacket tightly around his neck and endure it for the rest of the night.

The hours passed with agonizing slowness. Apart from the old man and an occasional glimpse of another villager passing along a nearby country road, Jimmy saw no one.

He missed the familiar sound patterns of his former life. The woods were silent except for birdsong and the occasional rustling of leaves by small forest creatures. His only other stimulation was the chimes from a bell tower in the nearby village. They tolled every hour and had a calming effect on him, particularly through the long nights.

Twelve o'clock and all's well.

Solitude wasn't all bad, he eventually decided. He just wasn't used to it. For all of his twenty-one years, he had been part of a family, or an athletic team, or a college club, or the air force. This was the first time he had ever been truly alone.

It gave him time to think about many things. He hoped his mother wouldn't be too distraught when she received the telegram that he was missing in action. He thought about the guys back in the 384th and wondered if they had already forgotten him, as he had quickly forgotten other pilots after they had gone down. In combat, one never dwelt on the past, only the next mission. He wondered about the existence of God, and found comfort in prayer.

If he made it back to England, he knew there would be no more combat missions, at least over Germany. It was strict air force policy that any pilot who successfully escaped from Nazi-occupied Europe was transferred out of the theater.

All he had to do was escape.

On Tuesday, September 14, eight days after Jimmy had been shot down, Gaston Viguier brought him his daily pan of food, along with some somber news. It was hard for Jimmy to follow it all, but the Germans had apparently searched the houses in the vicinity again, and Gaston's neighbor had come to see him after they left. He said he knew Gaston was bringing food to an escaped American, and that if the Germans asked him, he would tell them the truth to avoid being shot.

The old man said he must go.

Jimmy understood he had to go, but where?

"Paris," the old man said, pointing across the field, as if the city were just down the road. Jimmy took out his pocket compass and the handkerchief map. After glancing at the map, Gaston pointed southeast again toward the Seine River.

"Mersey bo-coop," said Jimmy in his slow Southern drawl.

Gaston had brought a small sack of food for the journey. They shook hands, and he headed off. After eight days, his right ankle now carried him with just a slight limp. His burned hands were still oozing fluid, but they were healing, too.

All he needed to do was reach the Seine River. It would take him straight to Paris. Once he was there, he hoped he would meet someone who could connect him to the French underground.

Regularly checking his compass, he followed a succession of paved and dirt roads for the rest of the day. No cars or trucks passed him by, and the occasional person he saw was far enough away not to take notice.

He passed through villages so small that they consisted of only a few stone cottages. They all appeared to be deserted. It began to strike him as quite amazing that a dirty, unshaven American pilot in his flight uniform could walk for miles across the French countryside without exciting the slightest curiosity. Maybe the Good Lord was looking over him after all.

As evening approached, he saw a large barn looming in the distance, and decided it would be a perfect place for a good night's sleep. It had been a long time since he had last slept under a roof, much less in a bed.

In the course of his travels, he had discovered something new and potentially valuable in one of the pockets of his coveralls. It was a single sheet of paper, and consisted of a list of phrases written in French, with an English translation underneath each one.

The first phrase was *"Je suis un aviateur américain."* I am an American pilot.

Jimmy couldn't wait to put it in the hands of the next person he met. Beyond the large barn was a white farmhouse. There were two small children playing in the front yard. When he began walking toward them, one of the children shouted. A few moments later, the front door opened and a woman came outside. Jimmy assumed she was the children's mother.

He thrust the phrase sheet into her hands. She examined it for several moments.

"Allez," she shouted at him, clearly frightened. *"Allez . . . allez."*

"Mersey bo-coop," said Jimmy, smiling as he moved off, praying she wouldn't report him to the Germans.

He spent the night in another grove of trees farther down the road.

Continuing his journey the following morning, he walked for most of the day before deciding to stop at another farmhouse near the road.

A man of about fifty was churning butter next to a small outbuilding as Jimmy walked up to him. Without trying to say anything, he placed the phrase page in his hands. It took no more than a few seconds to generate a reaction.

The man's face lit up with pleasure, and he began to dance around the butter churn. After he called into the farmhouse, a woman in her eighties came outside to join them.

In broken English, the man explained that they were White Russians, and their family had settled in France after the Russian Revolution. He gave Jimmy a glass of milk and told his mother to go inside and find suitable clothes for him. She came back with a black cap, an old white linen shirt, black trousers, and a patched black suit coat.

After Jimmy had changed out of his uniform, the man gave him some quick lessons in how to walk like a Frenchman. He mimicked Jimmy's long, sauntering stride, and shook his head that this wouldn't do. Then he began walking around the yard with short, mincing steps.

Jimmy practiced in step with him for a few minutes, and the man pronounced himself satisfied. His last gift was a few French coins, along with a small satchel filled with apples, onions, and bread.

"Mersey bo-coop," said Jimmy in genuine appreciation.

With evening approaching, he came over a hill and saw the Seine River valley stretching out below him. A town lay ahead of him at the edge of the river, and he walked toward it with the short, quick steps. Proud of his new disguise, he headed down the main street, which was filled with shops and people.

Stepping into the first café, he decided to buy a drink with the French coins to quench his thirst. A pretty young barmaid stood behind the counter. There were no other customers. He attempted to use sign language along with his phrase sheet to communicate his order.

He could see the growing alarm in her eyes. Suddenly, she began shrieking at him in French at the top of her lungs. A moment later, she was rushing out the front door into the street, screaming for help.

It was hard to know which of them was more frightened as he followed her outside. Maybe it was the eight days of growth in his beard and the hobo's clothes. Maybe she thought he was a thief.

By then, a man walking by the café had taken her by the hands and was trying to calm her. When she saw Jimmy coming, her fearful cries resumed with a vengeance. Jimmy was still gripping his French phrase sheet in his hand, and held it in front of the man's face.

The man glanced at the first line, *"Je suis un aviateur américain,"* and looked back at him with almost instant sympathy. Still holding the barmaid's hands, he motioned to Jimmy to move along.

With the short, mincing steps, Jimmy hurried down the street toward the river. He decided to forget about a cool glass of beer. He settled for another round of brackish water before resuming his journey to Paris on foot.

He spent that night in an orchard, finishing the provisions given to him by the White Russian Samaritan. The next morning, he began walking again. As the hours passed, he remembered another recommendation he had received from the intelligence officer who had conducted the escape classes back at Grafton Underwood.

"Make your approach to people or homes that are distant from any others," Lieutenant Celentano had told them. "If the people raise an alarm, you will have time to escape."

The next farmhouse was definitely isolated from its neighbors. When he approached the side door near the driveway, he looked through a kitchen window and saw a young woman peeling potatoes.

When she came to the door, he removed his peasant cap and said, "Bonn-jorr," hoping it wouldn't send the girl into a screaming fit. He heard another voice behind her in the kitchen, and a well-dressed matronly lady stepped forward to join her at the doorway.

Jimmy held up his crumpled phrase sheet, and in butchered French attempted to tell her he was an American aviator. She still seemed confused, and he showed her the dog tags hanging from his neck.

At that, the lady smiled. A few minutes later, he was sitting down to the best breakfast he had enjoyed since leaving the States. In broken English, the woman introduced herself as Madame Raymonde

Laurent, and told him that she had relatives in New York, and that she loved America. As he finished the meal, Jimmy's optimism about his chances for escape began to soar.

Madame Laurent dispatched the young woman to bring back "Madame Price," who apparently spoke fluent English. Jimmy was waiting in the side yard when a tall middle-aged woman arrived. In perfect English, she told him that her name was Annie Price and that she lived in the next village of Triel. She asked him to accompany her there.

Her small stone cottage was abutted by two others, but no one appeared to take notice of their arrival. While Annie cut up carrots and onions for soup, she told Jimmy that she had been born in Brighton, England. After completing her education, she had married a young Frenchman and moved to this village. She was now divorced; one of her sons was in the French army in Indochina, and another worked in Germany.

After supper, Annie told him that a man in the village named Edward Cotterell would be arriving shortly to interview him. Jimmy was naturally anxious, but she assured him that the old man was also English and had been imprisoned by the Germans until he was released due to failing health.

Later that evening, Monsieur Cotterell arrived with three men. The others looked like farmers, and were big, impassive, and uncommunicative. The interview turned out to be an interrogation, and the twenty-one-year-old soon realized that his life was at stake if he couldn't prove he was really an American.

After an hour of pointed questions about his training in the United States, his recent missions, and details about his air base at Grafton Underwood, the old man pronounced himself satisfied. If he hadn't been, the other three men were there to end the charade.

The next morning, another man arrived at Annie Price's house with the news that Jimmy would be leaving by train for Paris. He was a medical intern, and treated Jimmy's burns with a soothing salve. He also brought him a gray wool suit, white shirt, and red tie. While Annie set about tailoring the suit to his larger dimensions, Jimmy shaved for the first time in twelve days and enjoyed a cold bath.

On the afternoon of Monday, September 20, exactly two weeks after the Stuttgart raid, the medical intern escorted him to the Triel train station and handed him a ticket to Paris. Although he accompanied Jimmy in the rail car, he remained some distance away in case of the American's discovery or arrest.

When they arrived at Saint-Lazare station in Paris, he was instructed to walk straight to the exit gate. The intern told him that a few nights earlier there had been an insurrection in Paris, and the French gendarmes were now out in force checking identification papers. The fearful Jimmy began to imagine that every man in the station who looked at him was a possible Gestapo agent who would suddenly demand to see his papers.

But then he was through the gate and into the dark night. He followed the intern through the streets of Paris toward the apartment where he would be staying. At one point in the journey, he looked up and saw the darkened silhouette of the Eiffel Tower outlined against the starry sky.

He was on his way.

The Back of the Tiger

Monday, 20 September 1943
Eighth Air Force Command Headquarters
Bushy Park, England
Major General Ira Eaker
2100

S omeone had tipped off Hap Arnold to the Stuttgart fiasco, and he was livid.

As soon as the commanding general arrived back in Washington on September 9, he had sent a cable to Eaker requesting a full report on the mission. Eaker and Fred Anderson, who at Claridge's had assured Arnold the bombing results were "excellent," worked together on a more candid assessment.

On September 10, Eaker responded to Arnold's cable with a confidential memorandum entitled *Further information on Stuttgart mission as requested your A3517 September 9th.*

"*No further information available as to bombing results at Stuttgart,*" Eaker began, "*but pictures taken of Offenburg marshalling yards which were attacked by 1 part of formation show direct hits on at least three trains, an overhead bridge, dispatch control buildings, warehouses, and on single cars in area.*

"*Fighter opposition intense from time shortly after P-47s left formation until picked up again on return route. At least 200 fighters attacked,*" he wrote in reference to Luftwaffe opposition. "*Gunfire at Stuttgart intense and accurate.*"

As to losses, "*Because of size of force involved and intensity of enemy opposition, both fighter and antiaircraft, it is impossible to determine exactly the cause of losses even after thorough interrogation of crews . . . Of the 45 planes lost, 7 lost to fighters; 12 airplanes went down in Channel, damaged by antiaircraft and fighters and running short of fuel because of necessary use of extra power. Most of the others probably due to fighters but no definite determination can be made . . . 107 of returning B-17s damaged, 3 salvaged."*

Arnold remained incensed. Three hundred thirty-eight Fortresses had been sent to destroy two massive complexes of ball-bearing and magneto factories. They had apparently destroyed three trains. He concluded that the Stuttgart mission had been "a complete failure," and immediately began prodding Eaker to resume the air offensive against German industrial targets.

Eaker was well aware of Arnold's mercurial personality. In the course of a day, he might receive one cable overflowing with praise, followed a few hours later by another cable deriding his lack of commitment to advancing the air force's strategic goals.

He remained unmoved. Eaker refused to send the Eighth's heavy bombers back to Germany again until the Eighth had made good on the losses of planes and crews from the Stuttgart mission.

On September 7, 9, 15, and 16, bomber command dispatched the Eighth's depleted groups to attack lower-priority targets in France. None of the strikes were maximum efforts, and the bomber forces never exceeded three hundred planes. Increasingly inclement weather over Europe often precluded any mission at all.

As the days passed, Arnold grew increasingly frustrated at the lack of action.

Each morning in Washington, he met at 0830 with the other military chiefs of staff. Invariably, George Marshall would ask Arnold about the previous day's operations of the Eighth. More often than not, an infuriated Arnold would have to say, "Nothing to report."

The tone of his cables sharpened further. He simply couldn't understand why after sending the Eighth nearly a thousand Fortresses, Eaker could barely muster three hundred to attack.

"To us here in the United States," he cabled Eaker two weeks after the Stuttgart mission, "it looks as if the employment of large numbers of heavy bombers has not been followed through by your headquarters and staff."

An equally frustrated Eaker couldn't seem to make Arnold understand the cumulative impact of the heavy losses and battle damage the Eighth had sustained in attacking Germany without long-range fighters.

He could only try to stay on the back of the tiger.

Thursday, 23 September 1943
Eighth Air Force Bomber Command
Forty-first Combat Air Wing
Brigadier General Robert Travis

After reading the official reprimand he had received from General Eaker, Bob Travis wondered whether his air force career might be over before he ever had a chance to prove himself. What did they expect from a warrior?

The whole damn thing was pathetic, probably cooked up by some paper-pushing, brass-kissing bed wetter on Eaker's staff who had it in for him. Bob Travis was a combat commander, not a desk jockey.

On September 2, shortly after his arrival in England, he had sent a personal note to Colonel "Pop" Arnold, a senior officer in his former command, who was now at the Twenty-ninth Bomb Group, Gowen Field, Boise, Idaho. Travis had already asked General Williams, his division commander, to transfer Pop to his staff.

Travis had written the letter after flying as an observer on several missions to France, and a few days before he assumed command of the Forty-first Combat Wing. In addition to giving Pop a heads-up on some of the things he needed to bring with him when he left for England, Travis had taken a moment to comment on the deficiencies of the Eighth Air Force machine gunners:

Pop . . . anything said about gunnery in the past was not enough. The air is full of Bosche sometimes 2 to 300 and they are shooting real bullets. We have to fight our way in and out. We are paying with lots of crews because our gunners can't shoot. I could have got one bastard with a skeet gun that my nose gunner missed yesterday. They come close but the boys won't lead and swing through . . .

Nine days later, completely out of the blue, the official reprimand arrived from Ira Eaker, the commanding general of the Eighth Air Force, at Travis's Forty-first Combat Wing headquarters in Molesworth. Some bastard was obviously gunning for him.

HEADQUARTERS

EIGHTH AIR FORCE

ETOUSA

11 September, 1943

SUBJECT: REPRIMAND

TO: BRIGADIER GENERAL R.F. TRAVIS

Through Commanding General, VIII BOMBER COMMAND

1. Enclosed herewith is a letter which you apparently wrote and which was picked up by the ETO censors.
2. The censor showed good judgment in stopping your letter. It contained a base slander of the fighting men of the Eighth Air Force which was wholly unwarranted and unjustified. The wording of this letter is a very poor start for you in this air force and your sending of it indicates a lack of familiarity on your part with existing security and postal regulations.
3. I believe that you probably mean to imply that the state of qualification of our gunners is not as high as we would like to have it. We have always said that one of our gravest concerns is to improve the accuracy of our gunners and we have done everything possible in all echelons to improve it as rapidly as possible. But that is certainly not what you have said. The statement that our gunners cannot shoot is, of course, not true as is

demonstrated by the great success they have had in destroying a large number of enemy aircraft.

4. An acknowledgment is desired from you without delay upon receipt of this communication, and any explanation you desire to make will be carefully considered.

/s/ Ira C. Eaker
Major General, USA
Commanding

General Travis was still working on his response to General Eaker when the next blow fell. On September 18, he was charged with another violation of security by General Fred Anderson, the head of bomber command.

The new violation involved two more letters he had sent to officers who would soon be joining him at the Forty-first Combat Wing. The first was to Colonel Robert Warren at the Fifteenth Wing in Boise, Idaho.

Dear Bob,
Have asked for you. Will keep asking. You can let up on bombing and navigation . . . but for God's sake teach them to shoot. . . . Our gunners are not worth a damn. None of us have been impressed sufficiently with our weakness there. . . .

Travis's second letter had included equally provocative comments and had been addressed to Colonel A. F. Hegenberger, another former subordinate, who now commanded the Twenty-first Bomb Wing at Salina, Kansas.

The only thing that slows us up is the arrival of crews. We expend them as fast as you can send them. . . . Anything that has been said about our gunnery is an understatement. . . . If we do not teach them to respect our gunnery more, our losses will increase and they are too high now. Our fighters have been giving us rather poor support but we hope for better with Keppner at the helm. Best regards, Bob Travis

After personally reviewing those two letters, Fred Anderson, the head of bomber command, unloaded on him through his division commander, General Robert B. Williams.

HEADQUARTERS
EIGHTH AIR FORCE
APO 633

18 September, 1943

SUBJECT: Violation of Security
Hq. VIII Bomber Command, APO 634
TO: Commanding General, Hq. 1st Bombardment Division, APO
634. U.S. Army

1. The attached correspondence is self-explanatory. It is evident
    that Brig. General Travis does not appreciate the seriousness
    of his violation of security. His position in this Theater has
    become very precarious because of this and a previously
    reported violation. . . .

/S/ F.L. ANDERSON
Brigadier General, U.S. Army
Commanding

As far as Bob Travis was concerned, they were threatening to throw him out because he had told the truth, and it was increasingly obvious they didn't want anyone back in the States to know what was really going on. He would have to curb his tongue in the future.

In the meantime, he had to eat crow to save his job. On September 23, he officially responded to the charge of "base slander" leveled by Ira Eaker, as well as the other infractions that made his continued service with the Eighth Air Force precarious.

HEADQUARTERS, 41ST COMBAT BOMBARDMENT WING

APO 634, United States Army,

23 September 1943

TO: The Command General, Eighth Air Force

1. The letters referred to in the basic communication were addressed to a parent group commander and the executive officer of the 15th Wing, both of whom have been after my direct command. They are responsible for training a large portion of the crews arriving in this theatre. Anything I say on what phases of training should be given emphasis will bear great weight with these officers as they have had no combat experience and hold my opinions in respect, having served with me for two and three years respectively.

2. In the 2nd Air Force training facilities for gunnery, such requisites as two target ships, air to air ranges, instructors, etc., are still too limited to do the job. By my comments I hoped to spur these officers into making greater efforts in their procurement and to supply you with better gunners.

3. Doubtless you have sent back many letters in which you have stressed the type of training you desired your crews to get, yet I can assure you there is still a question as to where the emphasis in training should be placed.... It was my intention to write a voluminous letter to the staff of the 1st Bomber Command, which unit I last commanded, and enumerate all the weaknesses that our crews have. Should you have no objection I will still do this, but forward the communication through your headquarters for approval and to prevent any further breach of security measures on my part.

4. No slander was meant of 8th Air Force personnel. If criticism was made, it was of myself, as I trained the groups with which I have ridden.

5. If I have made a bad start in the 8th Air Force, I am sincerely sorry as I have never had an assignment on which I was more anxious to do my duty.

/s/ Robert F. Travis
Brigadier General, U.S.A.
Commanding

Travis's letter was forwarded through channels to the commanding general of the Eighth Air Force. A few days later, Bob Travis received a copy of the communication sent by General Fred Anderson to Ira Eaker. In it, Anderson outlined his recommended punishment, which was that no further action be taken since "his serious breach of security" had already resulted in an official reprimand by the commanding general, Eighth Air Force, and a verbal reprimand by the commanding general, First Bombardment Division.

That wasn't the end of it. Privately, several senior officers did not see Bob Travis as either a team player or an officer deserving of higher promotion. They had long memories, and the war was going to last a long time.

The official reprimand only inflamed Bob Travis's desire to do whatever was needed to achieve his goals for success in the army air forces. For now, there was only one way to accomplish it.

He would prove himself in air combat.

Interlude

Thursday, 23 September 1943
Tricqueville Air Base
Normandy, France
Jagdgeschwader 2 "Richthofen"
Major Egon "Connie" Mayer

C ould the bomber offensive against the Fatherland really be over?

Since the mauling the Luftwaffe had given the Eighth Air Force bombers when they attacked Stuttgart on September 6, the Americans had confined their raids to military targets inside France.

On the sixth, Connie Mayer had enjoyed one of his finest days in the air. As the fragmented bomb groups and squadrons that attacked Stuttgart tried to make their escape back to England, he had personally shot down three of them in less than thirty minutes. The victories had raised the total number of four-engine aircraft he had destroyed so far to twenty.

Now that the Americans were limiting their attacks inside France, the bombers were accompanied all the way to the targets and back by the growing arsenal of American and British fighter planes. It made the task of penetrating the fighter screens and knocking down the Fortresses more difficult. On the positive side, the Americans had obviously called off their air offensive against the Fatherland, at least temporarily.

On the evening of September 22, he and his staffeln had engaged a squadron of Spitfires that were escorting a force of American medium bombers near Évreux. It turned into an old-fashioned dogfight of the type he had excelled in before becoming the preeminent bomber killer in the Luftwaffe. In four minutes, he shot down two Spitfires, bringing his total number of victories to eighty-two, all of them on the western front against the British and Americans.

Although some of his fellow Luftwaffe frontline commanders wanted to believe that the Americans had given up their plan of attacking the Fatherland, Connie Mayer wasn't one of them.

He believed the Americans were simply licking their wounds, making good their lost aircraft and crews with the seemingly endless stream of replacements coming from the United States. They would be back, and once the Americans had long-range fighters, they would be unstoppable.

In the meantime, it was necessary for the Luftwaffe to husband its resources, continuing to inflict grievous wounds on the Americans whenever an opportunity presented itself.

Friday, 24 September 1943
Paris, France
Luftwaffe Military Hospital
Sergeant Olen "Reb" Grant

At first, Reb had no idea where he was.

When he regained consciousness again, his head was wrapped in several layers of white gauze bandages. They covered every part of his face except for his left eye and mouth. He cautiously opened his eye and saw that he was lying in a hospital bed in a sun-filled, high-ceilinged ward.

There were beds on both sides of him, and a man was lying in each one. For a few moments, he thought he might be back in England. Then he looked up and saw the photograph of a fierce-looking Adolf Hitler hanging above the entrance to the ward.

He tried to reconstruct the few fleeting memories he still retained of the last day he could remember. It was after *Yankee Raider* had gone down somewhere over France. He had been aboard all the way.

Reb remembered waking up in what he thought was someone's cellar. It was very cold in the room, and he had been as naked as a jaybird. Then he had fallen away again.

His next memory was regaining consciousness in an ambulance. It was very old, the kind they had in World War I, with a shrill, rackety little engine. He was lying on one of the stretcher racks, his head to the rear. A German soldier was sitting next to him on the bed of the ambulance with his feet hanging off the back. He was eating grapes. Seeing the bandaged Reb looking at him out of his left eye, he offered him one.

Reb faded out again.

His last memory was coming awake on a metal operating table. He was lying on his back surrounded by white-gowned figures whose faces were hidden by masks. He tried to speak as a nurse stepped forward and injected him in the upper thigh. Then he was gone again.

How long have I been here? he wondered. He could hear the wounded men lying in the beds next to him joking about something. He didn't understand the joke because they were both speaking German.

A nurse passed by and he called out to her. When she approached him, he asked her where he was, but she couldn't understand him. A German nurse who spoke English told him that he was fortunate to be in a German military hospital in Paris, where they treated captured soldiers as well as their own. He had been in a coma since being admitted to the hospital. It was a miracle that he was still alive, she told him, but he already knew that.

He had been unconscious for more than two weeks.

Later in the morning, the nurses transferred him from his bed to a hospital gurney, and he was wheeled out of the ward to a large elevator. It stopped on the main floor, and he was transported across an elegant lobby at least two stories high and draped with red swastika flags. Another angry portrait of Adolf Hitler, this one life-sized, dominated one wall.

They took him into an examination room, where a doctor began to gently clip off the bandages around his head. In fairly good English, the doctor explained that the cannon round had hit him between his right eye and ear, gone through his skull, and come out the front, taking his eye and most of his cheekbone.

It had become badly infected, probably because he had been wearing his leather sheepskin-lined helmet. Many of its fragments were still inside the wound, along with pieces of shrapnel. If they were unable to control the infection, the doctor told him that his prospects for survival weren't good. In any event, the hospital would be his home for the next month or two. Before putting on a new set of bandages, the doctor liberally dosed the open wound with sulfur powder.

Reb had no doubt he would live. After everything he had already survived, he was home free. His principal concern was his mother's weak heart. He hoped that when she received the telegram that he was missing in action, she would somehow know he was all right.

Saturday, 25 September 1943
Paris, France
Second Lieutenant Demetrios Karnezis

The morning after his first and only parachute jump, the Greek's coccyx was so sore he could barely move. If his benefactress had wanted to turn him in to the Gestapo, there was nothing he could do about it but lie there and wait.

He was willing to bet his life that she wouldn't.

Her name was Marcelle Andre, and both she and Marie Therese, her seventeen-year-old daughter, were unbelievably kind. He knew the two women faced a possible death sentence if he was found hiding there.

He thought Marie Therese might be a little sweet on him. The girl had spent a full day trying to help him learn basic French, although she might as well have tried teaching the bedpost. Learning a foreign tongue wasn't his forte.

It was a struggle for him to walk. It was a struggle to sit. He spent most of the first three days lying in the big feather bed that had been occupied by Marcelle and her late husband, who had been killed in a farming accident six months earlier. The soft down in the mattress took the pressure off his back and allowed him to rest comfortably.

Marie Therese brought him his first breakfast in bed. Real coffee was unobtainable, and she served him a brew made of roasted chicory that she poured from two small pots, one with the hot chicory and the other filled with warm cream and sugar. There was a garden omelet to go with it, along with freshly baked bread and butter.

A fellow could get used to this, he decided.

Four days later, another woman arrived. Her name was Suzanne Bouchy, and she lived in the nearby village of La Chapelle–Champigny. She spoke English with an appealing French accent.

Marcelle had called her on the telephone the day after the Greek had arrived at the farm. The Bouchy family was well known for its anti-German feelings, and Marcelle thought she was the best person to contact about her new problem.

"I have a stray rabbit," she had said to Suzanne over the party line connection. "Can you help me find a home for it?"

During her first visit to the farm, Suzanne Bouchy told the Greek that *Slightly Dangerous II* had crashed into a home on the south side of the village, killing the elderly woman who lived there. Five members of his crew had been found in the wreckage and buried nearby.

She said that she had tried to save his bombardier, Dick Loveless, from capture, but his leg had been badly broken in his jump, and the Germans had taken him into custody, along with Bill Frazier, the navigator, and Arthur Gay, the top turret gunner.

Suzanne said that a man would soon come to the farm to take him to get forged French identity papers. Once the papers were prepared, he would be escorted to Paris and turned over to an underground escape network that would deliver him to England.

Marcelle had put together a small wardrobe for him from the clothing of her late husband. On the day of his departure, Marie Therese came to wake him before dawn. After he was dressed and ready, she gave him a kiss good-bye on the mouth, saying she hoped they would meet again one day under less dangerous conditions.

The man was waiting for him downstairs. A tearful Marcelle

wished him good fortune on his journey, and the man drove him to the local train station, bought him a ticket, and boarded the same train. Thirty minutes later, they got off at the cathedral town of Sens, and went directly to the mayor's office.

These people are really connected, the Greek concluded after the mayor personally stamped the forged documents with his official seal. These people were all part of the French underground, he realized, not knowing how to adequately thank them for all they were doing.

The mayor introduced him to a Monsieur Maraceaux, who would be escorting him to Paris and hiding him in his home there. That afternoon, the two men boarded another train, this one filled with German soldiers. The Greek spent the whole trip staring out the window as the scenery rolled by, dreading the thought that someone would demand to see his papers.

After reaching Paris, it became obvious that Monsieur Maraceaux was an important man. His name was engraved on the façade of the imposing building that turned out to be his home. When the Greek climbed the stairs to the floor where he would be staying, two other escaped American fliers were already there. Warren Graff was a P-47 fighter pilot, and Frank Kimotek had been a gunner on a B-17.

They told him that the French underground was a big organization, and that hundreds of Allied fliers were hiding in every part of the city, awaiting their turn in the escape line.

For the Greek, the hours passed all too slowly. Monsieur Maraceaux had a large library, but the books were in French. Aside from eating and sleeping, there was little to do. Bored after several days of lethargy, the Greek and Warren Graff decided to explore the city. They both had excellent forged papers, and the risk would be slight.

Happy to be outdoors, they began walking the streets near their safe haven. The city was almost bare of automobiles. What vehicles they saw were powered by engines that burned charcoal. The cafés they passed served only table wine, and there were few patrons. Gay Paris was no longer gay.

Warren had stopped to look at a camera on display in one of the shops. The Greek had kept on walking. As he approached the next intersection, a German officer came around the corner and halted in front of him.

He was wearing a khaki uniform with polished calf-length brown boots. The Wehrmacht officer's uniform was clean and pressed, but well worn. An iron cross adorned his throat. He looked like a professional.

What an idiot I am, thought the Greek, realizing he had not only jeopardized his own freedom but that of the people he had entrusted his life to. What do I do now?

The Wehrmacht officer was demanding something of him in an imperious tone. The Greek thought he might be asking for directions. The fact that he was speaking German meant he didn't know any more French than the Greek did.

The officer was glaring at him, waiting for an answer. In response, the Greek threw up his hands in European fashion and began speaking Greek phrases he had learned around his parents' kitchen table in Norfolk. Disgusted, the officer clicked his heels and stalked off.

Warren Graff had watched the whole thing unfold from the camera shop and was sure the Greek was about to be arrested. After that incident, they decided to stay in the apartment.

It was the afternoon of September 15 when they heard a familiar rumbling overhead that sounded like distant thunder. A few seconds later, they knew it wasn't thunder. It was a big stream of heavy bombers, heading for Paris.

Going to the top floor, they watched them through one of the windows.

Even though the formation of Fortresses might soon be dropping their payloads right on top of them, the two Americans felt a thrill of pleasure at seeing them rumbling toward the southern edge of the city.

A minute later, the antiaircraft batteries deployed across Paris began opening up at the leading combat wing. It was the first time the Greek had ever been on the ground looking up at an attack. The German batteries were pumping hundreds of shells into the sky, turning parts of it almost black with explosions as the gunners tried to find the range.

The booming thunder went on and on, with the 88s shooting nonstop at the intruders. He saw a Fortress come shrieking down. It was on fire as it plunged toward earth, and exploded in a big fireball a mile or two away.

Suddenly it seemed to be raining jagged metal. Thousands of cannon shell fragments from the intense barrage, each one the size of his little finger, were raining down all over Paris.

Unlike hard rain, these drops were potentially lethal. He could hear them clattering like steel hail as they landed on the metal roofs and on the cobblestone streets below. This was no summer shower. It went on for at least fifteen minutes as the bomb groups came over to drop their payloads on the targets before turning for home.

As the last roar of the Wright Cyclone engines faded into the distance, the Greek wondered if the 388th, or whatever was left of it after Stuttgart, had been up there in the bomber stream. He grinned at the possibility he might have been bombed by his own group.

Four miles above him, Major Ralph Jarrendt and the rest of the 388th headed back to Knettishall, England, after bombing the Hispano-Suiza Aero Engine Works in southern Paris.

Jarrendt was in the lead wing of the bomber train, once more part of the low group to the 96th. Even though the 388th had lost eleven planes on the Stuttgart mission, new replacements had arrived to make up the difference.

Captain Robert Bernard was leading the high squadron of the 388th. He had taken over Ted Wilken's plane, *Battlin Betsy*. It was supposed to be a lucky ship, and so far it was living up to expectations.

Hitting the Road

Saturday, 25 September 1943
Sainte-Savine, France
Second Lieutenant Warren Porter Laws

The previous two weeks had proved to be both the greatest trial and the greatest adventure of his life. No longer was he the sheltered boy forced to remain at home on Halloween because of his mother's fears. Warren Laws had survived a horrific air battle and had so far escaped the Germans.

Following the fiery deaths of Ted Wilken and the rest of *Patricia's* crew, he and Joe Schwartzkopf had spent their first hours in France hiding in a dense thicket near the village of Montgueux. A dozen German soldiers had searched for them unsuccessfully for most of that day.

Warren had been carrying an escape kit inside his flight suit. In addition to chocolate, pain medication, bandages, and a pocket compass, it included a small map of Western Europe. While they hid in the thicket, Joe attempted to bandage Warren's arm wound as well as his burned hands and fingers. Afterward, Warren carefully examined the map.

In the escape classes Warren had taken at Knettishall, flight crews had been told that the two best escape destinations from France were Switzerland and Spain. He wasn't sure where *Patricia* had gone down, but the route they had flown appeared to be a lot closer to Switzerland.

When the German search party finally gave up and drove away in their trucks, the Americans waited two hours to be sure it wasn't a ruse, and then crawled out of their thicket.

A farmer was plowing a nearby field. Warren decided to ask the farmer where they were. He had taken two years of French in high school, and was carrying a pocket-sized French-English dictionary.

There was no need for a lengthy conversation. As soon as Warren showed him the map, the farmer pointed to a spot southeast of Paris. They were apparently near the town of Troyes, roughly ninety miles southeast of Paris and about 150 miles northwest of Bern, Switzerland. Spain was at least four hundred miles away.

Using the compass, Warren and Joe set off to the southeast.

Two miles away, Marcel Vergeot, a café owner in the village of Torvilliers and a member of the French underground, had seen *Patricia* falling to earth earlier that morning. By the time he reached the crash site on his bicycle, the Germans had recovered the bodies of eight crewmen, and they were lying on the ground near the plane.

Marcel Vergeot knew the American bombers carried a crew of ten. At the crash scene, a young man from Montgueux whispered to him that he had seen parachutes, and Vergeot concluded that there were at least two survivors. He assumed they would probably head for Switzerland, which meant they had to follow one of two routes southeast.

Vergeot wanted to help the Americans, but after three years of German occupation, he had learned to be very cautious. Other men had tried to help downed Allied airmen. They had been arrested and were never seen again. He wrote down the numbers on the vertical stabilizer of the plane: 349.

Still heading southeast away from the crashed *Patricia*, Warren decided they should keep walking as far as their energy allowed. After crossing a railroad track and a succession of fields, they came to a small orchard, and Joe stopped to fill his pockets with green apples. Farther on, they came to a macadam road heading southeast. Warren decided to follow it.

Aside from an occasional horse-drawn cart, there was no vehicular traffic in the French countryside. A few kilometers down the road, they passed a large farmhouse. Too late to hide, they spotted a group of men coming out of its tree-lined entrance. The Frenchmen's conversation immediately stopped. As the two fliers walked past, the Frenchmen stared at Warren's bloody flight suit.

The encounter filled him with foreboding. Any one of those civilians could easily turn them in for a reward. Crossing 150 miles of France on foot suddenly seemed hopeless.

Warren was now in agonizing pain from his burned hands and shoulder wound. As darkness fell he became feverish and told Joe he had to stop. Joe found a clump of bushes near the road where they could hide. Through the long night, Warren was wracked by chills. Joe gave him his own flight jacket to try to keep him warm.

Early the next morning, Marcel Vergeot told his twelve-year-old son, Daniel, to take his bicycle and ride out several miles along the only two roads that led southeast. If he saw any strangers along the road, he wasn't to talk to them, but to immediately return home and tell him their location.

As dawn broke, Warren's raw fingers were swollen like blood sausages. Weak from fever, he wasn't sure how long he could walk. He told Joe that he would have a much better chance to escape if he went on alone.

Joe shook his head. They would escape together or be captured together, he said, telling Warren he would look out for him as long as they remained free. After eating some green apples for breakfast, they crawled out of the thicket and began walking again.

They had barely traveled a mile when Warren was racked by chills again and had to stop. Once more, he told Joe to leave him. Again, Joe refused. The two men had begun walking again when they were overtaken by a boy on a bicycle. The boy stared at them as he passed by, then turned around and disappeared in the same direction he had come.

An hour later, two men on bicycles passed them and pulled off the road into a copse of woods. As Warren and Joe came up, one of the Frenchmen motioned for them to join him under the cover of the trees.

Marcel Vergeot asked them if they were American fliers, and

Warren said yes. Marcel showed him a piece of paper with three numbers on it and asked if they were the numbers of his airplane. The numbers were 329. Warren shook his head and said no.

In French, he told him the numbers were 349, the correct numbers. Marcel smiled and told Warren that after dark he would come back and escort them to his home in Torvilliers.

When he returned later that night, he brought along simple peasant clothing for them to wear on the walk back to Marcel's village. Inside the shuttered café, Madame Vergeot used scissors to trim the dead skin from Warren's hands and fingers before coating them with a greasy mixture of tannic acid, paste, and kerosene to prevent infection.

Marcel told them that hundreds of American airmen had parachuted into France the previous day, and that the underground was temporarily overwhelmed by the challenge of finding safe houses for all of them.

The following night the two Americans were taken to a small farm in La Rivière-de-Corps. It was owned by a middle-aged man named Leon Nelle, and his farm would be their home for several nights while long-term arrangements were being made for them.

Monsieur Nelle was a patriot, but quite eccentric. Each night before retiring, he would put on his be-medaled World War I uniform coat and sing "La Marseillaise" at the top of his prodigious lungs. It seemed odd behavior for a man who was housing two escapees and presumably trying to avoid notice.

Assisting Allied fliers wasn't Monsieur Nelle's only occupation. The second night after their arrival, a heavily armed man arrived at the farm in the early hours of the morning. He conversed with Monsieur Nelle in fluent French before turning to address Warren in English.

The man explained in an English accent that he was an operative of the British SOE (Special Operations Executive), which supported the French underground with weapons, explosives, and logistical support, while undertaking sabotage missions against German installations.

After getting Warren's and Joe's names and serial numbers, he said he would radio his controllers in England to report that the fliers were alive and well. It wasn't until later that Warren realized the agent was also looking to confirm that they were genuine.

They stayed at the farm for five days. On September 12, Monsieur Nelle told Warren that the underground had found a safer place for them to stay. That night they were taken on foot to a charcuterie in the village of Sainte-Savine, which sat on the main road to Troyes. The owner, Joachim LeDantec, lived on the second floor above the shop with his wife and daughter. Warren and Joe would share the attic.

Once they settled in, the days passed slowly. Warren spent his waking hours studying his French-English dictionary, and then practicing phrases with Madame LeDantec and her daughter, Anne Marie. He hoped that becoming fluent would enhance their chances of escape.

For his part, the perpetually hungry Joe Schwartzkopf was tormented by the aromatic smells of sausage, cheese, and roasting meat emanating upward from the shop below.

On September 20, Warren celebrated his twenty-fifth birthday. It was no different from any other day, although he found himself constantly thinking about his fiancée, Libby. He hoped she was weathering the news of his having gone missing with the same spirit and pluck she had demonstrated during their courtship.

It had not started well. After one of their first dates, Libby wasn't sure he was the one for her. "He's not my type," she confided to her diary. But his earnest sincerity had slowly won her over, and when she agreed to marry him, he took the next step in the old-fashioned way.

"I've got to go and ask your father," he had said.

Libby's father was a building contractor, and at that time he was constructing a new four-story house near Danbury. He was on the roof when the couple arrived at the building site.

"Mr. Minck, I'd like to talk to you," Warren shouted up to him.

"Can't you tell me from down there?" her father had called out to them, not wanting to descend all the way down the sets of ladders.

"I want to marry your daughter," Warren shouted up to the roof.

Mr. Minck came straight down the ladders.

"I think you should wait," he told Warren as soon as he was on the ground. Libby's parents were strict Catholics. Warren was Protestant. The Mincks had deep reservations about mixing religions.

Libby spoke right up to him. "When he comes back from the war, Dad, we're going to get married."

Sitting in the safe house, Warren only wished he could let her know he was safe.

One afternoon, he was studying French in the upstairs parlor when he heard the noise of a heavy vehicle rumbling slowly past the house in the street below. Glancing outside, he saw a huge truck and trailer filling the road that ran east through the village.

Strapped to the bed of the trailer was a wrecked airplane. From its shape and size, Warren knew it was a B-17. When he saw the painting of the half-naked girl on the fuselage, he knew it was *Patricia*. The Fortress was being hauled back to Germany to be melted down for new German weapons.

The sight of their destroyed plane brought home the loss of Ted Wilken and the rest of the crew like a fresh stab to the heart. When Warren asked Monsieur LeDantec what had happened to the dead crewmen, the Frenchman told him that Ted and the others had been temporarily buried near the crash site. Simple wooden crosses now marked their resting place. In the days since the plane had gone down, villagers had covered their graves with fresh flowers.

Eclipse

Since the birth of her daughter, Kathy, a month earlier, she had been staying at her mother's elegant ten-room apartment on Chicago's Lake Shore Drive. On September 9, Braxton was enjoying the stunning view of Lake Michigan when the doorman called up to say that a Western Union messenger was in the lobby to deliver a telegram.

Braxton had received another telegram from Ted just three days earlier. Dated September 6, 1943, it read, "CHECKING ON DAVE . . . WILL WRITE BETTY . . . LOVE TED."

The handful of words reflected everything that was fine and generous about Ted as a man. Dave was a fellow B-17 pilot in England. Ted had met him during bomber training and they had become good friends. Dave was married to Betty, who along with Braxton had trailed after their husbands from one installation to the next before the two pilots were deployed to the Eighth Air Force in England.

Dave's Fortress had not returned from a recent combat mission, and he had been reported missing in action. Ted's telegram meant that he wanted Braxton to let the distraught Betty know he would do his best to try to find out if Dave had survived before he wrote to her.

This latest telegram wasn't from Ted. It was from the War Department.

227

I REGRET TO INFORM YOU THAT THE COMMANDING
GENERAL EUROPE AREA REPORTS YOUR HUSBAND SEC-
OND LIEUTENANT RAY T. WILKEN MISSING IN ACTION
SINCE SIX SEPTEMBER. IF FURTHER DETAILS OR OTHER
INFORMATION OF HIS STATUS ARE RECEIVED YOU WILL
BE PROMPTLY NOTIFIED.

ULIO THE ADJUTANT GENERAL

First Dave and now Ted, both in the same week. She was devastated.

Braxton knew that Ted would want her to remain strong, both for herself and their new baby. On their last night together before he went overseas, he had spoken to her about the possibility he wouldn't come back. He knew the odds of surviving twenty-five missions in the summer of 1943.

She had already gone through the emotional agony of their parting in Spokane, Washington, after Ted left with his crew in their new B-17. She was pregnant with Kathy, and Braxton's stepfather had arranged a berth for her on the Northern Pacific to come back east.

Over the course of the two-day journey, she had cried without respite, leaving her sleeping berth only to go to the bathroom. It was as if she was enduring the grief of his loss without even knowing his ultimate fate. By the time she reached Chicago, Braxton was emotionally spent. She slowly recovered at her mother's home.

After hearing the news that Ted was missing, Braxton's stepfather was spurred to action. Chester "Red" McKittrick was the chief financial officer of the *Chicago Tribune* and the right-hand man of the aging newspaper baron Colonel Robert McCormick.

Red had plenty of friends in Washington and the Pentagon, and he now called on them to find out if Ted might have survived. As the days passed, none of his contacts came back with solid information. The family could only wait.

On September 18, Braxton received a v-mail letter from Gene

Cordes, the original bombardier on Ted's crew, who had been too ill on the morning of September 6 to go on the Stuttgart mission.

Gene was suffering from survivor's guilt, suggesting in his letter that the outcome might have somehow been different if he had been with the rest of them. He wrote that he had talked with many of the crewmen who had survived the mission to try to find out what had happened to *Patricia*. No one was certain, but one of them reported that he had seen parachutes from a Fortress that he thought was Ted's going down short of Paris.

Gene was sure Ted was still alive. It was impossible for him to accept that Ted wouldn't have made it. He urged her not to give up hope that he was in France and being sheltered by the French underground.

Whatever his fate, Braxton vowed that she would neither wallow in misery nor allow herself to become an object of pity. Their love was a private matter. It was between her and Ted. She would not share her grief with anyone else. He would want it that way.

For now, all she felt was a growing numbness.

Greek Holiday

"Your time has come," said Monsieur Maraceaux.

Since arriving at his benefactor's home in mid-September, the Greek had spent a month hiding on the top floor with P-47 pilot Warren Graff and B-17 gunner Frank Kimotek. The days and nights had passed uneventfully, but the Americans were anxious to leave.

The French escape routes were still badly clogged. Most of the men who had successfully made contact with the underground on September 6 had been sent on to Paris, where most of the escape lines were concentrated.

A recent series of arrests by the Gestapo of suspected Allied sympathizers had led to a number of confessions. Some underground members had been shot. Others had been sent to concentration camps in Germany.

Monsieur Maraceaux had become increasingly worried that his own underground cell had been compromised, putting both him and his family at peril of arrest and execution. The sooner the Americans could leave Paris, the sooner the pressure on him would be relieved.

In the weeks he had lived with the Maraceauxes, the Greek had come to admire the almost casual bravery of this man, his wife, and their only son, Jacques, a well-mannered teenager who had shown a great curiosity about America. The boy had studied English and hoped to visit the old west someday. He peppered the Americans with questions about famous American explorers.

The tedium of the Greek's stay had been relieved by a single visitor. On the afternoon he celebrated his twenty-second birthday, there was a knock on the door of his room. When he answered it, Marie Therese, Marcelle Andre's seventeen-year-old daughter, was standing in the hallway. She had come all the way from Champigny.

"Joyeux anniversaire, Jimmy!" she said, smiling up at him.

The Greek had told her that his family nickname was Jimmy. She pronounced it somewhat breathlessly with a softened "J." Along with fond greetings from Marcelle and Suzanne Bouchy, she had brought a birthday cake made with eggs and butter. It was obvious to the Greek's housemates that the French girl had lost her heart to him.

On the night of October 16, Monsieur Maraceaux came upstairs to tell them that they would be leaving Paris the next morning on a train going to Brittany. Their ultimate destination was the port of Brest in westernmost France. From there, the three Americans would be smuggled in a boat along with other escapees to England.

The Greek's forged identity papers identified him as a Breton fisherman. In fashioning his disguise, Monsieur Maraceaux had urged him to look as disreputable as possible. The Greek had allowed his beard to grow and had dribbled gravy stains all over his shirt and rumpled black suit.

At dawn the next morning, a member of the underground arrived to escort the three Americans to the train station. When the Greek said his final good-byes, he promised to come back at the end of the war and thank the Maraceauxes personally for their courage and generosity.

The Greek was aboard the train to Brittany when the Gestapo came for the Maraceauxes. The Frenchman denied that he had harbored Allied fliers. After thoroughly searching his house, they found sufficient evidence to arrest him along with his wife and son.

It took almost twelve hours for the train to reach its destination. It not only stopped in many of the towns but would sometimes come to a halt in the middle of a forest for fear of being strafed by Allied fighters.

Another member of the underground escape line met them on the platform in Brittany. He introduced himself as Raoul and led the Americans to a local village church. The floor of the church loft was covered with a layer of straw. It would be their resting place overnight.

The next morning they left to board another train for Brest, which was home to one of the largest U-boat bases in France. The train was packed with German U-boat crews returning from leave.

To preserve his good luck, the Greek reached inside his suit coat to rub his St. Demetrios icon. It was missing, and he realized it must have fallen out into the straw the previous night. He said a silent prayer to his patron saint.

Security was very tight at the Brest railway station. Every passenger had to go through a checkpoint manned by German soldiers. They would randomly stop travelers and request to see their papers. Perhaps St. Demetrios was looking over him, or maybe he looked disreputable enough to be a Breton fisherman. He was allowed to pass without incident.

Near the stone quay that rimmed the harbor was a street of ancient stone houses. The three Americans were led up a narrow staircase to the third-floor apartment of a retired French colonel and his wife. From there, the underground planned to smuggle them onto the boat that would carry them to England.

On the night chosen for their escape, they were taken to a fishing village on the north coast of Brittany along Camaret Bay. In the basement of a village bakery, the Americans met twelve other escapees who had also been brought to the village.

The Greek recognized two of them from the Stuttgart mission, including Dick Cunningham, the pilot of *In God We Trust*, and Art Swap, who was the copilot of *Lone Wolf.*

In the early hours of the morning, they were taken in groups of three to the quay.

A local fisherman rowed them out in a skiff to a twin-masted fishing boat that was anchored in the outer reaches of the harbor. Once aboard, they were led below by flashlight to a large storage hold filled with eel pots, coils of rope, and other fishing gear. The hold was pitch-black and reeked of fish offal.

Once they were all assembled, a British officer asked each man to identify himself along with his rank. There turned out to be sixteen escapees in all, including ten Americans, one Norwegian RAF pilot, four British airmen, and a New Zealander named Johnny Checketts, who was already famous within the Eighth Air Force for shepherding crippled Fortresses back to England in his Spitfire.

Checketts was a squadron leader in the RAF and had already shot down twelve German fighters. He had gone down on September 6 while escorting home a squadron of American B-26 Marauders that had flown one of the diversionary raids for the Stuttgart attack.

The Greek proposed that Squadron Leader Checketts become the group's de facto leader. No one objected. One of the Americans expressed his hope that they would be on their way at dawn.

Two days later, hope inside the hold was beginning to run out. Why weren't they going? What had happened? Tempers began to flare as the men were forced to remain in the clammy darkness through all the daylight hours.

Early each morning, a local fisherman would bring them out several loaves of bread and a cask of fresh water, but he had no news to give them. In response to Johnny Checketts's repeated questions about when the boat would depart from France, the fisherman professed total ignorance. They could do nothing but wait.

The following morning, a member of the French underground came out to tell them that one of the underground escape lines had been compromised from Paris to Finistère, and that the Germans were watching every boat that moved in the harbor.

It was the Greek's escape line. He asked about the Maraceauxes and was told that Monsieur Maraceaux and his son had been sent to a concentration camp in Germany. Raoul, the contact in Brittany, had also been taken.

The agent urged them to be patient. They would leave when it was safe.

There were slop buckets for their excretions, but the waste couldn't be emptied until after dark each night. The smell was appalling. In the unsanitary conditions, two men began to suffer from dysentery.

On the third day, the Norwegian RAF pilot began to vomit uncontrollably. That night, he slipped into a state of delirium and began crying out in the darkness. His cries became increasingly louder, alarming the others. If the Germans were patrolling the harbor, he was putting them all at risk. When the man's howling cries continued, one of the Americans crawled over to the Norwegian and began choking him. Two other men intervened and were able to help stifle the Norwegian's cries.

When the fisherman arrived on the fourth morning to give them their daily bread and water allotment, he handed Johnny Checketts a hunk of boiled beef. It was about the size of a grapefruit and wrapped in butcher paper.

"We're going to have to divide this among sixteen people," said Checketts, reaching into his pocket to pull out a penknife. As the men continued to stare ravenously at the meat, Checketts glanced around the compartment.

"I want the Greek to divide it," he said.

"Yeah, let the Greek cut it up," agreed Art Swap of the 388th.

The Greek felt like he had just been awarded the Distinguished Flying Cross. Leaning over to cut it, he did his best to make sure that each piece was close to the same size.

The rest of the men watched him like he was cutting the Hope diamond. When he was finished, each chunk was about the size of a grape. He passed the pieces of meat around to the others on the butcher paper. It went from man to man like they were receiving communion. The last chunk went to the Greek. It was mostly fat, but the morsel tasted heavenly.

On their fifth day in the hold, the underground agent came out to tell them that they would be departing early the next morning. Each boat leaving the harbor was required to go to a check station to receive a clearance. The underground had been waiting for a particular crew of German soldiers to man the check station. This crew was known for its laxity.

At dawn on October 21, 1943, two fishermen came aboard and fired up the boat's small diesel engine. Going below, they helped the sixteen men find hiding places behind and underneath the oilcloths, coils of rope, and other fishing gear. Leaving the compartment hatch open, they took their places at the wheel and began chugging over to the check station.

From his position in the dark hold, the Greek could see the open hatchway through the rungs of an eel trap. At the check station, he watched as a German officer and two Wehrmacht soldiers with rifles came aboard, clomping past the hatch in their hobnailed boots.

Like the other escapees, he waited with apprehension as the soldiers gazed down into the hold. Perhaps it was the appalling stench that greeted them, but neither one climbed below to search the compartment.

A few minutes later, they were under way.

Powered by the small diesel engine, the boat chugged along very slowly. Several hours later, they were out of sight of land, but the two fishermen refused to allow the men below to come topside until night had fallen. They finally raised the sail on the boat, and the boat began slashing through the roiling sea before a stiff ocean breeze.

After being confined to the hold for five days, the Greek was thrilled to feel the clean wind on his face and to smell the sea air. Picking out a spot on the deck, he sat and watched the top of the mast swinging back and forth across Polaris in the starry sky above them. He realized that the fisherman at the wheel was following the North Star.

The Greek stayed awake all that night, watching the stars and recalling everything that had happened to him since he had parachuted out of *Slightly Dangerous II*.

There were so many people to thank for putting their lives on the line both for him and the other fifteen men aboard the boat. Marcelle Andre, Marie Therese, Suzanne Bouchy, all of them. He prayed that the Maraceauxes would survive their imprisonment, and silently thanked them for their bravery.

They were still sailing north the next morning when one of the French fishermen shouted out and pointed into the distance. The Greek could make out a hazy landmass directly ahead.

A few minutes later, he spotted a small ship coming toward them at high speed. As it neared the fishing boat, he saw that it was a coast guard vessel. The Union Jack was streaming from its stern.

Reversing engines as he came alongside, the English captain of the ship called out to them through a bullhorn, demanding to know who they were. Johnny Checketts answered back, telling him that there were sixteen Allied airmen aboard, and that they had just come from France.

The Englishman grinned at them and pointed north.

"That's Penzance," he said. "You're home, lads."

Friends and Enemies

Saturday, 25 December 1943
Eighth Air Force Command Headquarters
Bushy Park, England
Lieutenant General Ira Eaker

In September, they gave him his third star.

He was now Lieutenant General Ira Eaker. After serving in the army for nearly thirty years, he had finally earned one of the top slots in the whole corporation, along with its finest job, commanding the Eighth Air Force.

Early in his career, he had hitched his formative star to Hap Arnold, and it had proved to be a wise decision. The invasion of Europe was coming, and he would be right at the center of all the action. Everything would now have to come through England.

One positive result of Hap Arnold's inspection tour back in September was that the old man had left for Washington finally convinced that the Eighth needed long-range fighters to protect the Fortresses. Stuttgart had proved that beyond any doubt.

With his customary sense of urgency, Arnold had ordered his senior staff to make production of P-51 fighters and jettisonable belly tanks one of the air force's highest priorities. Arnold's minions were expected to cajole and harass the companies responsible for making the weapons until his newly accelerated timetable was met.

Arnold could be a tyrant when his orders were not carried out with sufficient zeal. At one of his daily staff meetings, he became enraged when a member of his staff informed him that an order had not been carried out. Arnold dressed him down with such vehemence that the man had dropped dead of a heart attack in front of his desk.

Hap Arnold's new determination to deliver long-range P-51s to England did not mean he expected Ira Eaker to wait for their delivery before resuming the air offensive against Germany.

As September drew to an end without any resumption of deep-penetration raids, Arnold became increasingly aggravated at Eaker's lack of initiative. Based on the number of replacement bombers that were pouring into England, he couldn't understand why Eaker wasn't attacking Germany with at least five hundred Fortresses on every mission.

Eaker had been feeding the new planes and green crews into the groups that had been badly depleted by the Stuttgart fiasco. In the meantime, he was confining his bombing strikes to targets inside France, all of them within the range of his escort fighters.

On September 28, Arnold ordered a senior member of his staff to initiate a set of cables designed "to build a fire under General Eaker." In addition to exhorting him to attack targets in Germany, one of them included a snide insult to Eaker's fighter command:

"When our fighter groups in North Africa escort bombers it is a matter of honor that hostile fighters shall not be permitted to attack the escorted bombers. Do your fighters have that spirit?"

Eaker ignored the hectoring while he focused on making good the losses sustained on September 6. In the face of Arnold's relentless pressure, he reluctantly prepared to resume the German air offensive, but with the arrival of fall, the weather over the Continent became increasingly inclement, with the deep-penetration targets in Germany usually masked by heavy cloud cover. The last thing Eaker wanted to endure was a repetition of the Stuttgart disaster when none of the bombardiers could find their targets.

In early October, Eaker's meteorological team was able to predict a week of potentially good weather, and Eaker issued orders to resume the air offensive. Over the next six days, the Eighth Air Force bombed industrial and military installations in Frankfurt, Bremen, Münster, and Marienburg.

Although several of the targets received significant bomb damage, the cost of the campaign was ninety-five Fortresses and nine B-24 Liberators. With the loss of more than a thousand airmen in six days, the surviving crews began referring to it as "Black Week."

Arnold sent Eaker a cable praising the effort:

"Good work. As you turn your effort . . . toward crippling the sources of the still growing German fighter forces the air war is clearly moving toward our supremacy in the air. Carry on."

While the new losses rendered the Eighth Air Force incapable of mounting the five-hundred-Fortress raids that Arnold was demanding, Eaker decided to complete a piece of unfinished business.

While Arnold was in England, Air Chief Marshal Charles Portal of the RAF had asserted to him that the Schweinfurt ball-bearing complex, which the Eighth had bombed on August 17, was the most important strategic target in Germany. Based on new British intelligence, he told Arnold that another strike on Schweinfurt was needed to complete its destruction. Arnold had then told Eaker to go back and finish the job.

"I know you'll get to it as soon as the weather permits," Arnold wrote him.

On October 14, the Eighth went to Schweinfurt again.

The force of 291 bombers fought its way across France and Germany, confronting hundreds of German fighters along the route. Once more, the Fw 190s and ME-109s came in waves, using the frontal attacks with cannon and machine-gun fire perfected by Connie Mayer.

Joining the battle with the single-engine fighters were swarms of twin-engine Bf 110s equipped with rockets under their wings. Four and five abreast, they fired dozens of the rockets into the tightly packed combat boxes.

When the bombers finally reached Schweinfurt, they were greeted with an unprecedented barrage of flak from the newly reinforced 88-millimeter cannon batteries that now ringed the industrial works. In spite of these obstacles, the groups managed to deliver a devastating blow.

After the battle, the mission leader, Colonel Budd Peaslee of the 384th Bomb Group, estimated that three hundred German fighters had confronted them over the course of the day, making more than seven hundred separate attacks.

Sixty bombers had been shot down in the battle. The 305th Bomb Group lost thirteen of its sixteen Fortresses in less than thirty minutes. Five hundred ninety men had been killed in action.

The Stuttgart fiasco had proved that the Eighth could not sustain continued deep-penetration missions without long-range fighters escorting them. The second Schweinfurt attack was the final nail in the doctrine's coffin.

It marked the end of Ira Eaker's air offensive against Germany.

In Washington, President Roosevelt was asked about the extraordinary losses the Eighth was absorbing. For the first time, the president did not offer a strong defense of daylight precision bombing.

Hap Arnold publicly declared it to be a major victory, stating that the ball-bearing factories at Schweinfurt had been rendered "completely useless" and that "no moving machinery will operate without ball bearings."

It was a huge exaggeration, but one that underscored the fragile level of confidence by Arnold's fellow war commanders in his cherished goal of destroying Germany's capacity to make war with precision bombing alone. Desperate to make the case that the Eighth's efforts had now brought the Luftwaffe close to capitulation, Arnold fired off another cable to Eaker:

"It appears from my viewpoint that the German Air Force is on the verge of collapse . . . Can you add any substantial evidence of collapse?"

The suggestion was ludicrous. If either side in the air war was on the ropes at that point, it was the Eighth Air Force. One day after the battle, Ira Eaker responded to Hap Arnold's cable. His demands were explicit:

"Rush replacement aircraft and crews. . . . Send every possible fighter here as soon as possible. Emphasize early arrival of additional P-38s and Mustangs. . . . Give us 5000 auxiliary droppable tanks for fighters as soon as possible."

Arnold immediately complied with Eaker's requests, diverting the first shipments of P-51 Mustangs that had been slated to go to the Pacific and North Africa to England instead.

It would take nearly two months for them to begin arriving. In the meantime, Arnold demanded that Eaker resume the air offensive against German strategic targets with strikes of at least five hundred Fortresses on each mission.

It wasn't to be. In November, Eaker mounted only two raids with a force exceeding five hundred bombers, and neither was a deep-penetration raid. Arnold's legendary impatience reached a climax.

In early December, Hap Arnold met in Cairo with Air Chief Marshal Portal of the RAF to discuss the future of the combined bomber offensive in Europe. In assessing the American contribution, Portal made the case that Ira Eaker was doing everything he could to achieve the Allied bombing goals with the assets he had to work with.

His presentation fell on deaf ears.

Arnold declared to Portal that according to his inspectors the Eighth was utilizing only 50 percent of its available aircraft on combat missions, while the utilization figure in the other combat theaters was 70 percent. The failure of the air offensive against Germany, he said, was a direct result of Eaker not utilizing his planes in sufficient numbers to get the job done.

On December 4, the first shipments of long-range P-51 Mustangs began arriving in England. Eaker's urgent requests had finally borne fruit. His staff estimated that by early January, the Eighth would have enough fighters with jettisonable belly tanks to escort the Fortresses all the way to Germany and back.

That same day, President Roosevelt announced his decision to name General Dwight Eisenhower to be the supreme commander of the Allied forces that would invade Europe in 1944.

A few days later, Hap Arnold flew to Tunis to meet with Eisenhower. In the first planning session, Eisenhower told Arnold that he wanted General Carl "Tooey" Spaatz to be his senior air commander. Arnold agreed.

On December 9, Arnold flew to meet with Spaatz at his headquarters in Foggia, Italy. Together, they decided to recommend a shake-up of the air theater commanders. Ira Eaker would be transferred to the Mediterranean command. General Jimmy Doolittle, the hard-driving veteran of the daring Tokyo raid in 1942, would be given the Eighth Air Force.

Arnold now had to tell Ira Eaker he was out of his job. Months earlier, he had promised Eaker that if a change was to be made, he "would be the first one to hear of it." Dealing with unpleasant duties involving an old friend, however, wasn't one of Arnold's strong points. Instead, on December 18, he sent Eaker an official cable through channels:

"It has been decided that an American will take over command of the Allied Air Force in the Mediterranean now held by Tedder. As a result of your long period of successful operations and the exceptional results of your endeavors as Commander of the Air Force in England, you have been recommended for this position."

Eaker's shock after reading the cable turned to rage. With the invasion of Europe coming, the Mediterranean theater would become a backwater. This wasn't a promotion. It was a sacking. Arnold hadn't even had the decency to tell him in a personal communication. The cable had obviously been written by a member of his staff.

Eaker had personally built the Eighth Air Force from scratch. After all his months of requesting the long-range fighters that would change the course of the air war, they were finally starting to arrive, and no thanks to Arnold. Now that Eaker was poised to show what the Eighth could accomplish, Arnold was trying to take it away from him.

He had been as loyal a subordinate as any man could ask for, only to be humiliated in the end. He had often acceded to Arnold's demands against his better judgment and then watched his air crews pay the price for the mistakes.

They were his boys. He couldn't count the number of times he had gone to the base hospitals across southern England to pin medals on men who had had their arms and legs shot off.

After privately brooding about what to do, Eaker decided to fight for his job. He cabled Arnold his response. It was hard not to make the words sound like begging. He was.

"Believe war interest best served by my retention command 8th Air Force: otherwise experience this theater for nearly two years wasted. If I am to be allowed any personal preference, having started with the Eighth . . . it would be heartbreaking to leave just before climax . . . request I be allowed to retain command 8th Air Force."

That same day, Eaker sent a separate cable to Eisenhower, informing him that *"Arnold proposes new assignment for me,"* and requesting that he be allowed to remain in command of the Eighth.

Arnold's response to Eaker's cables preceded Eisenhower's. It left no doubt about the outcome. It also ended their twenty-five-year friendship. Eaker would never get over the betrayal.

". . . it is unfortunate that you cannot, repeat, not stay and retain command of the organization . . . the broader viewpoint of the world-wide war effort indicates the necessity for a change. . . . I cannot, repeat, not see my way clear to make any change in the decisions already reached."

On December 23, Ira Eaker received the official order relieving him of command of the Eighth Air Force. The following day, he cabled Arnold an equally impersonal reply:

"Orders received. Will be carried out promptly January 1."

On Christmas Day, Eaker finally received Eisenhower's reply to his cable asking to stay:

"Your personal message reached me en route to my base headquarters," it read. *"As you well know, I would be more than delighted to have you with me. I note that your orders have already been issued, but the fact is, as I have just informed General Marshall, your transfer was proposed to me specifically by General Arnold in a brief conversation in Sicily and I agreed because of the absolute necessity of finding an outstanding man for the post of Air CINC of the Mediterranean."*

He was going to the goddamn Mediterranean.

In Washington, Hap Arnold celebrated Christmas Day on General's Row at Fort Myer, Virginia. His estranged wife, Bee, had returned from her self-imposed exile to join him there for the holiday. She seemed to be less judgmental on his failures as a husband, and he thought there might be a chance for a genuine reconciliation.

Desperate Journey

Saturday, 25 December 1943
Girona, Spain
Second Lieutenant Warren Porter Laws

From his second-floor prison window, he could see men and women hurriedly crossing the sidewalk at the end of the narrow alley facing the boulevard. It was Christmas Day, and most of the people were rushing along with packages under their arms, probably heading home to enjoy the holiday with their families.

After a perilous climb across the snow-choked Pyrenees, Warren had made it to Spain, but now the authorities wouldn't let him contact the American consulate and were threatening to turn him over to the Germans.

It had been a long journey to reach his prison cell.

Warren had spent most of September and October holed up with Joe Schwartzkopf in a succession of safe houses around Troyes, about six miles from where *Patricia* had been shot down. German soldiers occupied the town, and after a week or two in one place, the two Americans would be moved at night to a presumably safer location.

Warren had occupied his six weeks of captivity as productively as he could, spending almost every waking hour studying the words and phrases in his pocket French-English dictionary, and then practicing colloquial French with their host families. By mid-October, the teachers' college graduate was not only completely fluent but spoke it with barely a trace of his American accent.

Joe Schwartzkopf was astonished. To him, it seemed like Lieutenant Laws had actually become a Frenchman, including adopting some of their physical gestures. Sometimes Warren would start talking to him in French, forgetting that he couldn't understand a word. Then he would stop and give Joe an apologetic grin.

They were staying with a family in Troyes when a Catholic priest came to see them. Introducing himself as Abbé Jean Bonnard, he told them that they were being sent on to Paris to join the Burgundy escape line, one of the many groups working to repatriate escaped Allied airmen.

On October 17, Warren and Joe, along with two other Americans who had been sheltered in Troyes, boarded a train for Paris's Gare du Nord. Upon their arrival, the four men had been instructed to wait on a specific platform until a woman wearing white gloves approached them with the correct code words.

When they arrived at the train station, Warren led them to the specified platform, but the woman in white gloves didn't appear. The Americans had no way of knowing she had been arrested by the Gestapo after leaving her house to meet them.

As the hours passed, Warren knew that something must have gone wrong, but their only recourse was to keep waiting. The nightly curfew hour was approaching when he finally concluded they would have to fend for themselves.

Warren was the only one in the group who could speak French, and the others asked him to try to find them a safe haven. He found it in the form of a scrub woman who was cleaning the stall of a food vendor in the waiting room of the station.

In escape classes back at Knettishall, Warren had been told that the safest potential ally was a Catholic priest. Next best was someone from the working class. Warren thought the cleaning woman had a sympathetic face.

In colloquial French, he described their situation to her and asked for help. Amazingly, she believed everything he told her. She said that her work shift was almost over, and that the Americans were welcome to spend the night at her one-room apartment.

In the morning, Warren proposed that they return to Troyes, and the other three agreed. Confident in his ability to now pass as a Frenchman, he bought their tickets and led them to the proper train. By midday, they were back where they started. Abbé Bonnard divided the men up again, and found new safe houses for them while another escape plan was organized.

Warren and Joe ended up at the farm of a man named Marcel Doré. It was the perfect place to hide. Monsieur Doré was an animal renderer and spent his days picking up dead horses, cattle, and other farm stock. After hauling the animals back to the farm, he and his men sawed them into large pieces that went into huge metal vats, where wood fires kept the carcasses cooking twenty-four hours a day.

A constant stench filled the air around the farm, and the Germans rarely came to search there. No one else came there, either, except British agents of the Special Operations Executive (SOE). It was their local base of operations.

In late November, Warren was recruited by the SOE operatives to participate in an upcoming resupply operation. A resistance unit near Troyes needed weapons, ammunition, and radio parts.

A single-engine Lysander airplane was coming from England and would arrive before dawn in the nearby countryside. The pilot would only land after he saw an agreed upon configuration of flashlight beams aimed at him from the ground. For this operation, the configuration was to be the French Cross of Lorraine.

At three the next morning, Warren was waiting in the pasture with a dozen members of the local Maquis, all armed with rifles and hand grenades. When they heard the plane coming, the men switched their flashlights on. The pilot landed the Lysander along the vertical line of the French cross. The precious cargo was quickly unloaded, and the plane took off again a few minutes later.

The Maquis' next mission was to be an attack on a local power station. Warren had agreed to join them again, but before the mission could be mounted, Abbé Bonnard arrived at the Doré farm to tell him that the Burgundy escape line was operational once more, and that he and Joe would be leaving for Paris right away.

They arrived there safely, and spent the next two weeks at a safe house near the Eiffel Tower. An underground agent came to tell Warren that he would be leaving on a train the next morning for Perpignan in the southwest corner of France. From there, he would cross the Pyrenees into Spain.

The agent told Warren and Joe that it would be necessary for them to split up. He said that another American they were harboring was having severe emotional problems. Because Warren had become fluent in French, he was the best choice to help the troubled American make it to Spain.

Before they parted, Warren again thanked Joe for staying with him after *Patricia* went down. They wished each other good luck, and agreed to get together for a drink back in England.

The troubled American, Henry Krueger, had been a gunner on a B-17 that crashed near Paris. He was the only survivor, and was now subject to severe mood swings. Warren stayed close to him all the way to Perpignan, and the trip passed uneventfully.

At the station, they were met by another underground operative. After exchanging the correct code words, he told Warren and Henry to follow him on foot. They walked several miles south until the buildings of Perpignan gave way to open countryside.

After hiking along a series of country lanes, they came to a small roadside café. Inside, Warren was introduced to the man who would escort them across the Pyrenees. He was a Spanish smuggler and intimately familiar with the trails they had to climb to reach the border. Human cargo was the principal commodity he dealt in, and he was regularly employed by the underground. To Warren, he looked like a man who sold himself to the highest bidder. He hoped the Germans hadn't raised their bounty on escaping Americans.

As the three men headed up into the foothills, it started to rain. Both Warren and Henry Krueger had winter coats, but they were wearing GI shoes and began having trouble climbing the slick, muddy trails.

The track soon became steeper, in some places heading almost straight up through the ancient rock-strewn canyons. The Spaniard told Warren that they needed to climb all night in order to reach the border the following morning. Crossing in daylight was too risky. Troops randomly patrolled the border, and often shot on sight.

As darkness fell, Henry Krueger began to drop behind, and the other two had to slow down. Henry Krueger was badly out of shape, and Warren's legs began to cramp up, too. The Spanish guide became increasingly angry at the slowness of their ascent. They were still hours from the pass, he said, and needed to hasten the pace.

The rain turned to icy sleet, and the rock defiles grew even more slick and dangerous. They were still an hour from the top of the pass when Henry Krueger told Warren he couldn't go on. Dropping to his knees, he began to sob.

The guide had no sympathy for his plight, and told Warren in French that they should leave him behind. Instead, Warren told Henry to climb onto his back. With Henry's arms around his shoulders, and Warren's hands under Henry's thighs, they continued the tortuous ascent.

With brief rest breaks, they finally made it to the top of the pass. After they reached the downward side, Henry told Warren he thought he could walk again. By then, the icy sleet had turned to snow. Night had finally given way to a gray dawn as they reached the bottom of a rock-strewn slope. That was when the guide gave Warren a wolfish smile and pointed ahead of them to a green meadow.

"*Espagne*," he said, baring his yellow-stained front teeth.

Before leaving them to their fate, the Spaniard pointed out a landmark to follow for the next few miles south, and urged Warren to get as far away from the border as possible. The closer they were when they were apprehended, the better the chance they would be handed back to the Germans.

The two Americans continued walking south in the rain into the Spanish countryside. Neither one had eaten since the previous afternoon, and they were ravenously hungry, but Warren refused to stop until they had left the border far behind.

In the afternoon, they reached a small village. An imposing Catholic church dominated the small square. Remembering how courageous Abbé Bonnard had been, Warren led Henry into the church sanctuary.

The village priest came forward and asked what they wanted. When Warren identified himself as an American, the priest ordered them to leave.

They were standing outside in the driving rain when Henry Krueger finally broke down completely from the physical and emotional strain of the previous two days. He began sobbing uncontrollably and saying he wanted to go home. Warren tried to assure him that everything would be all right as he helped him along the street. Now desperate for assistance, he stopped at the first house past the village square.

The man who answered the door couldn't speak French or English, but he gave them a welcoming smile and waved them into his warm kitchen. While his wife made them coffee, the man bowed and left.

The man was back ten minutes later with a squad of Spanish police. The two Americans were immediately arrested and sent by car to the prison in Girona, where they underwent several hours of questioning. The still disturbed Henry Krueger was sent to a mental hospital.

Warren would only give the Spanish authorities his name, rank, and serial number, while repeatedly requesting that the American consulate be notified that he was there. They ignored his request.

Confined to an eight-foot-square cell lined with stone walls and a barred window, he celebrated Christmas Day with a supper of thin soup, bread, and water. After everything he had gone through to get to Spain, he was grateful to have it.

There was a daily exercise period for each prisoner, and the next morning he encountered another man in the prison yard who spoke French. The man said he was there as the result of a false accusation, and told Warren that the Spanish judicial system was totally corrupt.

When Warren told him he was an escaped American officer, the man told him it would be necessary for the American consulate to bid for his freedom. The Germans would also bid, he said. Warren would go to the highest bidder.

The conversation left him confused. If that was true, why wouldn't the Spanish authorities have alerted the American consul that he was there? They couldn't make a bid if they didn't know he was in Spain.

The following day he was gazing out his second-floor cell window when a young man came walking up the alley from the boulevard. The first thing Warren noticed about him was that he was wearing American GI shoes, just like his own. Warren opened the casement window inside the bars and called down to the man, who immediately stopped.

"If you're an American, please tell our consulate that they are holding an escaped American pilot here," he shouted in English.

The man said nothing. A moment later, he was gone.

Maybe it was coincidence, but the following day he was released to the custody of an American military attaché at the United States consulate. He was driven to Barcelona, where he was debriefed for several days by an American intelligence officer who wanted to know everything about his adventures with the underground after he had been shot down.

After completing his debriefing, Warren was told that it would be a few weeks before passage could be arranged for him to return to England and then the United States. Warren had only one request. He asked to be provided with a Spanish-English dictionary. He thought three weeks might be enough time for him to become reasonably fluent in Spanish.

The Telegram

Friday, 31 December 1943
Scarsdale, New York
Braxton "Betsy" Wilken

The telegram from the War Department had arrived in November. It was from the adjutant general of the U.S. Army Air Forces. She knew what it would say before she opened the envelope.

DEAR MRS. WILKEN,

IT IS WITH PROFOUND REGRET THAT I MUST CON-
FIRM THE DEATH OF YOUR HUSBAND, LIEUTENANT
RAY T. WILKEN, 0-795,161, WHO HAS PREVIOUSLY
BEEN REPORTED MISSING IN ACTION. INFORMATION
HAS BEEN RECEIVED FROM THE GERMAN GOVERNMENT
THROUGH THE INTERNATIONAL RED CROSS THAT HE
WAS KILLED IN ACTION ON 6 SEPTEMBER 1943. I
REALIZE THE BURDEN OF ANXIETY THAT HAS BEEN
YOURS SINCE HE WAS FIRST REPORTED MISSING IN
ACTION AND DEEPLY REGRET THE SORROW THIS LATER
REPORT BRINGS YOU. MAY THE KNOWLEDGE THAT HE
MADE THE SUPREME SACRIFICE IN DEFENSE OF HIS
HOME AND COUNTRY BE A SOURCE OF SUSTAINING COM-
FORT. I EXTEND TO YOU MY DEEP SYMPATHY. SIN-
CERELY YOURS, J.A. ULIO, MAJOR GENERAL

From the very beginning, Braxton knew just how close to death he always was, even during training. When Ted was going through his B-17 trials, she and the other wives would gather near the control tower to watch their husbands bring the big Fortresses home. One afternoon, she had watched a B-17 come in to land with what seemed like a steeper approach than normal. When the plane hit the ground, it blew up, killing everyone aboard.

She could remember the words she had written to Ted's mother, Helen, soon afterward:

> I guess war has made us a very hardened and practical lot. We saw that when Mil Stevens was killed at George Field. You learn to be thrifty with your emotions. Teddy has a dangerous job to do and it must not be cluttered with emotions. That's the hardest thing all of us Air Corps families have had to learn—to accept—not to question. . . . It's an awful easy thing to die, but sometimes to live and do it gracefully is the seemingly impossible thing.

Shortly after receiving the formal confirmation of his death from the War Department, she wrote a letter to David Parry, another B-17 pilot in England and a good friend of Ted's. David and his wife, Edith, had gone through training with Ted and Braxton. After Ted went missing, David had written her to say that soon after the birth of Kathy, Ted had proudly brought the photograph of Braxton and the baby over to his quarters in Framingham, and they had shared a celebratory toast to his new family.

Now David was writing back.

> Dear Betsy,
> Edith has already written that she has seen you and that you have accepted the news of Ted's death with dignity and courage. I'm glad, not only for your sake but for Ted's, who would be the first to make a crack about widow's weeds if ever you should wear them. It's curious how tenuous in wartime that

line of demarcation becomes that separates the quick from the
dead. It's sometimes hard to remember just who in the group
has gone down and who has missed breakfast for a couple of
mornings. I can't offer you the solemn conventional condo-
lences because I know Ted would laugh at me. I wonder if you
feel the same way.

Two crews finished up the other day. I still have three to
go, which is like saying that if the black comes up three more
times at Roulette I'll break the bank. If I do get back, I am looking forward more than almost anything to seeing you again and
saying some of the things I can't now. The three of us will go
somewhere and talk about the fun the four of us had, and shall
always have, and we shall have a drink for Ted. Take good care
of Kathy. Love, David

There were no guarantees in life or love. Her principal regrets
were that they would never make more babies together, never grow old
together, and she would never have the chance to know what he would
have become if he had lived.

In early December, Braxton moved back to Scarsdale. She had
grown up there. Her friends were there. She rented a small furnished
apartment near the Bronx River and moved in at the start of the
New Year.

Her closest friend was Jane Eaglesham. They had gone to school
together. Jane had been one of the prettiest girls in their class, but she
had been in a terrible automobile accident and her face was horribly
disfigured. Aside from Braxton, her school friends no longer wanted to
see her.

In the wake of Ted's death, they began spending a lot of time
together. One of Braxton's new missions in life was to see that Jane had
dates like she used to in college before the accident.

Living alone with Kathy in the little apartment gave her a lot of time
to think about both the past and the future. She and Ted had shared so
many interests. In addition to being lovers, they were best friends. He
had been a whole man, and he had loved her.

She had admired so much about him, his intelligence, his natural leadership, his sense of the nonsense of life, and his generosity to anyone in need. If she were ever repaid the money he had lent to fellow officers and crewmen in their training days, it would pay for Kathy's college education.

At one point, Braxton remembered their last serious conversation on the night before he left. Ted had given her his thoughts on the things she needed to do if he was killed. He hadn't dwelled on it, but one meaning was clear. If anything happened to him, he hoped she would find someone else.

Get on with it, she thought as the days continued to pass. You will not be a moaning war widow. You still have a life to live the best way you know how. The New Year is at hand. You will find a new reason to live.

On the Run

Friday, 21 January 1944
Douarnenez, France
Second Lieutenant Jimmy Armstrong

He had survived enough adventures to last a lifetime.

There had been many times over the four months he had been on the run when Jimmy was sure he was about to be captured, and only a twist of fate had saved him from a prisoner-of-war camp, or worse.

He had arrived in Paris on the night of September 20, exactly two weeks after *Yankee Raider* had gone down. After spending two days at the tiny apartment of the medical intern who had brought him to the city, he was turned over to two young Parisians named Maurice and George. They picked him up in a wood-burning flatbed truck and transported him across Paris to the suburb of Drancy.

Maurice was the bartender of a café, and he celebrated Jimmy's arrival by pouring out three full glasses of cognac. He and George then demonstrated how it should be quaffed in one long swallow. The harsh liquor brought tears to the twenty-one-year-old's eyes, which engendered a good deal of laughter from the Frenchmen.

George brought out a pistol from under his belt, along with a wad of ration tickets he had stolen the night before from a government office. The coupons helped to supply the needs of their resistance cell.

Maurice's girlfriend, Monique, arrived shortly afterward and prepared

255

Jimmy's dinner. Later that night, she escorted him upstairs to the room he would be sharing with her and Maurice.

She pointed out the single mattress on the floor in the corner where he would sleep. It was only a few feet from the double bed she shared with Maurice. After falling asleep that night, Jimmy was awakened to the first of their many ardent sexual encounters. Each time he thought they were finished, the couple would somehow find renewed energy, and their bleating cries would rise to the next crescendo. He didn't get much sleep.

A few days later, Maurice escorted him to the studio of a local photographer, who took his picture for the false identity papers that were being prepared for him. On the way back to the café, they passed a massive building with high walls around it.

In mangled English, Maurice explained to him that it was once the Drancy prison, and that it now housed several thousand Parisian Jews who were being sent to Germany. Jimmy couldn't understand why the Jews needed to be kept in prison, or why they were being sent to Germany.

He was sitting in the café one afternoon when two young men accompanied by an attractive blonde sat down at his table. His nervousness receded when one of the men began talking to him in Americanized English with a distinct Southern twang. He said his name was Floyd Terry, and that he was a B-17 waist gunner from Dallas, Texas. The other man was an RAF bomber pilot who had been shot down on a night mission to Milan, Italy.

They were staying in the nearby suburb of Bobigny with the blond woman, who introduced herself as Theodorine Quenot. Maurice's café was a clearinghouse for escaping airmen, and she had come to replenish her food coupons. Like George and Maurice, "Madame Q" despised the Germans and was doing everything she could to drive them from French soil.

After Jimmy's long nights of enduring the amatory pleasures of Maurice and his mistress, Jimmy begged her to let him stay with the other escapees. She agreed and he moved in the next day. The three Americans were joined soon after by Andrew Lindsay, a red-haired American B-26 pilot from Monmouth, Maine.

The stolen food coupons allowed the Americans to eat well. In the evenings, they played hearts at the kitchen table while listening to the nightly BBC news broadcasts on her small radio.

The days passed by slowly.

In mid-October, Madame Q woke the airmen to tell them that they would be leaving Paris for the next stage of their journey to freedom. By then, Jimmy had new identity papers that identified him as Jean Riber, a pork butcher from Reims.

After packing their few belongings, the airmen were picked up in a canvas-covered truck. Inside, there were six more Americans, including John Heald, Jimmy's original bombardier, who had been shot down while flying with another crew on a mission to Paris in August.

That was when Jimmy realized how many French patriots must be involved in helping him and the others. Their courage in the face of possible execution by the Gestapo was astonishing to him.

At the Paris train station, the ten Allied fliers were divided into pairs and handed off to five members of the resistance who were to serve as their guides. Jimmy saw that his ticket was marked Quimper. He had no idea where it was, but once the train left the station, he knew they were traveling west. When he disembarked at their first destination with his escort, the platform was filled with German soldiers in bright green uniforms. He was so much bigger than the Germans that he worried he would stand out like a sore thumb.

Remembering the White Russian's tutoring of how to walk like a Frenchman, he made short mincing steps toward the exit and passed safely out of the station. The escort picked him up on the street and led him across the town to a large three-story house surrounded by a high brick wall.

Its owners were Jacques and Madeleine Mourlet. By day, Jacques was a wine merchant. At night he assumed the role of the Scarlet Pimpernel. Instead of helping French aristocrats escape the guillotine, his specialty was spiriting Allied airmen as well as Frenchmen seeking to join the Free French army out of occupied France.

Madeleine, who spoke fluent English, was stunningly beautiful, and Jimmy, along with his nine fellow guests, was immediately smitten.

On the night of their arrival, she served them all a delicious dinner accompanied by ample quantities of wine.

Looking around the table at one point, Madeleine focused her eyes on Jimmy.

"You look the least like a Frenchman," she declared with a charming smile. "You are strictly American." He took it as a compliment.

The next afternoon, another man arrived at the villa. He was wearing a long brown leather trench coat and matching wide-brimmed leather hat. To Jimmy, he looked like the archetypal spy.

Introducing himself as Fanfan, he informed the assembled airmen of their proposed escape plan. On a designated night, they would board a fishing smack and be transported by sea to a rendezvous with a high-speed British navy launch. Fanfan was waiting for the radio signal that would specify the night of the rendezvous.

Late that evening, Jacques received a hurried telephone warning that his house was about to be raided. A German collaborator in the village had informed the police that Jacques was harboring Allied escapees.

In a frenzied rush, the ten airmen gathered up their belongings.

The cars carrying the gendarmes were arriving at the front of the villa while Jacques led the ten airmen through a rear passage in the stone wall. After leaving them in a nearby copse of woods, he went back to his house.

It was well past midnight when he returned, saying that Madeleine had finally convinced the police that the accusation was false. He was sure they were still watching his house, so he had arranged another temporary hiding place for them until the radio signal came from England.

It turned out to be the small home of an elderly Catholic priest. After welcoming them with a short prayer, he ushered the ten men upstairs to a twelve-foot-square room, gave them blankets, and urged them to rest. The floor was soon crowded with snoring fliers.

They were confined to the room for four days and were only allowed outside at night to use the privy behind the house. Each day, the angelic Madeleine would arrive with baskets of bread, cheese, and fruit.

Once confined to the room, tempers began to grow short. One of the pilots began referring to the hulking Jimmy as "Li'l Abner," because his pants' legs barely reached the tops of his high-top GI shoes. When Jimmy asked the pilot if he would enjoy being hanged by his feet out the window, the officer quickly apologized.

On their fifth day in the small room, Fanfan arrived with bad news. The English launch was not coming. There would be no rendezvous. It was necessary for them all to return to Paris.

Arriving back at the Paris train station, Fanfan paired off the ten airmen again and sent them off with a new set of escorts. Jimmy and another pilot went with a man in his thirties named Gilbert Virmoux to an apartment building in the heart of Paris.

Two other Allied airmen were in Gilbert's apartment when they got there. They had been English machine gunners on a Lancaster bomber. Gilbert's apartment was on the sixth floor and consisted of one large room. The toilet was on the second floor and was shared by all the occupants of the narrow building.

One morning, Jimmy met a Jewish woman who was being hidden in an apartment on one of the lower floors. She spoke excellent English, and told him how fortunate she had been in escaping the roundup of Jews in her neighborhood. She told him that the Germans were arresting every Jew in France, stripping them of their possessions and property, and sending them to camps in Germany.

Her account of the German cruelty filled him with a desire to return to the war.

At the end of November, Gilbert Virmoux told Jimmy he was taking him and the others to be "toughened up" with a week of hard exercise at a place in the country. The following day, they traveled by rail to a small village in the countryside, and then walked several miles to an imposing French château.

Another group of Americans was already there. For the next ten days, he and the others sawed firewood and hiked forest trails, slowly regaining the fitness they had lost while in hiding. One of the fliers told Jimmy that they would be going out of France over the Pyrenees.

It was mid-December and the weather had grown sharply colder when Gilbert confirmed that he would be escorting them all to a town in southern France, from which they would hike across the mountains into Spain.

Boarding another train, they traveled south toward Carcassonne, a medieval fortress town near the Spanish border. Near the city of Toulouse, it began to snow. By the time they reached Carcassonne, it was nearly a foot deep.

How could they get across the mountains? Jimmy wondered. He didn't even have an overcoat, much less hiking boots. The question was almost rendered moot when he stepped down to the platform and headed toward the station exit.

Jimmy suddenly stopped short. Fifty feet away, a German officer was checking the papers of every traveler. Standing alongside him were three soldiers with unslung machine guns.

Slowly turning away, he saw Gilbert walking toward a small building that had a large "WC" painted on the door. When Gilbert disappeared inside, Jimmy followed him. Soon, six Americans were hiding in the reeking toilet urinals.

Urging them to remain quiet, Gilbert left them to meet the mountaineer who was to accompany them across the Pyrenees. He returned in an hour to say that the Germans had left, but that their mountain guide had been frightened off. It would be necessary to go to another village to find a replacement.

Snow was still falling hard as they boarded another train after dark and traveled through a valley to the village of Quillan. Soaring up behind it were the majestic snow-covered peaks of the Pyrenees. Spain and freedom lay on the other side.

In the frigid darkness, the men trudged through snow to a house on the outskirts of the village. When Gilbert knocked on the door, the shutters of an upstairs window creaked open. It was too dark for Jimmy to see the man's face, but after a brief exchange of words, he slammed the shutters closed.

A downcast Gilbert told the Americans there was no way to make it through the mountain pass, and they would have to go back to Paris. Thoroughly demoralized, Jimmy boarded the unheated train back to Carcassonne.

It was after midnight when they arrived at the station, and there was no place to go except the waiting room, where a wood-burning stove would at least keep them warm. Unfortunately, the waiting room was crowded with German soldiers who had also been stranded there for the night. Most of them were already gathered around the stove in the center of the room.

The cold, exhausted Jimmy no longer cared if he looked sufficiently French or walked like a Frenchman. Desperate to get warm, he crowded straight into the mix of soldiers until he could feel the welcoming warmth of the stove.

Gilbert was nearly out of money, but he was able to purchase tickets for them on a third-class coach leaving the following morning. After another twenty-hour journey, the train arrived in Paris after curfew, and Jimmy had to wait in the car the rest of the night before walking across Paris to Gilbert's apartment.

As he plodded through the deserted streets, Jimmy lost his faith that he would ever make it back to England. It was only a matter of time before he was picked up by the Germans and sent to a prisoner-of-war camp. It would be better to have the odyssey over and done with.

Twelve hours of sleep in the quiet of Gilbert's sixth-floor apartment helped to restore his flagging spirits. He felt ashamed of himself. Gilbert had done everything he could to help them escape, risking his life on their behalf for almost six weeks. He vowed not to lose hope again.

On Christmas Eve, Gilbert came home to give Jimmy the news that another escape attempt was being organized, and a man would soon be coming to escort him to the train station.

As a parting gift, he gave Jimmy a hand-painted Christmas card. The cover depicted St. Nicholas with a lantern in one hand. In the other, he was holding a gift-wrapped package. As he read the message inside, Jimmy realized that Gilbert was the true Santa Claus. The lantern represented hope, the gift-wrapped package his freedom.

Before Jimmy left for the next stage of his journey, the two men embraced. As he had done with his other benefactors, Jimmy promised to come back and visit him when the war was over.

The platform of the Paris train station was crowded with travelers on their way home to celebrate Christmas. When Jimmy's guide gave him his train ticket, he saw that the destination was Quimper, and he knew that the next escape attempt would again be by boat.

Three hours later, the train arrived in Le Mans, where it was necessary to change trains for Quimper. On the platform, he was given a slip of paper authorizing him to wait in the station during curfew hours for the next train. Finding space on a wooden bench, he fell asleep.

He awoke to someone kicking the soles of his shoes. He groggily looked up into the face of a French gendarme. The man was demanding something, and Jimmy had no idea what it was. With rising irritation, the policeman harshly repeated the same words.

Trying to appear calm, Jimmy pulled out his identity card and handed it up to him. Without looking at it, the policeman tossed it back and angrily repeated the same question. Jimmy suddenly remembered the slip of paper he had been given on the platform. He handed it to the policeman, who glanced at the pass and handed it back, then moved on to the next person.

The next train pulled into Quimper after midnight. He was about to get off when his guide, who was sitting in another row of the car, motioned to him to remain in his seat. A few minutes later, the train was diverted onto another track, where it continued west across the Brittany peninsula.

Early the next morning, the train stopped at a small seaside village. When the guide left the train, Jimmy followed him. In the basement of a house near the quay, he joined a group of more than thirty escapees. They were to leave France that very night. Christmas night. Without question, freedom would be the finest Christmas present he had ever received.

The escape boat was lying in a small bay near the village. At ebb tide, the escapees were to wade out to the boat and climb aboard. When the tide was full, they would sail for England.

He felt a rush of pure adrenaline as they divided up into small groups and headed toward the pier. Through one of the house windows along the street, he could see a family gathered in song in front of a piano, and heard the refrain of a familiar Christmas carol.

Suddenly, a patrol of German soldiers with flashlights emerged from the corner of a side street and came straight toward them. It was well past curfew, and they had no permit papers to be there if the Germans stopped them.

Jimmy and the others turned at the corner, desperately hoping they wouldn't be ordered to stop. Once more, an angel was riding his big shoulders. The Germans kept moving down the street.

At the water's edge, the tide had begun to rise. It was ankle deep, and Jimmy took off his shoes and socks to wade out to the boat. Most of the airmen were already aboard when he finally reached the darkened craft. He was about to pull himself over the transom when one of the Frenchmen in the boat said, "Turn around and go back. The escape is off!"

A disheartened Jimmy Armstrong made his way back to the house they had just left. A resistance leader was waiting there for them.

"We could not leave tonight," he told them, "but you will be in England soon."

Once more, the men were divided up. Jimmy and another airman were taken to an apartment in the nearby coastal village of Douarnenez. It was occupied by Madame Evelyn Malhomme, and had a spectacular view of the bay.

In the days that followed, Jimmy learned that her husband was in a German concentration camp called Buchenwald, and that her two sons were fighting with the Free French army under General de Gaulle. Jimmy turned out to be the same age as one of her sons, and it soon became clear that his presence was relieving the loneliness of not having her own sons at home.

One afternoon she came back to the apartment and told them that another boat had been readied to take them to England, and that they would be leaving the next night. As a keepsake of their time together, she gave Jimmy a small porcelain bell of a Brittany maid. Around the maid's waist, she had tied four tiny strands of red yarn. Jimmy didn't know what to say. He had nothing to give her back except his gratitude, then and for always. He tried to convey those words to her.

"*Au revoir*," she said to him. "*Bonne chance*."

The fishing boat was named *Breiz-Izel*. It was forty feet long and tied to a long dock at the edge of the harbor. As darkness fell, Jimmy and the other Allied airmen were brought to the boat in small groups. There were two holds, one fore and one aft. Jimmy was directed to the one in the stern.

When he climbed down into it, he was dismayed to discover that it was only a shallow crawl space. There was no room to sit up, much less stand. He hated confined spaces, and as one of the first aboard, he had to crawl farther and farther away from the hatch until he was hard against the outer hull. There were thirty escapees, and after they were all aboard, there was no room to move. Jimmy lay on his stomach in the pitch-black compartment and tried not to dwell on his fears.

Someone said that he now knew what it was like for a sardine lying in a tin can. No one laughed.

An underground agent arrived to tell them that the captain was planning to wait for the outgoing tide. Then he would release the dock lines and the boat would silently drift out into the bay. Once they were far enough away from shore, he would start the engine and head for England.

By now, Jimmy had learned not to get his hopes up. He could only rely on his prayers, along with the actions of the brave men and women who had saved him up to that point.

The minutes slowly dragged on into hours. One of the men became incontinent, and the air soon turned foul. Long after midnight, Jimmy heard footsteps clomping above him on the wooden deck. An escapee lying near the open hatch quietly announced to the others that the boat was moving.

Suddenly, the stillness of the night was rent by a loud scream.

"Halt!" someone yelled. "Halt!"

The voice was loud enough to raise the dead. Jimmy immediately imagined a German sentry standing at his post in the harbor as he aimed his rifle at the boat and pulled the trigger.

The escapee near the open hatch called out that someone onshore had turned on a searchlight. It was another failed attempt, thought Jimmy as he waited for the boat to stop or be turned around.

But this time the captain kept going. Jimmy heard the engine start, and the throttle was opened wide for full power. As the minutes ticked by, the men waited fearfully for a German patrol boat to intercept them.

When Jimmy felt the boat begin rolling back and forth from side to side, he realized they must be in the ocean. Soon the rolling action was joined by a rocking motion as the boat plowed into deep troughs and then came out of the crashing waves. The simultaneous rocking and rolling was nauseating.

After the first man began vomiting, it became contagious. A few of the men began spewing at both ends. As the hours passed, the sounds of men retching continued unabated. Jimmy no longer cared if he lived or died. He just wanted the motion to stop.

As the ferocity of the storm increased, cold seawater began sloshing through the open hatch and splashing the deck of the shallow hold. One of the French seamen shoved the hatch closed. Now we're trapped, Jimmy thought.

Fetid water from the bilge began soaking the deck they were lying on, soon rising a foot above the deck. He was about to scream out to the captain that they were drowning when he heard a diesel pump come on and the water level slowly began to recede.

The storm only got worse. At one point, the bilge pump stopped working, and the water level began to rise again. Jimmy heard the hatch cover being removed, and a flashlight beam lit the hold. One of the seamen crawled over the prone bodies of the airmen until he reached the pump. It had been fouled by food, clothing, and human waste.

The boat continued plowing through the raging sea all that night and into the next day. Eighteen hours after they had come aboard, the waves and wind finally began to subside.

One by one, the men were allowed to climb out of the hold onto the deck. Jimmy was completely spent. He could only sit with his back to the side of the hull and thank divine providence for his deliverance.

At dawn of their second day at sea, the captain called out that they were approaching a harbor. He hoisted two flags to the top of their mast, one French and the other English.

As they slowly chugged into the harbor, Jimmy was astounded to see a fleet of Allied warships, including destroyers, corvettes, and amphibious landing craft. They were in the vast port of Falmouth.

A patrol launch met them as they approached the pier, and an English officer came aboard. After the French captain explained that he was carrying thirty escapees from France, the Frenchman expressed surprise that he was allowed to enter Falmouth without being intercepted by a military vessel.

"We've been confined to port for two days because of the storm," said the English officer.

Against All Odds

In January, the American heavy bombers had begun hitting the Fatherland again, and in ever greater numbers. German intelligence estimates suggested that formations exceeding a thousand Fortresses would be bombing targets deep inside Germany in less than two months.

The bombers were now protected by a new American long-range fighter, an ominous development feared by Connie Mayer since the previous fall. The P-51 Mustang was a formidable weapon, and ideal for the job of escorting the Fortresses all the way to the deepest targets in Germany and back.

It was getting far more difficult for his Jagdgeschwader to penetrate the escort screens of American fighters to attack the bomber formations. The Focke-Wulf 190 could outturn the P-51, but the American fighter was faster. Overall, the performance of the two planes was about equal. The difference was in the skill and experience of the pilots facing each other in combat.

The American pilots were getting better all the time. Their training was long and arduous, and they came to Europe prepared to fight. The Luftwaffe's replacement pilots were relatively green and untested. Germany was losing the battle of attrition.

Connie Mayer had led Jagdgeschwader 2 without pause through

the fall and winter of 1943, enjoying his finest day in the air on December 1, when he shot down four American P-47 fighters and a B-17 in less than thirty minutes.

He achieved his ninetieth victory on New Year's Eve, shooting down a B-24 Liberator over Melun-Villaroche. On January 7, 1944, he had another brilliant day, downing four heavy bombers flying in the same formation.

On February 5, Connie Mayer became the first pilot in the Luftwaffe to achieve one hundred victories on the western front, destroying a P-47 fighter over Arguen. A day later, he shot down two more.

Mayer was emotionally and physically exhausted. He had been in almost constant air combat for nearly two years. He had flown hundreds of sorties, shot down twenty-six four-engine bombers, a dozen P-47s, and fifty-one English Spitfires.

Unlike the American fighter pilots, all of whom were allowed to return home after completing a combat tour, there was no going home for Connie Mayer. He was in it to the end.

On March 2, he led a formation of Fw 190s up to intercept a massive B-17 bomber formation heading for Frankfurt, Germany. It was protected by nearly two hundred P-51, P-47, and P-38 fighters.

Fifty miles northeast of Reims, France, Mayer confronted a large formation of B-17s. His staffel was badly outnumbered, but he had often fought against great odds with success. It was his trademark to take the offensive, regardless of the numbers.

While diving on one of the Flying Fortresses, he failed to notice a formation of twenty-nine American fighters poised to attack him from above. A P-47 flown by Lieutenant Walter Gresham of the 358th Fighter Squadron found Mayer's Fw 190 in his sights and he fired a short burst of .50-caliber machine-gun bullets into the German's fuselage.

Mayer's fighter turned over onto its back and plunged over into a steep dive, blowing up when it hit the ground near the village of Montmédy. The Luftwaffe pilot who had owned the skies over France was dead at the age of twenty-six.

Cloak and Dagger

After Andy's encounter on the train to Zurich with Allen Dulles, the head of the American spy network in Europe, Andy's first day as an internee in Switzerland became increasingly unpleasant. In Zurich, he had been taken under armed guard to the office of the head of Swiss military intelligence.

The tall, austere army colonel motioned Andy to a chair in front of his desk, and curtly requested a full briefing from him on his mission to Stuttgart. Andy politely responded that he could say nothing until he met with an American military attaché.

The colonel flew into a rage. Picking up a sheaf of Swiss newspapers from his desk, he held them in front of Andy's face and shouted, "What do you mean you can't tell me anything about your mission? It seems you people are perfectly willing to talk to our journalists!"

For the first time, Andy learned that four other American bombers on the mission to bomb Stuttgart had also ended up in Switzerland. Glancing at the newspapers, he could see long passages of quotes from some of the American crew members who had spoken freely with Swiss reporters.

"I can't answer for their actions, Colonel," said Andy, "but I am not at liberty to say anything connected with U.S. military matters."

The colonel angrily dismissed him, saying, "I would advise you not to try to escape, Lieutenant. Our soldiers are very good shots."

Along with the rest of the crews interned after the Stuttgart mission, Andy and his crew spent the next two months in a temporary holding camp in the Jura Mountains. Morale fell quickly. Some of the pilots shared Andy's sense of guilt at having flown out of the war, particularly those whose planes had been undamaged. Others began to realize they might have to languish in an internee camp for years.

Andy committed himself to helping raise the men's spirits, as well as his own.

Using the small library of books provided by the Salvation Army, he began teaching courses in English literature, history, and geometry. In the afternoons, he taught English to Swiss children in the village. There was a shortage of texts, so Andy wrote stories for the children to read. It all helped to pass the time.

In November, Andy's crew was transferred with several others to a new camp at Adelboden. Morale immediately improved when the Americans arrived on a bus and saw their new home.

The evergreen-dappled village of Adelboden was nestled in a beautiful sun-drenched valley in the heart of the Bernese Alps. A ski resort before the war, it had elegant hotels, picturesque Swiss chalets, good restaurants, and well-stocked shops.

As a neutral country, Switzerland was required to keep its internees from escaping. They had chosen Adelboden as a permanent internment camp because there was only one gap in the high peaks that surrounded it. The place was a natural fortress and completely isolated from the outside world.

For the arriving crews, it seemed as if they had somehow been transported into a Brothers Grimm fairy tale. From the flak-torn skies over Germany, they were now living in Shangri-la.

Their arrival also turned out to be a boon to the local economy. After the war began, tourists had stopped coming to Adelboden. Now, the United States government had agreed to reimburse the hotel keepers and restaurant owners for their internees' room and board. The fliers had money and little to spend it on. Many of the local girls were both attractive and available.

It was no German stalag.

Andy's crew moved into the seven-story Nevada Palace Hotel, which had been built as an exclusive spa in the late nineteenth century. All the upstairs rooms had balconies that faced the alpine peaks. The resort had its own skating rink, and the ski slopes were within easy walking distance. Glittering glass chandeliers lit the hotel's bars, lounges, library, and piano recital room.

Adelboden soon began to fill up with new internees. Hundreds of British soldiers and airmen also began arriving from prisoner-of-war camps in Italy, from which they had been set free after Benito Mussolini had been driven from power. Soon, the Americans were enjoying the spectacle of Indian Sikhs and Nepalese Gurkhas promenading along the town's snow-clogged streets.

While the spirits of most of the men skyrocketed, Andy found himself increasingly demoralized. He hadn't volunteered to fight so that he could spend the war schussing on ski slopes, or relaxing in the hotel spa, or lounging at a restaurant with one of the local girls. He could only imagine the privations of all the fliers who had ended up in German prisoner-of-war camps. It was embarrassing.

In February, Andy was granted a chance to get back in the war.

One afternoon he was teaching English to the village children when a telegram arrived for him from Bern. It was from Allen Dulles. He requested that Andy visit him there immediately. The Swiss authorities agreed to give Andy a pass to do so.

When Andy arrived at the rail station in Bern for his appointment, Dulles escorted him back to his apartment through a street lined with dense linden trees, the branches of which helped to obscure them from view.

The spymaster was living in an undistinguished apartment building at 23 Herrengasse in the oldest part of Bern. It was from here that he operated a network of scores of spies across occupied Europe.

"I am being constantly watched," he told Andy, adding that both the German Gestapo and Himmler's SS were well aware that he was a spy, and that they often had him under surveillance.

Once inside the apartment, Allen Dulles told the young lieutenant that he had been impressed with the way Andy had refused to divulge any information after his plane came down in Switzerland the previous September. He thought Andy was discreet and intelligent, two qualities that were important for an important undercover assignment he wanted him to undertake.

He told Andy that he had arranged a direct exchange of seven German officers interned in Switzerland for seven interned American airmen. If Andy agreed, he would be one of them. The exchange would serve a higher purpose.

For months, Dulles had been gathering vitally important intelligence information from his network of agents in anticipation of the Allied invasion of Europe. He had also recruited a source in Germany who was privy to the most secret cable traffic between the Wehrmacht high command and the German foreign ministry. There was far too much material to send by encrypted code and he needed a courier.

Allen Dulles wanted Andy to memorize the information and carry it back in his head to OSS headquarters in Virginia. An admiral on the OSS staff would debrief him when he got there.

Dulles said that the intelligence could save the lives of countless Allied soldiers, and Andy immediately agreed to help. It was a daunting intellectual challenge, but one perfectly suited to his cerebral gifts. He remained in Bern for a week while studying page after page of documents.

The catalogue of intelligence data included the force dispositions of every German division in France, detailed descriptions of specific fortifications along the French coast, recent German production figures from its armament industries, and the code names and real names of important Germans who were secretly spying for the Allies.

A week later, Andy told Allen Dulles that he was confident he could remember everything he had been given to memorize, and Dulles proceeded to schedule the exchange.

Under the terms of the agreement, the Americans would travel by train across Germany and France to the French village of Hendaye, where they would cross a bridge into Spain. The seven German internees would not be released until the Americans were safely across the border.

On the morning of March 3, 1944, the seven American officers, dressed in civilian clothing, were escorted to the Basel train station. Half the station lay in Switzerland, and the other half in Germany.

The cavernous waiting room was deserted when they arrived. Looking toward the German half of the station, Andy saw that they had adorned the walls with massive red banners and swastikas. Several German officers were waiting for them at the other end.

As the Americans approached, one of the German officers marched toward them. He was a major and wore the black uniform of Himmler's SS. A death's-head symbol was emblazoned on his peaked cap, and he carried a dagger at his side. Stopping short, he gave the Americans a stiff-armed salute and shouted, "Heil Hitler!"

This one is a true believer, thought Andy, as the officer began barking a torrent of German at them. Andy suddenly remembered Allen Dulles telling him in Bern he was under constant surveillance by the SS. What if Andy had been covertly photographed with Dulles, and the Germans matched that photo to the one in his identity papers?

If the Germans chose to detain him once he was across the border, there would be nothing the Swiss could do about it. The Nazis had routinely broken their promises since the war began. Once he was in the custody of the SS, they could do anything they wanted with him.

For one of the few times in the war, he felt a jolt of unreasoned fear. It was one thing to fly twenty-five bombing missions in a Flying Fortress, and quite another to be carrying secrets in one's head that might affect countless lives in the upcoming invasion.

The SS officer completed his harangue and stepped back. A Wehrmacht captain moved forward to take his place. He accepted charge of the prisoners, and ordered them to follow an armed guard of several more soldiers.

They were marched to a waiting train on one of the platforms. Several of the cars were fortified with batteries of antiaircraft guns to defend the train against fighter attacks. Three military escorts would be going with them, the captain who had taken charge of them in the station, a sergeant, and a corporal. The seven Americans and three Germans occupied two compartments in one of the passenger cars.

After leaving Basel, the train moved north along the Rhine Valley, stopping at a number of rail stations along the route. At one of them, a young woman was walking along the platform, carrying a basket and pleading for donations to the German Red Cross. Andy gave her his last Swiss franc note.

More German soldiers came aboard as the train continued north. By the time it crossed the Rhine, hundreds packed the cars, with many of them returning to their units along the west coast of France.

Word quickly spread that there were American fliers aboard, and curious German officers stopped at their compartment. One was serving with a German tank regiment in Russia. He spoke excellent English and told Andy he had gone to Western Reserve University in Cleveland, Ohio. He seemed wistful about his days living in the United States.

Another officer was both arrogant and confrontational. He was a Luftwaffe fighter pilot, and wore the Knight's Cross around his neck. He declared that the American bomber pilots were barbarians and that the German people detested President Roosevelt. One of the pilots laughed at him and said that was nothing compared to how the American people felt about Hitler. The officer stalked off.

Andy had brought a carton of Swiss cigarettes with him and had given several packs to the Wehrmacht sergeant accompanying the Americans. He was the only German in the escort who spoke English, and his name was Albert. He smoked incessantly.

"Albert," Andy said, "you're going to have a very sore throat by the time you leave us."

"Ah, yes," he replied with a grin, "but it will be the first sore throat I've had from smoking good cigarettes in five years."

As the train continued on through the night, Andy talked with a Wehrmacht colonel who commanded an infantry unit along the

Normandy coast. He kept assuring Andy that the German defenses in France were impregnable.

"Look," he said, "we Germans cannot defeat you, but you cannot defeat us. Why don't we come together and fight the Russians?"

Andy's fears about being revealed as a spy subsided once they were in France. If the Germans had any suspicions that he was a secret courier, he assumed they would have taken him off the train in Germany.

In Paris, two Wehrmacht officers picked up the seven Americans in two Dodge station wagons with swastikas painted on the doors. One of them spoke English with a Scottish burr. He had been a peacetime lawyer in Edinburgh, Scotland, and enjoyed regaling Andy with quotations from Wordsworth.

After a ride across the city, they boarded another train that took them south through Bordeaux before finally reaching Hendaye, a town that bordered Spain along the southwest coast of France. From there, they were scheduled to walk across a small bridge over the Bidasoa River to Irun, Spain.

Aboard the same train as the Americans were about forty survivors of the Spanish Blue Division that had been fighting alongside the Wehrmacht in the Russian campaign. They had taken terrible losses, and were intensely bitter.

Somehow, they learned that the American pilots were crossing into Spain at the same time. On the bridge, they began screaming insults at the Americans. Many clearly wanted to fight.

The Spanish police intervened, and a Swiss diplomatic courier arrived to take the Americans by car to Madrid. There they were delivered to the U.S. embassy. Andy was immediately put on a plane to Gibraltar, and then on to Casablanca before crossing the Atlantic from Lisbon.

In Washington, he was met by an OSS agent and taken for his debriefing with the retired navy admiral. He was first asked to write down everything he had memorized from the documents Allen Dulles had given him. It took several days to complete the account. Afterward, the admiral and his staff spent another day going over additional questions with him.

When the admiral finished debriefing him, he took Andy aside and thanked him for taking on the perilous assignment. Andy said he hoped some of the information would make a difference, and the admiral told him it undoubtedly would.

"And now, Lieutenant, I want you to do something else for me," he said. "I want you to forget everything that happened. I want you never to mention to anyone that you ever met or talked with Allen Dulles. Believe me, Lieutenant, it's just as easy to forget as it is to remember."

The End of a Tour

21 September 1944
Molesworth, England
Forty-first Combat Bomb Wing (A)
Brigadier General Robert F. Travis, Commanding

General Robert Travis was flying his final combat mission.

At the pre-mission briefing before the Stuttgart raid a year earlier, he had told the boys of the 303rd that he would finish his combat tour of twenty-five missions just as they were required to do. He had kept his word.

Bob Travis was now the only general officer in bomber command to finish a full tour.

His last mission was to Mainz, Germany. It would be his twenty-ninth. He had not taken the milk runs. Bob Travis had led many of the toughest combat missions of the war.

He had asked for them.

Travis was now one of the most highly decorated wing commanders in the Eighth Air Force. Over the course of his combat tour, he took great pride in sharing each new citation with his father, Major General Robert Travis (Ret.).

* * *

14 October 1943
Major General R. J. Travis
16 Commercial Building
Savannah, Georgia

Dear Dad,
My last raid was considered to be the most successful one ever conducted against German targets. . . . I have been notified by General Williams that I have been put up for both the DFC and the Silver Star. They mean something anywhere. . . . My love to you, Bob

23 December 1943

Dear Dad,
Citation for award Silver Star reads, "For gallantry in action while serving as Air Commander of a Task Force of Flying Fortresses on a mission over Anklam, Germany, 9 October 1943. . . . En route to the target, the bombers were subjected to fierce and persistent attacks by enemy fighters. . . . General Travis had his force over the target and wrought vast destruction on vital enemy installations. The gallantry, skill and superb leadership displayed by General Travis reflect the highest credit upon himself. . . ." I'm afraid there isn't much other news. The food has been particularly lousy lately. . . . I must be getting old. Whenever I take a hard workout in squash it takes me two days to get over it. Much love . . . Bob

On January 6, 1944, General Jimmy Doolittle had replaced Ira Eaker as commander of the Eighth Air Force. Less than a week later, he ordered his first maximum-effort mission. It was to be the biggest deep-penetration raid ever undertaken.

Six hundred fifty heavy bombers would participate, and for the first time in the air war, a fighter escort of hundreds of P-51s, P-47s, and P-38s would accompany the bombers all the way to the targets and back.

Bob Travis was chosen to command the First Air Division, which included 174 Fortresses and would lead the entire bomber train. The First Division's target was an industrial complex in Oschersleben, Germany, which was then producing nearly half of the Fw 190 fighter planes built for the Luftwaffe.

When Travis's division took off, the weather was clear over the Continent.

It didn't remain clear over England. By the time Travis's division was on its way to Germany, a dense cloud front gathered over the British Isles, preventing most of the fighter escort groups from assembling with the bombers.

With the weather continuing to deteriorate, General Doolittle ordered a recall of the bomber forces already in the air, as well as the fighter groups that had been assigned to escort them.

The First Division was closing in on Germany when General Doolittle's recall order was issued. If Bob Travis ever heard the order to return to England, he never acknowledged it.

Most of the fighter groups assigned to escort Travis's division opted to return to England with the other two. Only forty-nine P-51 Mustangs remained with the First Division as it continued on toward Oschersleben.

None of the American fighters were up front with the lead group.

General Travis was flying in the 303rd's 8 *Ball*. It was the lead plane of the lead squadron of the lead group of the division. When he realized there were no friendly fighters covering his formation, the general radioed Fighter Control. He told them that he was without support, and asked for assistance. There was no response to his message.

Waiting for Travis near Oschersleben was the largest force of enemy fighters assembled since the October 1943 attack on Schweinfurt. Most of the German pilots were flying Fw 190s, which seemed fitting since the Eighth's target that day was the largest industrial complex producing them.

The German fighters focused on Travis's lead group. They attacked from every direction, nine o'clock, ten, eleven, twelve, one, and two, flying in combinations of three to eight planes at a time. Once the attacks began, there was no lull. As one wave came through the formation, the next wave was already positioning itself.

One enemy fighter even attempted to ram the *8 Ball*. A crash was only averted when pilot Bill Calhoun lifted his left wing at the last moment, preventing the imminent collision.

On the intercom, Bob Travis kept calmly calling out the attack vectors of the incoming fighters. It became a nonstop commentary. One of the machine gunners was finally exasperated enough to interrupt him, shouting, "Don't call 'em so fast, General. I can't shoot 'em all anyway."

Jack Fawcett, the *8 Ball's* bombardier, was manning the machine gun in the nose compartment. Between attacks, he watched as the Fortresses of the 303rd Bomb Group began to fall around them. One of the first to go was *Baltimore Bounce*, the Fortress flying on the *8 Ball's* immediate left. One of its wings separated from the fuselage just before it blew up.

Approaching the target, Fawcett was able to recognize the topographical features he had memorized in the prestrike photographs. After a short bomb run, he dropped his bombs squarely on the factory complex. The rest of the bombers followed suit.

As the *8 Ball* turned from the target and headed for home, the Fortress flying directly behind it was set on fire by the next wave of enemy fighters. It spiraled downward, out of control.

Dozens of Fortresses went down under the relentless fighter attacks as the division fought its way back across the Continent. When the surviving planes finally reached the channel, England was still enveloped in thick fog.

Using homing beacons, the pilots of the 303rd were able to find Molesworth, but when they arrived, the field was completely socked in. From then on, it was every plane for itself.

In the *8 Ball*, Lieutenant Colonel Bill Calhoun finally broke through the fog bank at an altitude of three hundred feet. Other bombers were descending through the low ceiling all around him, and he narrowly avoided two collisions before safely reaching the ground.

After emerging from the plane, Bob Travis had a photograph taken with Bill Calhoun. From the two men's casual demeanor, one might have thought they had just flown a training mission to Scotland.

The mission had been one of the epic air battles of the war. In three hours, the Luftwaffe had launched more than four hundred attacks against the Eighth Air Force bombers, destroying sixty Fortresses and five escort fighters. Ten planes in the 303rd Bomb Group had been shot down around the 8 *Ball*. In spite of all the obstacles, the Fortresses had wrecked the Fw 190 factories at Oschersleben and destroyed thirty-nine enemy fighters.

Bob Travis pronounced it a successful mission.

That was no solace to many of the pilots in the 303rd. They were outraged that the general had not turned back with the five hundred bombers of the other two divisions when the recall order had been issued.

One day later, the First Division's group and squadron commanders met to discuss the mission. General Travis was the senior officer at the meeting. One of the squadron commanders asked him directly why he hadn't turned back with the other two divisions.

"I received no recall," he said, ending the discussion.

For the Oschersleben mission, the First Bombardment Division was awarded a Presidential Distinguished Unit Citation. Bob Travis wrote to his father two weeks later about his own most recent commendation.

28 January 1944

Dear Dad,
My DFC citation reads, "For extraordinary achievement while leading a mission over Germany, 26 November 1943. . . . The high degree of success achieved on this mission can be attributed to the courage, unyielding determination and skillful leadership of General Travis." . . . Have no news . . . Love, Bob

His reward for leading the Oschersleben mission would be a second Silver Star.

4 April 1944

Dear Dad,

A copy of the citation for the Oak Leaf Cluster to the Silver Star reads as follows: "For gallantry in action while leading a heavy bombardment division on a mission over Germany, 11 January 1944. . . . In spite of relentless attacks by hostile fighters, General Travis maintained perfect air discipline and maneuvered the formation over the assigned target. A crippling blow was dealt to one of the enemy's most important units of war production. The outstanding success achieved is attributable to the tenacity of purpose and brilliant leadership of General Travis, whose gallantry was an inspiration to all members of his command." The weather has been bad for days and we are stood down temporarily. Love, Bob

On April 29, 1944, Bob Travis led the First Division in an attack on Berlin. More than seven hundred Fortresses participated in the raid, supported by sixteen fighter groups. Three hundred German fighters attempted to defend their capital.

It was the only time he was wounded in combat.

He was flying with the 303rd again, this time with Lieutenant Don Stoulil in the lead plane of the lead squadron. They had dropped their bombs on Berlin and were heading home when the group encountered an intense flak barrage over Hannover, Germany.

Fifteen of the seventeen bombers in the 303rd received serious flak damage. Two were blown out of the sky, including *Spirit of Wanette*, which had been tucked in behind the left wing of General Travis's plane.

As 88-millimeter cannon shells exploded all around them, Don Stoulil fought to control the plane amid the buffeting flak bursts while an unruffled General Travis sat in the copilot's seat writing mission notes on his legal-sized clipboard.

Suddenly, a jagged two-inch-square hole materialized on the right side of the windshield, directly in front of the general. A moment later, shards of glass were swirling around the cockpit.

Without a word, General Travis slumped forward, his head coming to rest on the clipboard. Seconds later, blood began trickling down the general's left cheek. He sat motionless as the bomber continued to careen through the bumpy sky.

Oh, shit, thought the young pilot. The old man is dead.

He was still wrestling the plane through the stormy air when General Travis slowly raised himself back up to a sitting position. Stoulil called on the intercom for his waist gunner to come up to the cockpit with a first aid kit.

They were at twenty thousand feet, and the gunner used one of the plane's "walk around" oxygen bottles to reach the cockpit. After dressing the general's flesh wound, he wrapped a white gauze bandage around his head.

When they arrived back at Molesworth, Stoulil fired off a red flare to signal "wounded aboard" and brought the plane straight in to the hardstand. The general's staff car was waiting for him.

Ten minutes later, Don Stoulil was sitting in the cockpit filling out his after-flight "Form 1" on the postmission condition of the plane, when he looked down and saw that the general was still there, pointing out the hole in the windshield to a member of his staff. It couldn't have been too serious, the young pilot decided.

That night, the general came over to the squadron's officers' club. He was still wearing the heavy gauze bandage Don's gunner had wrapped around his head during the mission. They all celebrated the general's good fortune with a free round of drinks.

He received his third Silver Star in May.

17 May 1944

Dear Dad,
I thought you might be interested to know that I have received my second Oak Leaf cluster to the Silver Star, the citation for which reads as follows: "For gallantry in action, while serving as Air Commander of a Heavy Bombardment Division on a mission over Germany, 9 April 1944. Extremely adverse weather

conditions over England made assembling of the units almost impossible. . . . It was not until General Travis was more than an hour's flying time from the English coast that he was able to form a tight combat wing formation. . . . He led two combat wings along the briefed route to the target knowing full well that a serious shortage of fuel would develop later. . . . Determined to accomplish his assignment, General Travis maneuvered the formation through vicious attacks by enemy fighters and bombed the objective with excellent results. . . . He accomplished this so expertly that losses were held to a minimum. The gallantry and will to fight on against all odds displayed by General Travis inspired all units under his command."

Though there is much news, I must again apologize for being unable to pass it on to you due to censorship. . . . A letter from Uncle Jack states that your health is much improved and that you and Mother are both well. Your son, Bob

5 July 1944

Dear Dad,
My latest Distinguished Flying Cross Citation is as follows: "For extraordinary achievement while serving as Air Commander on a heavy bombardment mission over Germany, 20 June 1944. On this date General Travis directed the formation on a successful attack on a vital enemy objective. For six minutes prior to the release of bombs, the aircraft in which General Travis was flying was subjected to an intense barrage of flak. The rudder controls were badly damaged and an engine shot out by one burst. Another hit destroyed the aileron controls and successive bursts further crippled the airplane. In spite of these obstacles, General Travis led the formation in a straight bombing run, insuring an accurate release of bombs. The unwavering determination . . . courage, coolness and skill displayed by this officer reflect the highest credit on himself. . . ."

As I write this, my boys are landing from a morning mission. I see some red flares going up which means "wounded aboard." Love, Bob

The general's final combat mission was to the marshaling yards at Mainz, Germany, on September 21, 1944. As always, he flew in the copilot's seat, this time with Captain William E. Eisenhart of the 303rd. Their plane led the entire Eighth Air Force that day.

Unlike so many of General Travis's missions, the Mainz raid was relatively uneventful. The 303rd's bombs were dropped squarely on the target. They were on their way home when something untoward occurred that would soon become a permanent part of group lore.

A directive had recently been issued that pilots should not leave their cockpits to urinate if their piss tubes were frozen during a high-altitude flight. It was recommended that the pilots crack open their side window, get on their haunches, and pass the urine through the open window, where it would be carried away by the slipstream.

When Captain Eisenhart experienced an urge to urinate on the way back to Molesworth, he opened his window and attempted to comply with the directive. Unfortunately, General Travis was smoking a cigarette, and had cracked his own window open to release the smoke.

Caught in a cross draft, Captain Eisenhart's urine swirled across the cockpit, hitting the general full in the face. As soon as they landed, the general began dressing the pilot down, calling Captain Eisenhart an embarrassment to the Eighth Air Force. The tirade concluded with the general demanding that the directive about cockpit urination be removed from the bulletin board.

In the following days, Captain Eisenhart became widely celebrated within the 303rd Bomb Group as the only junior officer to ever piss in the face of a general and not be court-martialed for it.

Now Bob Travis was going home.

For thirteen months, he had lived a charmed life in the air, surviving some of the most dangerous missions to Germany while one plane after another around him was blown out of the sky.

Before Bob left England for a well-earned family leave, Major

General Robert Williams, the commanding officer in the First Division, declared him to be the finest wing commander in the Eighth Air Force. He had done well, winning a chest full of combat decorations.

Decorations usually led to promotions.

Bob Travis was aiming for the top.

Reb

Monday, 25 December 1944
Krems, Austria
Stalag 17
Barracks 18B
Sergeant Olen "Reb" Grant

Dearest Mother,

It's night here, but you probably haven't sat down to eat Christmas dinner yet. We had plenty of snow this morning and the sun came out nice and bright. By noon it had clouded up again. I sat up until three o'clock last night thinking of you and Sis and Dad and Hugh and Lamar. . . . A man does a lot of thinking here and I have found all the mistakes I have made and I'll see that they don't happen again. Mother, when I get home we will celebrate Christmas all over again. Until then God bless you all and keep well and safe. All my love, Olen

The 1944 Christmas dinner menu at Stalag 17 was neither mouthwatering nor expansive. It consisted of cabbage soup, raw carrots, a slice of coarse bread, and cold tap water. The prisoners enjoyed the same meal almost every day. On special occasions, the soup was flavored with small chunks of horse meat.

Reb Grant was celebrating his second Christmas at Stalag 17. Since November 1943, he had lived in Barracks 18, a one-story woodframe building that housed five hundred men. They slept in three-tiered bunks that ran along the rough-board walls. After six months of captivity, he had secured a prized second-tier bunk near the center of the building, which remained slightly warmer during the harsh winters.

The barracks had no stove. Warmth was provided by the body heat of the men. There was a wash room in the center of the long building that had a half dozen cold-water taps. There were no sinks. The water ran into an open trench beneath the barracks floor.

A walkway ran down the center of the building. With the snow and mud, it had several inches of packed dirt along much of its length. There were no brooms or mops to clean up the mess.

Lice, fleas, and bedbugs ran rampant. Most of the men hadn't been able to bathe in months. The smell of their bodies was ferocious and constant. Dysentery was common, and the latrines were some distance away. If a man needed to relieve himself at night, there was a two-seat privy at each end of the building. No man left the barracks at night. Several had been shot doing so.

For Reb Grant, the conditions weren't all that intolerable. He was used to hard living. During the Depression, his whole family had lived in a single tent with no running water after his father, Eli, had gotten a job wildcatting at an oil field near Longview, Texas.

Aside from the stinging cold, he hated the boredom more than anything else.

In one important way, this Christmas was different from the last one in 1943. According to the camp rumor mill, there was a big battle going on in the Ardennes Forest, with the Germans claiming they had driven the Allied army back to the sea. Of course, one couldn't accept anything they said at face value.

It was clear to all of them by then that the Germans had lost the war. It was only a matter of time before either the Americans or the Russians broke through. The prisoners simply had to survive until that day came.

Their principal fear stemmed from another rumor that Hitler had ordered the execution of all the captured bomber crews that had wreaked so much death and havoc on the Fatherland. There was no reason to doubt that this order could still be carried out.

All in all, Reb thought he was pretty damn lucky. It was a miracle that he had survived the crash of *Yankee Raider*. After regaining consciousness in the Paris hospital, he had slowly regained his strength. Once he was able to sit up, the nurses transferred him to a chair next to his bed. He had spent many hours gazing out the window of his ward.

The converted military hospital was located next to the Seine River. A soccer field separated the hospital from it. Every day, the Luftwaffe air defense units that manned the antiaircraft batteries around Paris would be marched to the field for calisthenics and soccer games.

The Germans would always arrive in marching order singing military songs so loudly that the music carried straight up to his window. After the games and exercise periods were over, they would reassemble to march back to their units, still singing. Reb decided that they were the singingest people in the whole world.

There was one German nurse who he found very attractive. She was the blond assistant to the doctor who was treating his wound. Even with the right side of his face blown away, he thought there was something going on. The old rebel still had it, he decided.

"Here is the Englander," she would always say in a sarcastic tone when he arrived to have his dressing changed.

"I'm not English," he would reply hotly. "I'm an American."

Behind all the sarcasm, Reb was sure she liked him.

In October, they brought in two American pilots from a downed B-24. The fliers had been splashed with leaking hydraulic fluid inside their burning plane, and the fluid caught fire before they bailed out. Their bodies were terribly burned. To Reb, it looked like their faces had melted away. When the first one regained consciousness, he glanced at himself in a hand mirror and said he could never go home again.

In late October, Reb's doctor told him that the infection in his head wound had been stabilized and he would soon be able to leave. A few days later, he was escorted to the main entrance of the hospital to join three other Allied airmen who were being released the same day.

They were loaded into the back of a truck and taken to Saint-Lazare train station.

On the train platform, a shoe shine boy, as black as the children Reb had grown up with in El Dorado, Arkansas, came scrambling through the sea of passengers. He stopped at Reb's feet and, using sign language, asked if he wanted his shoes shined. Looking down at the little boy's searching eyes reminded him of home, and he found himself crying.

It was snowing by the time the train left the station, and they traveled all night. When the train arrived at Frankfurt, Germany, Reb smelled the smoke before he saw the fires that were raging across the city. It had been bombed the night before, and panic-stricken Germans were lined up at the station, waiting to take the same train he had just arrived on.

The four Allied prisoners were being escorted by four German soldiers, all of them armed with light machine guns. Reb had made a joke in the train about the need for four Aryan supermen to escort four invalids who had just left a hospital.

On the platform, his thinking changed.

The fear on the faces of the Germans turned to rage when they saw the men under guard, including an RAF flier in his flight suit. Word coursed through the crowd that these were some of the men who had bombed Frankfurt.

The mass of frightened people suddenly became a raging mob. They surrounded the small group and began screaming for vengeance. The German guards shoved their way through as the mob kicked and clawed at the airmen.

Two men began dragging Reb out of the slow procession and into the clutch of the others. He knew they would beat him to death. It was a close result. He was only reprieved when one of the German soldiers opened fire with his machine gun into the air.

The four were taken to a holding camp outside Frankfurt. It was surrounded by barbed wire. Inside the camp, he was placed in an unheated five-by-eight-foot cell with an iron door.

In his first interrogation, he was told that since he wasn't wearing a dog tag when he was first captured, the Germans had to assume he was an American spy. Spies were shot.

Reb tried to explain why he didn't have his dog tag: that he had taken the tag off back at his base in England before taking a shower. The interrogator said he didn't believe him.

The next morning, Reb heard the sound of gunfire and his imagination began to run wild. Along the cell block, the iron doors were being opened and slammed shut. Were they taking men out into the field and executing them?

In his next interrogation, the interrogator again demanded to know who he really was. Over the next few days, he kept repeating the same story while continuing to give them his name, rank, and serial number.

By then, his facial wounds had become infected again. The dressing over his eye had not been changed since he left Paris. An RAF doctor who was also a prisoner in the camp finally changed it a week after he arrived.

Reb was being held in another cell when he saw that some of the recent Allied prisoners had scratched their names on the wall. His good eye was drawn to one of the names.

"Sgt. A Valcour," it read. "384th BG."

Al Valcour had been shot down on the Hamburg mission back in July. Finding his name on the wall was like a letter from home. Old Val was still alive. Maybe Reb would even catch up to him. The discovery gave him a new injection of hope.

After a week of solitary confinement, he was finally released from the holding camp. Another train took him through the bomb-devastated cities of Nuremberg and Regensburg before crossing over the border into Austria.

His new home of Stalag 17 was located in Krems at the confluence of the Danube and Krems rivers. A German army garrison was quartered in the same town. When Reb and about fifty other prisoners arrived at the rain-swept camp, its "Main Street" was lined with hundreds of American airmen, all hoping to recognize a new arrival who might have fresh news of crewmates or friends.

One of them was Eldore Daudelin, the other waist gunner on *Yankee Raider,* who had left Reb for dead aboard the plane before he bailed out and was taken prisoner by the Germans.

Awestruck, Daudelin gazed at him like he was Lazarus risen from the grave. His pleasure at Reb's survival was quickly replaced by a sense of guilt at what he had done. Reb told him to forget about it, but the other man continued to blame himself for leaving him behind in the doomed bomber.

In February 1944, Reb's facial wound became infected yet again. The right side of his face became paralyzed, and he lost his sense of smell. Considering the ever-present stench in the barracks, that wasn't all bad, but the infection continued to grow worse.

He was sent under guard to a military hospital in Vienna. There, a surgeon told him the infection would continue to fester unless he removed the shrapnel embedded in the bone of his nose and the shattered eye socket. He proposed to remove some of the shrapnel, and then cut away a large section of skin on his forehead and fold it over to cover the eye socket. He would leave a tiny opening in the skin so that Reb could use an eyedropper to suction out the ongoing drainage from the wound.

In the weeks he was there, continuous trainloads of wounded German soldiers arrived from the Russian front. When Reb left, they lined the floors of all the corridors and anterooms.

On April 5, 1944, he turned twenty-one years old.

Six months later, word began to spread through the camp that representatives of an international repatriation commission were coming to Stalag 17 to interview prisoners whose wounds and injuries rendered them incapable of serving as future combatants. Prisoners who met these conditions were to be exchanged for German prisoners currently held by the Allies.

Reb added his name to the list, and after several interviews, the doctors working for the commission approved his participation in the exchange. In late December, he joined the fortunate few who would be leaving for America.

They traveled by train to Leipzig, passing one desolate, bombed-out place after another. At a former officers' training school, he was issued new clothing by the International Red Cross and permitted to take a bath, the first one he had enjoyed in more than a year. Reb reveled in the hot soapy water for more than an hour, only emerging when the aroma of roasting meat drew him toward the nearby mess hall.

From Leipzig, the prisoners traveled by train to Marseille, where the exchange took place near the port. Reb watched the downcast faces of the German prisoners as they filed past. He didn't think they were very thrilled to be going home.

Reb and the other American prisoners were ferried out to the Swedish ocean liner *Gripsholm*, which was waiting for them in the harbor. Soon, they were on their way across the Mediterranean Sea.

On February 20, 1945, the *Gripsholm* arrived in New York. Many of the returning Americans had predicted that the dock would be thronged with cheering crowds, but the huge pier was almost completely deserted.

At the foot of the gangway, they were greeted by three GI musicians who played "Yankee Doodle Dandy" and "When Johnny Comes Marching Home" over and over while an officer checked off their names on his clipboard. They were herded onto several buses and driven to Halloran General Hospital in Queens.

Two days later, Reb received his first pass. Howard Wood, a friend of his from Stalag 17 who had been repatriated to the United States a year earlier, picked him up at the hospital with his new wife and drove him into the city for a night on the town.

They had also arranged a blind date for him.

Her name was Priscilla Hutchinson, and she was a slim, lovely, strawberry blonde. Twenty years old, she worked as a receptionist at an advertising agency on Madison Avenue.

She wasn't at all put off by his facial disfigurement.

"You have the look of eagles in your face," she told him later that night.

They had two more dates over the next two nights. Then he received his travel orders. The army was sending him to O'Reilly Army Hospital in Springfield, Missouri, for the first of many operations to rebuild his face.

That night, Reb told Priscilla he was in love with her, and asked her to marry him. Priscilla told Reb that she had also fallen in love with him, and tearfully accepted his proposal.

On Monday, February 26, 1945, six days after his return to the United States, Olen Grant and Priscilla Hutchinson repeated their marriage vows at John Street Methodist Church. Reb's best man was Sergeant Tom McDonald, who had spent a year with him in Stalag 17.

As soon as he got out of the army hospital in Missouri, he was planning to head west with Priscilla. In his long months of captivity, Reb had often dreamt of roaming the high country in Colorado and California. Wherever they ended up, he planned to savor each and every day for the rest of his life.

EPILOGUE

T here are few traces left of the air bases in England that once served as home to the Eighth Air Force bomb groups that took the air war to Germany in 1943. The author had a chance to visit a number of them in the course of researching this book. They would be unrecognizable to the Americans who were stationed there during the war.

Most are quiet, windswept places, stripped clean of the concrete runways, hardstands, repair hangars, and half-cylindrical Quonset huts with their distinctive corrugated metal roofs.

Small granite commemorative monuments, similar to the ones erected by postwar generations at Gettysburg and Antietam, mark the empty airfields that once launched intrepid flight crews on their missions to Germany.

Grafton Underwood, from which the 384th's Jimmy Armstrong and Reb Grant took off on their last combat mission, is now a landscape of woods and pasture, with a few concrete perimeter tracks being the last hints of the airfield that once was.

The 388th's base at Knettishall, where Ted Wilken, Warren Laws, and the Greek were stationed, was newly constructed when they got there, with fifty-yard-wide runways and enough concrete hardstands for two groups. Some decaying buildings are all that is left.

Thurleigh, the home of Andy Andrews's famed 306th group, is now a business park, although it also hosts a small museum dedicated to the men who served in the bomb group.

Molesworth, where the 303rd Bomb Group was based, remains a U.S. Air Force facility, although there are few reminders of the base from which Bob Travis and Bud Klint completed their combat tours.

The Eighth Air Force in Europe is a distant memory, but an indelible one.

Its battle losses were astonishing. According to Donald Miller in *Masters of the Air*, the casualty rate among the American bomber crews in 1942 and 1943 was in excess of 50 percent. Only one man out of five was able to complete the original combat tour of twenty-five missions.

The author agrees with Donald Miller that the deep-penetration raids into Germany in the fall of 1943 should not have been launched until the bomber forces were large enough to accomplish the task and could be protected by long-range fighters.

Combat losses in the bomber crews dropped dramatically after these goals were achieved. It is a tribute to the courage of the Fortress crews in the first year of the air war that they kept on going in the face of tremendous odds, and with little hope of ultimate survival.

For those readers interested in what happened to the group of individuals whose stories were chronicled in this book, a brief account of their subsequent lives after the Stuttgart mission follows.

Martin "Andy" Andrews

After delivering his trove of top secret military intelligence to the admiral at OSS headquarters in Virginia, Andy enjoyed a brief family leave before being assigned to the U.S. Army Air Forces' Transport Command. He spent the rest of the war piloting new military aircraft from the factories where they were manufactured to the active war fronts across the globe.

In the course of his travels, Andy spent his free time writing a stage play that he was sure would find glory on Broadway. Discharged from the army at the end of the war, he headed straight for New York and the Great White Way. Although his play failed, it led to a job as a writer for Paramount News, which then made the newsreels that ran at all the movie houses in the years before television. Aside from the radio networks, the newsreels were the only electronic medium for millions of Americans to learn the news.

In 1948, the Republican Party produced an expensive ten-minute propaganda film in support of its candidate for president, Governor Thomas Dewey, who was running against President Harry Truman. In every national poll, it appeared that Dewey was going to whip the unpopular Truman in a landslide, and Paramount News, among other companies, ran the film as if it was their own independent newsreel in movie houses all over the country.

The outraged White House press staff demanded "equal time" for Truman, and Andy was assigned to write and narrate a newsreel about him. It had a production budget of $1,200. Most of the footage came from Paramount's film library, but Andy was granted an opportunity to interview Truman at a campaign event at Madison Square Garden.

Knowing that the president was ill at ease in front of a movie camera, Andy urged him to speak off the cuff on anything he wanted. Truman then gave his famous denunciation of the "do-nothing Congress" in Washington. In the week that the newsreel was shown in theaters across the country, 60 million theatergoers saw the newsreel. Truman narrowly won reelection a few weeks later in the greatest political comeback in history. Andy likes to think his newsreel might have helped.

A few years later, he was selected to become head of the documentary division of Hearst Metrotone News, eventually writing, producing, and directing nearly two hundred films. In 1956, shortly after Dwight Eisenhower was elected president of the United States, Andy was at home one evening mucking out his barn when he received a telephone call from his boss, who told him that five thousand feet of film had just arrived in New York. It was raw footage of the first bloody days of the Hungarian Revolution. He needed Andy to come into the city to cut it down to nine hundred feet and write an accompanying script for a newsreel that was to be shown to President Eisenhower the next morning. Two film editors were waiting for him at the Hearst studio in New York City, and a courier was on hand to take the finished film to Washington that night.

Andy had less than three hours to do the job.

Reaching the studio an hour later in his overalls, Andy had time to screen the raw footage once, and then told the editors what to open with, what to keep in the body of the ten-minute film, and what footage to close with at the end. There was no chance to write a script. After ad-libbing a ten-minute narrative to go with the footage, he gave it the title "A Nation in Torment." The courier put it in his pouch and was on his way.

Convinced it was a disaster, he went to a local bar with the two editors and they proceeded to finish a bottle of whiskey together. The following morning, President Eisenhower invited the leaders of the House and Senate to watch it with him. After the screening, Senator James Mead of New York was quoted in the *New York Times* as saying, "This film should be shown around the world."

It was. "A Nation in Torment" was screened in eighty-two languages and dialects, becoming the most successful propaganda film ever released by the United States Information Agency.

After winning numerous awards for his work, Andy established his own film company, going on to produce and direct numerous documentaries on the New York State park system and many environmental subjects.

Along the way, Andy's first marriage ended in divorce, but he and his second wife, Jean, have been together since 1977. They share five children, along with five grandchildren.

After his friend Preston Bassett, the former president of the Sperry Gyroscope Company, reached the age of ninety, he told Andy, "You know, when you get to be ninety years old, you slow down. There are some things you can't do anymore."

Still high on life, the ninety-two-year-old Andy Andrews is now wheelchair bound, and lives in a veterans' nursing home. The move there was a jarring experience for him. He felt a great sense of isolation living apart from his wife and family. To cope with his loneliness, he has embarked on a rigorous program of physical exercise, and dedicated himself to rereading the classic books of Western civilization.

James E. "Jimmy" Armstrong

After completing an account of his five months behind enemy lines to intelligence officers in England, Jimmy was granted home leave, and arrived to a joyful celebration with his parents and grandparents in Bradenton, Florida. It seemed like the whole town turned out to greet him when he got there.

"Jimmy, you are so pale after living underground for so long," his grandmother told the twenty-one-year-old.

He quickly regained both his tan and his strength after three weeks of sun and swimming at the public beach. When his leave ended, Jimmy was assigned to the gunnery school at Buckingham Army Base in Florida. There, he was awarded his Purple Heart by the base commander.

Upon receiving his discharge from the army in 1945, he entered the University of Florida under the GI Bill and studied agriculture. In his sophomore year, he attended a dance, where he met a lovely young woman named Nita DesChamps. For Jimmy, it was love at first sight, and they were married two years later after his graduation.

In 1945, Annie Price, the Englishwoman who had sheltered him in Triel, France, and put him on his way to eventual freedom, wrote to him in Florida. He had sent her a letter saying he hoped to return to France to thank her in person.

"Dear Jim," she wrote. "Are you serious about coming back? Are you thinking of trying to make Paris gay once more? You'll have a job, for Paris is like myself—we have had all the stuffing knocked out and the beauty knocked off. . . . We're a couple of ruins the Germans left behind. . . . Annie Price."

As the years passed, the happy-go-lucky Jimmy slowly transformed himself into a more serious Jim. After an unfulfilling business career, he decided to enroll as a student at Columbia Theological Seminary in Decatur, Georgia, where he earned a master of divinity degree. In the years after his ordination, he served as the pastor of three churches, drawing the admiration and respect of all the congregants he served. His last church family before his retirement was in Thomasville, Georgia, where he still lives.

In 1981, Jim made the first of four trips back to France to thank the people who had sheltered and protected him for the five months he evaded capture by the Germans. He met with Madame Laurent, who was still living in the same house where she had served him breakfast before turning him over to Annie Price. Annie had died in 1951. The medical intern with whom he had stayed initially in Paris was now Dr. Alec Prochiantz, and was serving on the medical staff at the American Hospital in Paris.

He had no luck finding the underground reprobates Maurice and George, with whom he had stayed above their Paris café, or Theodorine "Madame Q" Quenot, who had sheltered Jim and three other Allied escapees, or the brave Gilbert Virmoux, who had tried to help him escape over the Pyrenees.

In Quimper, he learned that his hosts Jacques and Madeleine Mourlet had continued to help Allied escapees to leave France until Jacques was arrested and imprisoned in 1944. They had both died after the war.

"Fanfan," the French underground agent who had arranged Jim's escape aboard the *Breiz-Izel*, and was a leader of the "Dahlia" resistance network, had been arrested by the Gestapo a few months after Jim's escape. After weeks of torture, he died in a railroad car on his way to Dachau. The Catholic priest who had housed the escapees in his upstairs bedroom disappeared in a German concentration camp.

After his first visit, Jim continued to make trips to France to pay homage to the members of the underground networks who had assisted Allied airmen, and to provide support to those who were in need.

In 2008, Jim and Nita Armstrong celebrated their seventieth wedding anniversary. They have three children, Alice, Jim, and Jean, seven grandchildren, and a vast circle of friends.

Jim still plays golf and loves spending hours each week in his garden. He has made one concession to his age as he closes in on ninety. Jim no longer climbs an extension ladder to pick the oranges at the top of the fruit-laden trees in his backyard. A recent fall reminded him all too painfully of his parachute landing in France in 1943.

Henry H. "Hap" Arnold

In August 1945, his B-29 bombers delivered the nuclear payloads to Hiroshima and Nagasaki that ended World War II. Six months after the Japanese surrender, Hap Arnold resigned as the commanding general of the U.S. Army Air Forces. He had survived four heart attacks during the war while overseeing the disposition of two and a half million airmen and seventy-two thousand military aircraft.

One of his first priorities after leaving the army was to rebuild his shattered marriage. During the war, Bee Arnold had developed an acute nervous condition and had lost a good deal of weight. At one point, she accused Hap of being unfaithful. He had become increasingly bewildered by her shifting moods.

In February 1946, the Arnolds moved out of Quarters Number 8 on General's Row at Fort Myer and headed for California. A few years earlier, while Arnold was at a military conference in Cairo, Egypt, Bee had found a small, unimproved ranch property in the Valley of the Moon near Sonoma, California, and decided to buy it for their future home. Although the price was only $7,500, Hap did not have enough money to pay for it. After overseeing billions of dollars in procurement contracts, he had to borrow most of the down payment. It would be the only land he would ever own.

After the war, Arnold had commissioned the construction of a modest house on the property. With a tiny kitchen, living room, and three small bedrooms, Arnold looked at it as a future guesthouse after he had the money to build his real home.

That was never to be. He was still suffering the lingering effects of his fourth heart attack, and his legendary stamina began to ebb. Hap's doctor recommended increasing his alcohol consumption, and Arnold doubled his daily ration of two old-fashioneds.

Isolated from his old friends, he and Bee settled into a quiet retired life. He bought some woodworking tools and made the redwood furniture for their patio. The couple usually spent their evenings sitting on the patio gazing out at the surrounding hills.

In early 1948, he had his fifth heart attack and was forced to remain largely bedridden for months. Worried about Bee having sufficient means to support herself in the event of his death, Hap began working on a war memoir called *Global Mission*. Based on the success of similar books written by his contemporaries, he hoped it would sell at least one hundred thousand copies. The book came out to excellent reviews, but sales were less than ten thousand.

In May 1949, he received a letter from Harry Truman that temporarily lifted his spirits. The president had just signed an order retroactively making Arnold the only five-star general to have ever served in the air force.

At Christmas, Hap's son gave him a light bar to use with his handheld movie camera. Hap was too weak to hold up the bar. A few weeks later, he sent a confused telegram to the editors of Encyclopedia Britannica, for whom he had hoped to write an article on the history of aviation.

"Help. Have been working on rewrites for Britannica and am all at sea. . . . What's the score before I strike out and the game is called on the account of darkness?"

Hap Arnold died on January 15, 1950, at the age of sixty-four.

Ira C. Eaker

In January 1944, Ira Eaker was named commander in chief of the Mediterranean Allied Air Forces, having under his command the Twelfth and Fifteenth U.S. Air Forces and the British Desert and Balkan air forces.

Although the Mediterranean theater was soon to become the relative backwater he had feared, Ira Eaker deftly employed airpower to assist the Allied forces seeking to defeat the German forces in Italy. One of his decisions led to controversy after the war. Under pressure from Allied ground commanders in Italy who were attempting to eliminate a German garrison at the fourteen-hundred-year-old Abbey of Monte Cassino near Rome, Eaker reluctantly signed off on the decision to destroy it with fourteen hundred tons of bombs. In the wake of its total destruction, the ruins provided even better defensive positions for the German garrison.

On April 30, 1945, weeks after the war in Europe ended, General Eaker was named deputy commander of the army air forces and chief of the air staff. He retired on August 31, 1947, having logged twelve thousand hours in the air during his thirty-year military career.

In his later years, Ira Eaker remained active in the aviation field, going to work for Howard Hughes at Hughes Aircraft, and later for Douglas Aircraft. He and his wife, Ruth, settled in San Angelo, Texas, southwest of Fort Worth. Until 1982, he wrote a weekly column for the *San Angelo Standard-Times* that was syndicated to newspapers across the country.

In 1985, Congress passed legislation that awarded General Eaker with a fourth star, and the law was signed by President Ronald Reagan. It left him with one less than Hap Arnold. The two men never reconciled.

Ira Eaker died in 1987, and was buried at Arlington Cemetery. He was ninety-one.

Olen "Reb" Grant

The first of the many reconstructive surgeries on Reb's face took place at O'Reilly Army Hospital, where surgeons removed the last of the shrapnel that was embedded in his nose and cheek. While he was recuperating, Reb found his first postwar job washing cars at a local automobile dealership.

Moving on to Cushing Army Hospital in Framingham, Massachusetts, he received several bone grafts to rebuild his right cheek and eye socket. New eyelids were grafted from the large flap of skin his Austrian surgeon had stretched across his empty eye socket. In another procedure, mucous membranes from his mouth were used to line the inside of the eye socket, so that fluid would be secreted to allow movement of a future prosthesis. Reb asked the doctor if this meant that his new eye would be able to taste apple pie.

He went to Valley Forge Army Hospital in Pennsylvania, where doctors constructed the prosthesis for his right eye socket. The new eye fit all right, but there was no muscle left around it to keep his eyelid from drooping shut. His doctor inserted a tiny shelf beneath the eyelid, but that meant the new eye always remained open. It's the best we can do, the doctor told him. He's worn a patch ever since.

While he was hospitalized, millions of returning veterans had begun using their GI Bill benefits to seek a college education, and few colleges had available space when he was ready to go. Olen aspired to be a journalist, and he was finally accepted at the small college of Colorado A&M in Fort Collins. He and his wife headed west.

Priscilla wasn't happy there, and Reb attempted to enroll in college in California, only to learn there were no available openings in their state school system. Returning to New York, he worked at a number of jobs, including wrapping gifts in Macy's basement and selling paper products.

One day he returned home from work to discover that Priscilla had moved out. She left him a note saying that she was moving back with her mother and would seek a divorce.

In the fall of 1948, Reb was accepted at the University of Arkansas, where he went on to earn a double degree in journalism and political science. Unable to find a newspaper job, he went to work for Beech Aircraft in Wichita, Kansas, writing technical catalogues. After marrying a second time, he and his new wife raised three daughters, Terry Lynn, Brenda Jo, and Janet Leigh, who was named after Reb's favorite actress.

When a bout with tuberculosis put him back in the hospital for six months, Reb emerged to find his position gone, but eventually found a job drafting contracts and specifications for the Army Corps of Engineers at Fort Bliss in El Paso, Texas. He remained with the corps until his retirement.

Since then, he has kept busy with a variety of activities, including building a mountainside cabin in Ruidoso, New Mexico, and imbuing his grandchildren with the importance of reading. His favorite authors include Somerset Maugham, Ernest Hemingway, and Larry McMurtry.

In 2008, his daughter Janet visited France to thank the people who had saved her father's life, including Robert Artaud, who drove the local ambulance in Entrépagny and brought Reb to the local hospital after he had been removed from *Yankee Raider*. In England, Janet left a poem Reb had written near the monument to the men who served with the 384th Bomb Group at Grafton Underwood.

Always a free thinker, Reb believes that nature is the driving force behind life. The reward for human beings is how we live our lives here on earth, but nature is always the immutable power. Reb, who now lives in Hot Springs, Arkansas, once saw a tornado pick up a neighbor's house and carry it into the next state. At eighty-seven, he recognizes power when he sees it.

Demetrios "the Greek" Karnezis

After returning from England to the United States in early 1944, Jim Karnezis became a B-17 instructor pilot at Hobbs Air Force Base in New Mexico. When the war ended, he decided to make his career in the air force, and received a regular commission as a captain in 1946.

That same year, he married Versamee Vandouris, whom he had first met while attending basic flying school in Chico, California. Back then, Versamee was attending a nearby teachers' college, and they met at an officers' club dance. She gave him her address and they began corresponding when he was in England with the Eighth Air Force. Their bond drew closer when Versamee's brother was killed piloting a B-24 bomber later in the war. After marrying in 1946, the couple began their new family a year later with a son they named Ted. Three more boys were to follow, Arthur, Ivan, and Alec.

After a year of intensive study at the Army Language School in Monterey, California, he became fluent in Greek, and attended Princeton University's School for Near Eastern Studies. Upon graduating from the program, he was assigned to the U.S. Joint Military Group in Greece, serving three years there as an adviser and instructor at the Royal Hellenic Air Force Academy, where he introduced night-flying procedures into their curriculum.

While in Europe, he returned in September 1953 to Champigny, France, where he reunited with Marcelle Andre and Suzanne Bouchy, and visited the graves of his five crewmen, who were buried in the small cemetery close to where *Slightly Dangerous II* had crashed. After the war, the people of the village had created a memorial to the crew. Each September 6, they held a somber commemoration of their loss. On his first visit, Marcelle Andre confided to Jim that her daughter Marie Therese had never married, hoping that he would someday come back for her.

Returning to the United States, the newly promoted Major Jim Karnezis spent the next three years at Moody Air Force Base in Georgia, first as its operations officer, and two years later as a squadron commander training interceptor pilots.

From 1958 to 1960, he went overseas again as an exchange officer with the Royal Air Force in England, responsible for advanced jet fighter training in RAF Meteors, Vampires, and Hawker Hunters. In the early sixties, he was assigned to Lackland Air Force Base, where he led the command's aerobatic team.

Promoted to lieutenant colonel, his last posting was at the Alaskan Air Command, where he was director of operations. He retired from the air force after thirty years of service as a full colonel. His decorations include the Legion of Merit, Order of the Purple Heart, two Air Medals, and the Air Force Commendation Medal.

In 1993, he returned once more to Champigny, France, to attend the fiftieth commemoration of his crew's loss there. Jim was moved to see that hundreds of people had come to pay homage to them. He had memorized two French sentences that summed up his gratitude to those who had put their lives on the line for him, including Marcelle Andre and Suzanne Bouchy. "You are my second family," he told them in French, adding tearfully, *"Je vous aime très beaucoup."*

Today, "the Greek" lives with Versamee in Sacramento, California, where he grows citrus fruit and enjoys quiet time with his children and seven grandchildren. The only physical reminders of the Stuttgart mission lie in an old footlocker out in the garage next to his house. Inside it are the cracked leather GI brogans he was wearing when he was shot down.

Wilbur "Bud" Klint

After surviving the ditching of *Old Squaw* in the English Channel on September 6, 1943, Bud returned to the 303rd's air base at Molesworth the following day. By then, his clothing, personal effects, and bedding had been removed from the officers' hut where he had been living along with the rest of the officers in the crew. It wasn't easy to get it back.

Bud and the rest of his crew received a forty-eight-hour pass after the Stuttgart mission, which was his sixth. He had nineteen more to go before completing his combat tour.

The remaining missions included some of the toughest in the history of the Eighth Air Force, and he came to believe that a higher power was somehow looking out for his welfare. Over Münster, he experienced the most intense flak barrage of his tour. Thirty Fortresses went down that day.

On October 14, he went back to Schweinfurt a second time. On the first Schweinfurt mission in August, thirty-six bombers had been shot down. On the second raid, it was sixty. Both times, his plane was rocked by enemy flak and cannon fire, but it somehow got through.

In early 1944, Bud was made a pilot of his own Fortress and assigned a new crew. His twenty-fifth and final mission was to Bernberg, Germany, after which he returned to the States, where he finished out the war.

After being discharged, he returned to his hometown of Chicago. Prior to the war, he had worked as a sales clerk for a local candy company. He was offered a junior executive position with the same company. Shortly after resuming his civilian career, he met and fell in love with his future wife, Mary.

After raising three children, he and Mary moved to Fort Worth, Texas, where he became the marketing director for King Candy Company. Retiring from business life in the early 1980s, Bud focused his time and attention on his children and grandchildren, while pursuing an interest in creating a lasting memorial to the men he flew with in 1943.

In 1998, he participated in a ceremony in Schweinfurt, Germany, along with a few of the surviving German veterans of the city's Luftwaffe antiaircraft batteries, to honor the men of both sides in the conflict. Inscribed on the stone monument are the words "Dedicated by some who witnessed the tragedy of war, now united in friendship and the hope for lasting peace among all people."

Surrounded by his family, Bud Klint passed away in July 2009.

Warren Porter Laws

From Barcelona, Spain, Warren flew back to the United States in February 1944. After a thirty-day home leave, he was sent on a lecture tour of army air force bases. The purpose of the tour was to educate flight crews on how to escape from occupied Europe if they were shot down.

It was also designed to boost morale by proving that if a man was shot down in occupied Europe, he had a good chance of evading capture.

Upon completing the lecture tour in April 1944, Warren returned to Connecticut to marry Libby Minck. Deciding to remain in the air force, he became an instructor pilot in B-17s. In March 1946, seven months after the war ended, Libby gave birth to their son, Warren, Jr. In the years afterward, they had three more children, Lisette, Laurie, and Lynn.

In the late 1940s, Warren was assigned to lead the Reserve Officer Training Corps (ROTC) program at Cornell University in Ithaca, New York. After that posting, he was transferred to an Air-Sea Rescue Unit in Greenland, where he flew B-17s equipped with inflatable lifeboats that could be dropped to distressed ships and crews.

He was then ordered to Wright-Patterson Air Force Base in Ohio, where he helped to establish the air force's Institute of Technology. That was followed by a two-year tour at an intelligence post in Germany. While in Europe, he visited France several times with his son to visit many of the people who had helped him during his four months evading capture by the Germans.

One of his last tours of duty was as the supply squadron commander at Beale Air Force Base in California in 1962. An incident occurred there that may well have cost him further promotion.

One day a black noncommissioned officer asked to see him. In the privacy of Warren's office, the noncom told him that his black airmen had no time to eat lunch. At lunchtime, they had to catch a bus several miles across the air base to their own mess hall. By the time they got there and sat down to eat, there was no time to catch a bus back to their workstations on the other side of the base.

"Why don't your men eat at the mess hall over here?" Warren asked.

"We're not welcome over here," the noncom told him.

It was an unwritten law on the base that the black airmen ate in segregated mess halls. Although segregation was illegal under air force code, the base's senior commanders did not want to arouse the resentment of the older, white, noncommissioned officers who had lived and

worked under segregated conditions for most of their careers. It was easier to look the other way.

"From now on," Warren told the black noncom, "you tell your men to
eat at whichever mess hall is closest to their work area. If you run into any
problems, you have that mess sergeant call Major Laws. I'll take care of it."

That ended it.

Warren had done what he thought was good for the air force. His
decision earned the admiration of the black airmen under his command, but it did not lead to further promotion.

He retired in 1963, and moved back to Danbury, Connecticut. After
taking graduate courses at Columbia University, he began a job teaching in the Danbury school system.

In 1969, his son, Warren, Jr., graduated from the U.S. Air Force
Academy, and followed him into a military career. Warren, Sr., swore
him in to active duty at his commissioning ceremony.

That same year, Warren was diagnosed with colon cancer. Shortly
before he died at West Point Hospital in 1970, he dictated a detailed
account of his mission to Stuttgart, Germany, in 1943. He was fifty-one
years old.

Braxton Wilken Robinson

In 1944, Braxton's friend Jane Eaglesham began dating an Australian
army officer who was temporarily stationed in New York. At one point,
he told Jane that a friend of his was about to arrive from Europe.

His name was Ivor "Rob" Robinson, and he also served in the Royal
Australian Air Force. His most recent assignment had been doing secret
work adapting the Norden bombsight for the Dutch air force in England. When Rob reached New York, he contacted Jane, who invited
him to come for dinner. Jane also invited Braxton.

The tall Australian was unlike anyone Braxton had ever met, an
untamed outdoorsman who had lived in the outback and regaled her
with tales of his fabled land of Oz.

Rob had been assigned to work with U.S. Army Air Force engineers on improvements to the Norden bombsight, and he planned to remain until the project was completed. As the project drew to an end, he proposed marriage to Braxton and asked her to go back to live in Australia with him. Although it meant leaving behind everything she had known, she never hesitated in her decision.

On a chilly fall afternoon in October 1946, the football field at Choate School in Wallingford, Connecticut, was dedicated in Ted Wilken's honor. As the Choate and Lawrenceville football teams stood in formation along the right sideline, Choate's headmaster, Seymour St. John, spoke to the crowd assembled for the dedication ceremony.

"There could be no occasion more fitting than this to do honor to one of Choate's greatest athletes, Ray Theodore Wilken. Ted excelled in every pursuit he undertook to learn. The men of Lawrenceville knew what it was to meet the teams captained by him. Today, Ted Wilken lies with his fellow crew members in Épinal military cemetery in France. But the spirit of Ted Wilken is here at Choate. We dedicate ourselves to all that Ted Wilken stood for—to his respect for a worthy opponent, to his sense of fair play, to his complete self-sacrifice to a cause he believed in. In honor then of Ted Wilken, a name and an ideal, we dedicate this field."

Braxton and Rob were married for almost seventy years, living in Perth, Australia, before moving back to the United States. They had three daughters together. Rob passed away in March 2009. Kathy Wilken married University of Michigan professor Bill Ribben, and they have two children. Kathy inherited the life-size oil painting of her father commissioned by Ted's mother shortly after his death.

Joe Schwartzkopf

After his successful escape from Europe on the same escape line used by Warren Laws, Joe returned to the United States and enjoyed a month of home leave in Buffalo, New York. For the remainder of the war, he served as a radio instructor at Drew Field in Tampa, Florida, training young radio operators on multiengine military aircraft.

With the end of the war, he went to work for the General Electric Corporation, staying with the company for seventeen years. In 1962, he moved back to Tampa, Florida, and finished his career as a company supervisor at the Treasure Isle Seafood Co. in Plant City, Florida.

Of Hungarian ancestry, he loved to cook spicy family recipes, and was also partial to pickled eggs, Limburger cheese, and pickled pig's feet, which horrified his six daughters.

Joe didn't trust medical practitioners any more than parachutes, and refused to go to a doctor when it became obvious he was suffering from the onset of heart disease. He lived life on his own terms, and often said he was living on borrowed time. He died of heart failure in 1979. According to his youngest daughter, Lori, he died a happy man.

He was fifty-seven years old.

Robert Falligant "Bob" Travis

After completing his combat tour with the Eighth Air Force in September 1944, Bob Travis enjoyed a month of home leave before being named commanding general of the Seventeenth Bomber Operational Training Wing, at Grand Island, Nebraska.

Shortly after the war, General Travis received a coveted appointment to the National War College at Fort McNair in Washington, D.C. Only officers expected to be promoted to the most senior ranks were selected. After graduating from the college in June 1947, he became the chief of staff of the Seventh Air Force at Hickam Air Force Base, Hawaii.

While serving in this command, he received disturbing news. After holding the temporary rank of brigadier general since 1943, Bob Travis learned that he was about to be demoted to the regular rank of colonel again. It was tantamount to a death blow to his ambitions.

The first step he took was to write a letter to his father.

23 December 1947

Dear Father,
I have some additional information about my probable reduction, and I must warn you that this information was given to General Wooten as top secret, so if you pass it on to the congressman or other influential friends, I ask you to caution them. . . .

General Wooten states that Lt. General Idwal Edwards, who heads Personnel of the Air Force, made this statement to him. "The chief reason why Travis is being reduced is because he was relieved of his command for cause." As you know, the record of my 41st Combat Wing, which I built from nothing, was the outstanding record of any such unit in the Eighth Air Force.

I am writing a letter to General Williams asking him to immediately write to General Edwards and straighten out the misunderstanding. . . . I am certain that I can get the record straightened out, but I greatly fear that it will be too late for my reduction as the announcements are intended for publication prior to 1 January. Dearest Love from your son, Bob

Bob Travis had clearly made some enemies in the air force, and they were at work behind the scenes. In spite of his having been the only general officer in the Eighth Air Force to complete a combat tour, and his being its most decorated senior officer, the detractors were making the specious case to General Edwards that he had been relieved of his command "for cause." If General Wooten, Travis's commanding officer in Hawaii, had not confided the false charges to him, his career would have been derailed.

In a follow-up letter to his father four days later, Bob Travis wrote:

General Wooten is scared because he gave me the info on my demotion. He says it was "secret" and that I should have told no one. Let me caution you again to take any actions very cautiously. . . . Bob

By then, Bob's father, retired Major General Robert Jesse Travis, had written a three-page single-spaced letter to U.S. Senator W. Lee "Pappy" O'Daniel of Texas, as well as five other members of Congress. It was neither cautious nor discreet.

My dear Senator:
The state of Texas, on account of the Alamo, owes my family an obligation . . . and I am calling on you as a Texan to take immediate steps from preventing a terrible mistake being made. . . .

My son, Robert F. Travis, who has been a Brigadier General (temporary) for over four and a half years . . . has had his name removed from the promotion list and will be reduced in rank because the board found that just before Germany folded up he had been relieved from his command. . . .

An investigation of his record will disclose that no officer contributed more to the success of the Air Force than he. . . . From this government, he received the Distinguished Service Cross, the Silver Star . . . several times, and the DFC several times, the Purple Heart. . . .

You have the reputation of fighting for Texans and their families. Please see to it that no injustice is done in this matter. . . . Sincerely yours, Robert J. Travis

The matter of the promotion was settled when General Robert Williams, who had been Bob Travis's division commander in England, took up his cause in a letter to General Edwards.

Dear Idwal,
It is not my desire to interfere in any way with the personnel policies of the U.S.A.F., but in order to clear the record of an officer who performed brilliantly in combat, I believe this erroneous statement should be cleared up.

General Travis is the only general officer I know who completed . . . a combat tour. He didn't pick the milk runs, either.

He led some of the toughest and most successful missions conducted by the Eighth Air Force. His 41st Wing . . . was certainly
the most outstanding wing in my division . . . with the best
operational results in the entire Eighth Air Force.

That would have been the end of it except for the fact that several
members of Congress were now demanding to know why the injustice
had occurred. The congressional interference infuriated General Carl
"Tooey" Spaatz, who had replaced Hap Arnold as commanding general
of the army air forces.

There was no way to deny promotion to Bob Travis. Instead, the
retribution fell on General Ralph Wooten, who had confided the news
to Travis about his demotion. General Wooten was passed over for
promotion.

In September 1948, Bob Travis was appointed commanding general of the Pacific Air Command. Less than a year later, he became the
commanding general of the Ninth Strategic Reconnaissance Wing at
Fairfield-Suisun Air Force Base in California.

Late on the night of August 5, 1950, Bob Travis took off on a training mission in a B-29 Superfortress. The pilot at the controls of the
bomber was Captain Eugene Steffes. Travis was commanding the mission from the copilot's seat.

Just as the plane was about to lift off the runway, the left inboard
engine propeller malfunctioned and Captain Steffes had to feather it.
Once in the air, he attempted to retract the landing gear, but the activating switch was inoperative and the wheels would not retract.

Due to the increased drag of the landing gear, and with his thrust
reduced to three engines, Captain Steffes turned back to land at the
Fairfield-Suisan air base. Coming in, he had to maneuver the Superfortress away from a trailer park located near the field.

The B-29 struck the ground at a speed of 120 miles an hour with
its left wing down. The subsequent explosion killed ten crewmen and
passengers in the rear of the plane. All but two of the ten crewmen and
passengers in the forward compartment escaped with minor injuries.

Bob Travis was one of the two men killed. Twenty minutes after his body was removed, high explosives in the bomb casings inside the bomb bay ignited. The subsequent blast was felt more than thirty miles away.

On August 14, 1950, General Robert Travis was laid to rest at Arlington Cemetery. An honor guard of two hundred soldiers and an army band escorted his coffin from Fort Myer Chapel to the grave site.

Six months later, the Fairfield-Suisun Air Force Base in California was renamed Travis Air Force Base in his honor. At the official ceremony marking the dedication on April 20, 1951, a life-size oil painting of the general was unveiled by his wife and Governor Earl Warren at the officers' club.

One night after the club had closed for the evening, the painting was slashed to pieces by a vandal. The lower half of the painting could not be restored. After the upper half was repaired and hung again in the club, the painting disappeared. It was eventually found in a storeroom on the base.

Bob Travis was forty-five years old at the time of his death.

Readers are invited to contact the author at rjmrazek1942@gmail.com if they have any questions or comments related to the people and events recounted in this book.

APPENDIX

No one will ever know why General Robert Travis decided to lead his bomb wing around Stuttgart three times on September 6, 1943, or whether he might have gone around a fourth time if his lead bombardier hadn't accidentally released their bomb load.

Certainly, the decision led to important consequences for the crews flying the mission behind him, particularly those whose Fortresses were not equipped with Tokyo tanks. Some of the pilots who flew with him that day never forgave him for a decision they believe contributed to the loss of so many crews.

Some of the pilots who flew with him on subsequent missions had equally negative impressions of his "press on, regardless" brand of combat leadership. It led to a bitterness toward him that lingered long past his death in August 1950.

After leading a bombing mission to Oschersleben, Germany, on January 11, 1944, in which sixty bombers were lost, General Travis wrote a letter describing the mission to the wife of Second Lieutenant William A. Fisher, the copilot of a Fortress named *Bad Check*, who was killed that day along with his pilot.

General Travis's account provides some valuable insight into his personality. Considering the level of detail in the letter, it's clear that the ultimate audience was intended to be greater than a single widow. In letters to his father while serving as commander of the Forty-first Combat Wing, General Travis indicated that he had drafted similar accounts of other important missions. To the author's knowledge, they have not been published.

OSCHERSLEBEN — January 11, '44
by Brigadier General Robert F. Travis

We were seated on hard chairs in the base movie at Molesworth. It was a cold damp evening and darkness had come on prematurely due to the overcast, which was now breaking into low scudding clouds, and giving some promise of improving weather for the morrow. The theater consisted of a Nissen hut with a concrete floor, and was unheated and poorly ventilated; the only heat coming from the bodies of the military personnel present, which also exuded a distinct masculine odor. Seated next to me were Lt. Colonel William R. Calhoun, Operations Officer of the 41st Combat Wing; Major William R. Thompson, Intelligence; and Captain Dan E. Baker, Adjutant and Aide-de-Camp.

The picture had just gotten well started when one of our interruptions occurred, being caused by a Sergeant who shouted above the sound of the movie, "All maintenance and gunnery personnel of the 341st Squadron report to your organization immediately." Cal turned to me and said, "It looks like we're up for tomorrow." Other such interruptions occurred successively as each organization was called to duty.

For some time we had been expecting orders to make our first attack on Berlin, and the weather map indicated a possibility of this mission being put on on the succeeding day. I knew that the men had been called out on the Alert Order and that the regular Field Orders would not arrive for some time; yet, I lost interest in the movie and shortly thereafter departed with my staff for our headquarters to see if any premature information had been released.

With our headlights dimmed, we drove a mile and a half over narrow roads beneath concealing trees to the oblong one-story brick building which served as our headquarters. The duty officer had only received the Battle Order and bomb and gasoline loadings, but from this information we could see that it would be a deep penetration, a visual target, and that my Combat Wing was to lead.

I immediately got on the phone and called "Chuck" Merwin, Operations Officer of the Division, and asked if there was a possibility of my leading the division. He could not give me the target over the telephone, but indicated that it was extremely important; and he believed that General Williams would let me go as it was about my turn. There was nothing more that we could do until the Field Orders began to arrive so I stepped out into the darkness to look at the weather. Stars were beginning to break through and the scud was only a few hundred feet thick in patches. Activity was apparent over the entire area covered by our dispersal aircraft. Portable electric units furnished light for the maintenance crews who were feverishly trying to get the maximum number of aircraft available for the morning mission. Trailers loaded with 500-pound demolition bombs were creeping slowly toward the aircraft that would swallow up their loads. Overhead one or two Mosquitoes could be heard droning as they climbed toward altitude and reconnaissance flight over the Continent. Far off to the east could be seen occasional flashes, where the British were practicing night bombing or a Jerry was putting on a nuisance raid. Search lights came on for short periods, fingered the sky, and disappeared into oblivion.

I was recalled to the office by the sudden chattering of the Teletype machines as the Field Orders began to arrive. Looking over the shoulder of the operator, I obtained the code letters from which I could look in the Intelligence File and pick out the target. It was to be the Focke-Wulf plant at Oschersleben, just south of Berlin, which so far had been untouched by our bombers. To reach this objective meant breaking through the concentric rings of fighter interceptors which the Hun had placed about Berlin and her important industries. We were to have some fighter support, but not nearly enough. Flak was sure to be intense and accurate at many places along the route as well as in the target area.

As soon as I had grasped the essentials of the mission and seen my name commanding the division, I went home to get a few hours' sleep before the early briefing, leaving the essentials of getting our Supplementary Field Orders to my staff.

From experience I had found it necessary to lay out all the equipment which I intended to use the succeeding morning where I could quickly get into it and not forget some necessary item. On the table I placed my escape kit, emergency rations, identification tags, silk muffler to protect my face from freezing should the windshield be shot out, cigarettes, and a clean handkerchief. On the floor I piled a clean suit of winter underwear, my electric flying suit, boots, gloves, special helmet with oxygen mask, flak helmet, and vest. Alongside of this flying equipment was a special target folder in which my

Intelligence Officer had placed a route to and from the target with check points and fighter rendezvous points marked thereon. Also was included aerial maps of the area and large scale identification photographs of the actual target.

Warning Sgt. Deldoso to awaken me at 3:30 I climbed into my G.I. bed and started my usual battle with sleep. This is the time when I get scared, not on the mission. Lying there in my bed and attempting to relax, my imagination runs wild. Being aware of the opposition and the problems of such a mission, I start thinking of all the things which can go wrong. I remembered that I volunteered for the damn mission and that it was not necessary for me to go at all as I had already done more than my share. I remembered my duty to my wife and children and how little money they will get in case I am killed. I wonder whether my sense of duty has caused me to go, and not just the desire for excitement and adventure. The net result is that I never sleep soundly but toss from one side to another in the bed until I hear the approaching feet of the Charge of Quarters to tell me it is time to arise.

Once I wash and dress this is all behind me. I am then ready and eager, and my only worry is that the mission will be scrubbed at the last moment due to adverse weather.

I left my quarters and drove to the 303rd mess. As a special treat for the combat crews going on the mission, fresh eggs were served. I always eat a hearty breakfast, for once forgetting my tendency toward obesity, as I am pessimistic enough to realize that it may be a long time, maybe the duration of the war, before I get another good meal.

Driving through the darkness, I arrived at the briefing room of the Group. The crews ahead of me had assembled in front of the big wall map where the briefing would be given. The target and route are temporarily concealed by a curtain and much conjecture is going on as to where we are to be sent. One young pilot saw me enter the room, and realizing that I only went on visual missions of great importance that involved deep penetration, said, "We have had it. The Old Man is going." Everyone took their seats with a sense of expectancy. The room was bitterly cold and damp. In the far corner one Sibly stove struggled valiantly against the winter climate of England. Many of the crews were suffering from colds as was apparent from their almost constant coughing. Colonel Lyle, Operations Officer of the 303rd, took his position and raised the curtain. Immediately a sigh of intense expectancy and trepidation arose from the entire room as they saw our route northeast across the North Sea, Holland, and on into Germany. All data pertinent to the mission were given to the crews; escape procedure, in case they were shot down, was covered in detail; methods of assembly; identification flares; what they should do in various emergencies; and every conceivable question which might be in their minds was answered. Slides showing the initial point, route to the target, and the target itself were thrown on the screen and discussed in detail. Great emphasis was placed upon the importance of destroying this target. An explanation was made to the crews as to what great bearing it would have upon the ultimate defeat of Germany. We knew that to get this target would cost us a great price and these boys must be convinced that the loss of life and aircraft was well worth what we hoped to accomplish.

There was one hour between the end of briefing and "stations time," which is the hour set when all members of the crew must be in the proper position in the aircraft with all essential equipment aboard and ready to go. During this period, Group, Squadron, and Flight Leaders are given last-minute instructions. Airplane commanders gather their crews about them in the dispersed aircraft positions, check their equipment, and give special instructions.

I drove out through the darkness on the perimeter until I reached dispersal area No. 25, and as my headlights swung on the nose of the "8-Ball," the ship I was to fly, a guard who had been standing in the darkness challenged me and made me identify myself. About the aircraft I could see some 25 or 30 men checking the fusing on the bombs, topping off the oxygen, loading flak vests and miscellaneous equipment aboard the aircraft, and wiping off the pilot's and bombardier's windshields.

Though there was little snow on the ground, the night was bitterly cold and I remained in my warm car until approximately ten minutes before "stations," when I descended and shook hands with the crew. I particularly cautioned the tail gunner to keep me informed of any straggling or difficulty which the elements of my formation might be in while en route to or from the target.

As usual I found considerable difficulty in working my large body with all of its winter flying equipment and paraphernalia up through the emergency exit and into the copilot's seat. Calhoun, who is to be my pilot, followed me and seated himself on the left.

We both spent several minutes arranging such things as binoculars, maps, parachutes, and so forth, at conveniently located spots about us in the cockpit.

On my left front a white rocket shoots skyward and bursts in a shower of small stars, which is the signal to start engines. Immediately the entire airdrome throbs to life with the powerful deep-throated roar of 160 engines. Normal checks are made, wheel blocks removed, and the crews stand back in readiness for us to taxi.

At the second rocket the brakes are released and our heavy laden aircraft lumbers forward. The ground crews, whose faces and bodies are illuminated by the light from the cockpit, hold up their right arms with forefinger touching thumb in the form of a circle to wish us good luck and a safe return.

Our progress through the dark on the narrow perimeter track is necessarily one of caution, for should we drop a wheel off the concrete, the aircraft would immediately bog down, obstruct the runway to following aircraft, and prevent our departure on the mission.

We swung into position on the main takeoff runway and lined up two abreast in our proper order. The sky was just beginning to lighten and in the gray light I could see our 36 aircraft and 4 spares all taxied into proper position with their engines idling.

At the green flare, Cal fed full power to our B-17 and we slowly gained momentum as we rushed into the dark. It always seems as though these ships will never leave the ground and the last few moments are anxious ones as we approach the end of the runway and see ahead of us a line of trees, which we never clear by more than a few feet.

Slowly we climb in circles while each succeeding airplane cut short their turns and fill into proper positions until we have a group of eighteen ships flying a normal combat formation several thousand feet in the air. Beneath me the snow-covered fields looked like a jigsaw puzzle cut by the black lines of hedge rows and rock fences. Smoke from the tall chimneys in the nearby industrial town hung close to the ground and stretched out like a river toward the sea. All about me I could see other groups rising from their fields and firing identification flares which floated earthward as twin brilliant balls of green, red or yellow. The first rays of the rising sun struck the metal wings and reflected pink light. Radio calls were being made by the Unit Commanders for identification and request for position reports.

Slowly the entire division assembled into Groups, then into Combat Wings, and finally into a Division Formation which proceeded towards its departure point on the English Coast.

I looked behind me and as far as I could see came a mass of B-17s, stretching from horizon to horizon, which gave me a great sensation of the strength and force of our mighty nation.

The "8-Ball" is the leading aircraft of the entire force and on our ship are the picked members of the lead crew, each a specialist and the finest that we can produce. On their shoulders will rest the responsibility for the success of the entire mission. All the blood, sweat, tears and effort that have gone and will go into this mission will be futile unless each and every one of them performs his task perfectly.

As we approach the coast, I called Ground Sector Control and informed them that we would be on course on time. This was to aid our fighters who were to support us in making proper rendezvous with us at the enemy coast.

The channel can be seen through broken clouds which increase in density until we are flying over a solid undercast. The sun is now up and shining brightly in our eyes; all aircraft have worked themselves into proper position; radio conversation has ceased; and the formation proceeds like a well-drilled Army, as it climbs toward altitude and the enemy.

Well out over the North Sea I give the order to check our guns. Even though I expected the firing, I always jump when the twin .50-caliber machine guns of the top turret fire just above my head. The whole cockpit vibrates violently while they discharge. Dust floats down through the rays of the sun and the shadow of the twin barrels swings across the nose of the aircraft as the gunner tries out his turrets.

This is our last period of relaxation. All preparations have been made that are possible and just before going on oxygen we all smoke one last cigarette. The outside air temperature is rapidly dropping as we ascend, and as the needle passes minus 20 degrees, I plug in my electrically heated flying suit and adjust the rheostat to a comfortable temperature. All members of the crew relieve their bladders, as this is also the last opportunity for many hours of cold flight ahead of us.

The navigator announces our progress as the result of dead-reckoning and checks through the radar equipment which can see the enemy coast even though it is beneath a solid cloud cover. After several hours we are approaching the Dutch Coast and the Zuider Zee. Ahead of me I can see many pursuit aircraft and, though they are too far for me to identify even through my field glasses, I believe them to be friendly. Our cruising speed is tremendous and as I count them I have a greater trepidation of troubles to come, for there are several times too many. Only one group is supposed to make rendez-vous with us at the enemy coast with other groups further along the route. Obviously some of the friendly fighter cover has arrived too soon, meaning that their endurance will be curtailed when we get further into Germany due to gasoline shortage.

Over the interphone I said to Cal, "There are too goddamn many of them. I don't like it."

As is customary the navigator kept the crew informed of our exact position to aid in escape procedure, should we be shot down, and he now informed us that we were just flying over a fringe of land on the Dutch Coast. Almost immediately I saw five ME-109s diving toward us out of the sun. All gunners were alerted and tracked the approaching aircraft, holding their fire until they were in range. We had little to worry about with this first attack as our friendly fighters had also observed them and were right on their tails giving them so much difficulty that they were never able to press home their attacks. Our entire friendly cover was drawn off behind these five aircraft, and almost immediately engaged by another large force of enemy fighters from the south. This was the last I saw of any effective fighter support.

As we drove toward the heart of Germany at 300 miles an hour, I began to feel mighty lonesome, and searched vainly in all directions for a converging force of friendly fighters. I called Fighter Control and told them that I was without support and asked for aid, but was never able to ascertain whether my message had been received.

Five minutes later I could see large numbers of small black objects rising on both sides of the formation and flying parallel of our course. It was not necessary for them to get close enough for positive identification—I knew them to be Huns, as they soon proved themselves. From this time on action became so violent and combat so exciting that it is difficult to tell a cohesive story. The enemy aircraft continued to climb and pull ahead of us until there were two columns of pursuit ships of approximately twenty-five each, strung out just outside of machine-gun range. Drawing ahead of us four or five miles the ends of the columns turned in 90 degrees across our course, peeled off in elements of five, which flew in abreast wing tip to wing tip head-on to our formation; successive waves of fighters being so close that when our gunners fired at the first wave, the next two waves would get through unmolested. Every gun in the formation was firing continuously. As the waves of fighters would dive toward me, my eyes would be fastened to the leading edge of their wings, waiting for the first burst of 20-millimeter fire. Suddenly the entire wing would burst into flame as all of their guns bore upon us. 20-millimeters would leave a chain of white doughnuts hanging suspended in the air, and within a matter of split seconds after the firing had started, the pursuit ships would be to and through the formation. These first attacks were made with no effort whatsoever at evasion. They flew into the B-17 formation, firing as they came. Such suicidal attacks effectively driven home are sure to obtain results.

Both our aircraft and the enemy's were going down in great numbers. Normally the tail gunner reports losses, gives the position and time that B-17s are shot down, but the action was too fast and everyone was too busy. One of my wing ships was seen to burst into flames [2Lt Henry J. Eich, 1 KIA 9 POW]. He dove away from the formation and almost immediately exploded—a blind flash of red flame and smoke. Nothing could be seen of debris and only a black cloud hung temporarily in the air to mark where the ship had been. Fighters could be seen spinning earthwards and portions of wings, segments of their control surfaces, and miscellaneous gear flew off as they attain greater speed and plummet to the ground. There seemed to be no end to the Hun fighters and as we shot them down, others rose and took their place.

Not once did the intense attacks let up or dwindle. Most that I observed came from head-on, but it was obvious that we were under attack from all directions as no gunner ceased firing. The Hun had decided that we were going to Berlin as our course was straight for this important target, and he had airborne every available aircraft in the Reich. Among the ships attacking us were not only ME-109s and Focke-Wulfs, but also night fighters and other twin-engine aircraft.

I was heartsick and yet proud as I saw the terrific pounding my boys were taking and the valor and determination they exhibited as they closed their dwindling formation, flew even closer, and fought their way on to their target.

Repeatedly we were under fire from antiaircraft batteries on the ground as we passed principal cities in Germany, but compared to the fighter action, this flak was of no interest and caused us not even enough alarm to record or remember its position or accuracy.

While still under attack I made a rapid survey of the remaining aircraft in my lead wing. I called "Cowboy Baker," my Low Group Leader, and asked him how he was doing. He answered that he only had five aircraft left of his original eighteen, and since the Low Squadron of the Lead Group had been entirely wiped out, he moved what was left of his group into the position originally held by my low squadron.

Just then my attention was distracted by my second wing ship being shot down [2Lt William A. Purcell, 10 KIA]; this position being immediately filled by another aircraft in formation [2Lt Vern L. Moncur]. Diving toward me now was another formation of Fws. One of these seemed determined on knocking us out by collision. Cal rolled our aircraft to the left in almost a vertical bank and the FW shimmed over our wing, missing us by so little that the distance was impossible to estimate. My top turret gunner without thinking yelled over the interphone, "That was too goddamned close." As we rolled back to the horizontal, I perceived a huge hole in my right wing where a 20-millimeter had passed through, but it appeared to have missed the gas tank.

Losses by both the enemy and ourselves had now reached such proportions that the fighting was either becoming less violent or we were becoming immune. Long before this I had decided that this was one mission from which I would never return. Our opposition had been such and our losses so great that survival seemed impossible. Never has the 8th Air Force been turned back from a target by enemy opposition, and not one of my boys was willing to let this be such an occasion.

Combat had become so violent and we so occupied that no contact had been made with succeeding units to determine how they were faring for a period of over an hour and a half.

We were now within 10 or 15 minutes of our I.P., where we would turn on course toward the target. The radio operator contacted me by interphone and told me that the Division had scrubbed the mission for many of the Combat Wings due to weather conditions at their targets. Though we had received no instructions, I was left with the decision as to whether to proceed on to the target or return to our bases with the main force. I fully realized that should I proceed I would become the sole target of all that remained of the Luftwaffe and their undivided attention would almost certainly wipe out what was left of my force. Visibility was excellent and it appeared that the target would be visual. I felt that our losses had been so great that success of the main mission must be accomplished. I informed the Combat Wing and my crew that we would continue and attack as briefed.

Turning from the I.P. toward the target we observed one lone P-51 diving into the midst of our attacking enemy and fight with glorious disregard to his own safety and determination to break up their murderous attacks upon us. As he rolled and dove through their formation with all his guns blazing, we saw him shoot down successively five enemy aircraft, and though he could never hear our encouragements, cheers went up from every American in formation. Out of ammunition and nearly out of gas, this lone fighter finally had to leave us and return to his base with our prayers and hopes for his safety. He made it and later each of us had the opportunity to extend our personal thanks for his brave assistance.

On our bombing run we stopped all evasive action. The bomb bay doors were open, the interphone was turned over to the bombardier and navigator, and no more fighter attacks were called. A red flare was fired to announce the approach of the target and caution the Wing Men to close up into a tight bombing formation. Ahead lay the town of Oschersleben. On its outskirts was a compact, distinctly marked factory area, the goal which we had come so far and fought so hard to reach. A juicy target presented itself just before we reached Oschersleben, for underneath us was a large enemy airdrome with aircraft of many descriptions, but we would not be distracted from our main goal. With our reduced numbers not one bomb could be spared from the main target.

Enemy attacks had never ceased, but now our goal was so close attention was concentrated on its success and all of our opposition that was made to the fighters must be made by the gunners alone, as no evasion was possible. Slowly over the interphone came the voice of the bombardier, "Three Minutes to go, Two Minutes, One Minute, Bombs Away!" As much as we wanted to turn and proceed toward home, evading enemy fire, we held our course and heading momentarily until we were assured that all bombs had departed toward the target.

I watched the open bellies of my wing ships as the 500-pounders dropped in close succession and descended as rapidly disappearing black dots toward the target. We turned toward home, and looking back I could see the entire factory suddenly burst into a huge cloud of dirty black smoke which blossomed upwards for 5,000 feet and then mushroomed out to a white edge cloud with a dark center. Our destruction could be seen when we were a hundred miles on our way toward home. Opposition still continued, but by this time it was spasmodic and by single aircraft instead of large formations. Occasionally a B-17, which could no longer struggle on toward home due to the punishment which it had received, would drop down and descend earthwards.

We were far from being safe yet, but after what we had gone through and the success we had obtained, we felt elated and justifiably proud.

I sent a WT Message to the Division reporting the target bombed visually with excellent results. A quick survey was made to determine the number of aircraft still with me, their condition, and the ability of the stragglers to keep up. Four ships could be seen with feathered props. Many were having difficulties in conserving what gasoline was left to get home. Despite my reluctance to remain over Germany any longer than necessary, I reduced power, slowed down the formation to keep it compact, and started a gradual let down as we again approached the North Sea. Once over the channel we felt relatively safe, for the Hun has repeatedly shown himself to be a coward when fighting over water.

Our let down continued and at 10,000 feet we yanked off our oxygen masks, grinned at each other and shook hands with a heartfelt warmth, and lighted cigarettes.

At the English Coast the setting sun had turned west into a glorious mass of color shading from the pale pinks to the deeper reds, purples and blues, as though to welcome us home safely to a green peaceful countryside which lay beneath us and seemed well worth fighting for.

Oschersleben might be classed as just one of many such battles fought by the 8th Air Force, but there was something a little special about this mission. It was the turning point in the battle between our forces and the Focke-Wulf. Up to that time, if anything, the Germans actually had a slight edge on our fighters, but never again after January 11 was he able to put up large opposition to any of our missions.

Our route across Germany into the target and back was well marked with tragic reminders of the conflict. It was a steady and unbroken trail of crashed airplanes, white parachutes, and dead soldiers, both from our forces and the Germans.

Once and for all we proved that the American lad has the guts and the determination to reach his goal, regardless of the opposition; and the spirit exemplified on January 11th at Oschersleben is the same spirit which will win this war and keep America victorious so long as she keeps the principles of our free land high like a torch and our flag unfurled.

(General Travis's letter appears courtesy of Gary Moncur. It was first published by the 303rd Bomb Group Association.)

ACKNOWLEDGMENTS

The principal source of inspiration for *To Kingdom Come* was my friend Martin "Andy" Andrews. I first met Andy when I was a college student looking for a summer job. By then, he was an accomplished independent filmmaker. After he hired me as his gofer, we spent many hours together traveling from one film location to another.

Over that summer, I learned that he had been a B-17 pilot during World War II, and had flown some of the Eighth Air Force's most harrowing missions in 1943 with the famed 306th Bomb Group, the unit that served as the model for the book and motion picture film *Twelve O'Clock High*. While always self-deprecating about his own accomplishments, Andy's stories about the bravery of his fellow pilots and crew members instilled a sense of awe in me. Andy became an important role model in my life.

In the course of researching *To Kingdom Come*, I had an opportunity to travel across the country to meet the pilots and crew members whose stories I hoped to tell. Researching and writing this book has been one of the most rewarding professional experiences of my life.

The men whose stories are in this book were not unique. There were tens of thousands of young Americans just like them who put their lives on the line flying the early deep-penetration raids into Germany when the Luftwaffe fighter command was at its peak strength.

It was my goal in this book to ennoble their sacrifice by focusing on a small group of men who flew one of the many tough missions. Through their eyes, I thought, the reader would have a chance to understand what it might have been like for many of the airmen in those perilous times.

In order to tell this story, I reviewed more than twenty-five hundred pages of official documents specifically related to the Stuttgart mission. A compendium of the military sources I found is catalogued in the bibliography section of this book. Studying these documents, along with the cables and communications of the senior commanders before and after the battle, enabled me to develop a reasonable understanding of why this mission was ordered, what happened during the course of the battle, the results of the mission, and the impact of those results on the prosecution of the air war against Germany.

The challenge in finding some of these answers was complicated by the fact that the Stuttgart mission was the most calamitous defeat sustained by the Eighth Air Force in the war. Military historians who have commented on the mission have referred to it as a "fiasco" and a "disaster."

The two missions to Schweinfurt in August and October 1943 may well have been more savage air battles, but in both those cases most of the pilots and crews located their intended targets and achieved significant success in destroying them.

Not one of the 338 Fortresses that set off to bomb the industrial targets around Stuttgart on September 6 was able to find its mark. It is not surprising that the Eighth's senior commanders initially attempted to cloak the disastrous results from General Hap Arnold. Not only were their jobs at stake, but so was the fate of daylight precision bombing itself.

The Stuttgart mission was a turning point in the air war against Germany. It was that rare time in history when wholesale slaughter was required to force a fundamental change in a poorly conceived strategy, in this case the doctrine that unprotected Flying Fortresses could defend themselves while destroying Germany's capacity to wage war. General Arnold would never again assert as he did at his press conference in London two days before the Stuttgart mission that Fortresses alone could get the job done.

The Stuttgart mission was also historically important because it finally convinced General Ira Eaker that a *sustained* air offensive against Germany could not be carried out without long-range Allied fighters capable of going all the way to the targets and back.

After Stuttgart, General Arnold also realized that the Eighth needed long-range fighters, and he went back to Washington determined to accelerate the production of the P-51, along with jettisonable gas tanks for the fighters already deployed.

The difference in Eaker's and Arnold's conclusions after Stuttgart was that Arnold continued to believe a sustained offensive against Germany's important industrial targets could be resumed with the assets at hand. Eaker disagreed. After Stuttgart, he ordered only one additional maximum-effort deep-penetration raid to Germany before he was relieved of his command in December 1943.

I want to express my appreciation to the many people who assisted me in writing this book. The list begins with Andy Andrews, Jim Armstrong, Olen Grant, Jim Karnezis, Don Stoulil, Bill Eisenhart, Bud Klint, Clifford Hammock, and Wilbert Yee. I am deeply grateful to them for sharing their stories with me. Although I never met Ted Wilken and Warren Laws, I am indebted to their widows, Braxton Wilken Robinson and Elizabeth "Libby" Laws, for helping me to hopefully bring them alive again on the printed page.

I also owe a big debt to Warren Laws, Jr., who was not only of great assistance in providing important details of his father's story but also helped me to verify that it was Egon "Connie" Mayer who shot down *Patricia* six kilometers west of Troyes. Mr. Laws confirmed the site of the crash with the assistance of a local Frenchman using a metal detector, and reviewed all the evidence presented to him. Warren, a former U.S. Air Force pilot himself, has made a number of trips to Europe to follow the path his father took in escaping from occupied Europe, and meeting many of the people who helped him. Lori Sarnese, the youngest daughter of Joe Schwartzkopf, provided me with helpful information about her father.

As all World War II students know, negotiating the labyrinth of the National Archives is a daunting challenge. I was thankful to have the assistance of an extraordinary researcher, Tim Frank, who found reports I was unable to locate at the National Archives and Records Administration in College Park, Maryland.

Yvonne Kinkaid, the senior historian at the Air Force History Support Office at Bolling Air Force Base in Washington, D.C., was very helpful in securing other material I needed, as was researcher Tom Berkey (Col. USAF-Ret.), who volunteers at Bolling to assist the occasionally inept through their vast trove of official records. I am also grateful to C. R. "Dick" Andregg, the Director of the Air Force History and Museum Programs at the Pentagon, for smoothing my difficulties in retrieving information on the Stuttgart mission.

Another important source in telling this story were the many fine Eighth Air Force bomb group Internet Web sites, all of them dedicated to the men who flew in them. In particular, I would like to thank Gary Moncur, the historian and Web site designer of the 303rd Bomb Group Web site. His father, the late Vern Moncur, delivered one of the lines I included on the epigraph page at the beginning of this book. Another important Web site was the 388th BG Database, created by Dick Henggeler, whose father was a squadron leader in that group. It was very helpful to me, along with the Web site of the 384th BG. I particularly want to thank Ken Decker, whose magnificent contribution can be found in the "Memories" section.

I am deeply grateful to Professor Tami Davis Biddle at the U.S. Army War College in Carlisle, Pennsylvania, for sharing with me her insights into the simmering conflict between Ira Eaker and Hap Arnold, and how the pressure on General Eaker affected the course of the air war. Along with transcripts of two important interviews conducted with General Eaker, she provided me with a lengthy excerpt of an unpublished memoir by Major Richard Hughes, who served on Eaker's staff as the senior officer in the Enemy Objectives Unit, and whose recollections shed a good deal of light on the internal workings of target selection, as well as the pressure the Eighth Air Force was under to prove the value of daylight precision bombing.

In undertaking this project, I received valuable advice from three superb military historians, Donald Miller, Rick Atkinson, and Brian D. O'Neill, all of whom generously provided me with important leads in finding answers to the riddles I was faced with at the start of my research.

In the process of securing valuable information about the life of General Robert Travis, I received help from Erica Bruchko and Elizabeth Stice at the Manuscript, Archives, & Rare Book Library (MARBL) at Emory University in Atlanta, Georgia.

I also want to thank Vivian Rogers-Price, the Research Center Director at the Mighty Eighth Air Force Museum in Savannah, Georgia, for her assistance, as well as Nick Siekierski at the Hoover Institution Archives at Stanford University in Stanford, California. Also at Hoover, researcher Jenny Fichmann found important information related to this story in the papers of General Frederick Anderson, Jr.

Don Patton, who is a director of the World War II History Roundtable in Edina, Minnesota, was very helpful in locating several Eighth Air Force veterans who gave me assistance on another part of the story. Stephanie Balls at Claridge's Hotel provided information on the formal dinner held in General Arnold's honor on September 6, 1943.

I want to also express my appreciation to Gary Hodges for restoring many of the photographs that had become badly faded since the war. He did an incredible job. For transcribing more than a hundred hours of author interviews, I would like to thank Dawn Ryan.

As always, I am indebted to my gifted literary agent, David Halpern, for his continued wisdom in helping me to choose worthwhile projects. Ian King at the Robbins Office also gave me valuable assistance. Finally, I am grateful to my able editor at Penguin Books, Mark Chait, for his role in shaping and structuring the final version of the book. It is stronger for his insights and recommendations.

SOURCES

Prelude

Hap

The primary source for the events and incidents described in this chapter was General Henry H. Arnold's personal diary, in which he chronicled his daily activities on his inspection trip to England during the first week of September 1943.

Hap Arnold's complete wartime diaries, which were edited by retired Major General John W. Huston and published in two volumes under the title *American Airpower Comes of Age*, provided the author with a host of fascinating insights into the character of this remarkable, hard-driving war leader. In the diary, Arnold is always direct, often pungent, and occasionally quite funny. His words do not spare those under his command who did not live up to his expectations.

In recounting the contentious marital situation between Henry and Eleanor "Bee" Arnold while living in Quarters Number 8 at Fort Myer in the fall of 1943, the author relied on Thomas Coffey's excellent biography *HAP: The Story of the U.S. Air Force and the Man Who Built It*. The descriptions of Arnold's precarious health situation, his daily routines, Arnold's early life, and his prewar career in the army were also largely drawn from incidents described in Mr. Coffey's book.

The account of General Arnold's brief visit to Gander, Newfoundland, his recorded observations while there, his subsequent flight across the Atlantic, and the dramatic events that occurred at Prestwick, Scotland, when he arrived in dense fog were drawn from Arnold's diary. The excerpts of the speech he was to deliver on September 4 appear in the final version of the statement that he read in London before an assemblage of Allied war correspondents on September 4, and which is included with the general's papers at the Library of Congress.

General Arnold's unwavering views on the importance of daylight precision bombing, his unyielding commitment to making certain that the Eighth Air Force's offensive against Germany would be pursued without delay, his efforts to counter the continued British opposition to his plans, his deft maneuvering in Washington on behalf of the air force, and his concerns about the lack of aggressiveness on the part of the senior commanders in the Eighth Air Force are richly explored by Mr. Coffey in *HAP: The Story of the U.S. Air Force and the Man Who Built It*, as well as in James Parton's fine biography of Ira Eaker, *Air Force Spoken Here*.

Ira

Ira Eaker's worries about being relieved of his command of the Eighth Air Force are documented by both Parton and Coffey. The burgeoning confrontation between the two longtime friends in 1943 resulted from the pace at which the Eighth's daylight precision bombing campaign was being prosecuted against Germany.

Arnold was convinced that Eaker was moving too slowly with the assets he had at hand. Eaker thought that Arnold wasn't taking into account the impact of the losses of so many bombers on the long-range missions to Germany, the time required to train replacement crews before they could be sent into battle, and the difficult maintenance challenges resulting from the severe battle damage being sustained by so many Fortresses on the deep-penetration raids.

Also at the heart of the conflict was Eaker's view that the bombing raids to strategic targets inside Germany could not be long sustained without the assistance of long-range fighters to protect the bombers on their way to and from the targets. Arnold disagreed.

In writing this chapter, the author also relied on official military sources to document the increasingly bitter disagreements between Arnold and Eaker over how to employ the Eighth Air Force. In early June, Arnold began sending a series of cables demanding to know why Eaker was not aggressively pursuing the bombing campaign against Germany, and recommending that Eaker replace several of his senior commanders.

These cables initiated a blizzard of communications over the next month in which Arnold and Eaker continued to trade verbal body blows. The author reviewed these letters and cables at the National Archives and Records Administration (NARA) in College Park, Maryland. "We get nowhere with recriminations," Eaker wrote back bitterly at one point. His frustration culminated in a June 29 confidential letter to Arnold in which he wrote, "I do not feel . . . that I am a horse that needs to be ridden with spurs."

At one point, James Parton, Eaker's aide and future biographer, wrote, "It began to look as if Generals Arnold and Eaker were devoting more time to fighting each other than to defeating the Germans."

The sections of this chapter recounting Ira Eaker's early life and his prewar career in the army's fledgling air corps were principally drawn from *Air Force Spoken Here*. The increasingly close personal and professional relationship of Arnold and Eaker as they pursued their careers prior to World War II was chronicled in both *HAP* and *Air Force Spoken Here*, as were the factors that led Arnold to eventually choose Eaker to command the Eighth Air Force.

Eaker's change of heart about the Flying Fortress's ability to defend itself without long-range fighter protection evolved over the early months of 1943, and is fully explored by Parton, as well as his urgent but initially unsuccessful campaign to convince Hap Arnold to make the delivery of long-range fighters a high priority.

The author utilized official military records at NARA to relate the events of July and August 1943, including the launching of the air offensive against Germany on July 25, 1943, and the attacks on Schweinfurt and Regensburg on August 17.

In describing Arnold's arrival in England, and his subsequent visit to High Wycombe Abbey on September 2 for meetings with Ira Eaker and his senior staff, the author relied on General Arnold's diary comments, his personal account of the meetings in his book, *Global Mission*, the diary of General Frederick Anderson, and General Eaker's interview with Joe Green on January 28, 1972.

Although in most of his interviews after the war General Eaker remained largely circumspect in describing his internal battle with Hap Arnold at this time, he was quite candid with Green in describing the pressure that Arnold put on him to resume the air offensive against Germany.

Eaker referenced Arnold's rhetorical demand in the wake of the Schweinfurt mission as, "Why don't you send them out the next day?" Eaker's rhetorical response was, "Well . . . we would have no bombers left."

Eaker added in the same interview, "I said to General Arnold that it was going to be my policy to conduct our operations at such a rate that we will always be growing and therefore a more menacing force. I will never operate at such a rate that I will be a diminishing and vanishing force. Well, this argument was—quite intense, quite bitter."

In the same interview, General Eaker commented on the fact that in private, General Arnold referred to him as "Son." In *Air Force Spoken Here*, Parton documented several instances in which Eaker, whose own father was a remote figure to him, nurtured father-son relationships with other senior commanders in the army.

His father-son relationship with Arnold was by far the most important of his professional life. But as the "son" in the relationship, Eaker never directly challenged Arnold, even when he was sure Arnold was wrong. Loyalty always overcame his better judgment. He also knew that Arnold didn't hesitate to fire anyone who opposed him in air force matters, regardless of their personal relationship. It left Eaker in a serious quandary in the days before ordering the Stuttgart mission.

It is impossible to know if General Eaker would have ordered the Stuttgart raid if Hap Arnold had not been in England pressuring him to resume the air offensive. Some military historians doubt it.

In a June 25, 2009, article for the Air Force Research Institute at Maxwell Air Force Base, Alabama, retired USAF Brigadier General Richard Baughn asserted that the first Schweinfurt-Regensburg raid in August 1943 was planned without Eaker's knowledge, and that he "protested it bitterly" upon learning that it was to be undertaken. Eaker's opposition was ostensibly based on his strongly held view that the losses going deep into Germany without fighter escort would be unsustainable. At the same time, Eaker knew that failure to comply with Arnold's demands to resume the deep-penetration raids would lead to his removal as commander of the Eighth Air Force.

In relating the events that transpired on General Arnold's inspection tour on September 3, 4, and 5, the author relied on his diary entries, along with his detailed account of those three days in *Global Mission*. The odd movie-screening incident was recounted by General Arnold in one of his diary entries.

The Warriors

Reb

The primary source for the events in this chapter can be found in the author's taped interviews with Olen "Reb" Grant. His recollections of his relationship with Estella, the story of his early life in Arkansas, the account of his being picked up by military police on the morning of the Stuttgart mission, his experiences with the 384th Bomb Group during its training phase at Wendover, Utah, including the machine-gun incident that led to his being demoted, and his belated introduction to Jimmy Armstrong shortly before the takeoff to Stuttgart were all recounted over the course of more than fifteen hours of interviews.

Olen Grant also provided the author with a lengthy reminiscence of his experiences in the war entitled *For You the War Is Over,* and the author used it to fill in many of the details of the story. Also of value in describing the 384th Bomb Group's training phase at Wendover Air Force Base was the book *Heritage of Valor: The Eighth Air Force in World War II.* It was written by Colonel Budd Peaslee, who commanded the group during the time that Olen Grant served in it.

The Greek

The principal sources for the incidents and anecdotes in this chapter were the author's interviews with Demetrios "Jim" Karnezis. In these interviews, Colonel Karnezis described the morale of the pilots after the group's heavy combat losses in the previous weeks, and vividly recalled the ways that flight officers dealt with their fears through alcohol and gallows humor, including the amusing anecdote he witnessed involving bombardier Sid Alford.

The physical descriptions of the air base at Knettishall in September 1943 were provided by Mr. Karnezis, although the author also drew valuable assistance from the photographs in the outstanding book *The 388th at War,* written by Edward J. Huntzinger. The preflight rituals performed by Colonel Karnezis, including his carrying of the icon of his patron saint, Demetrios, in his flight suit, also came from author interviews.

The details of the premission briefing to the 388th's flight crews came from the operation staff's actual briefing notes and sketches, all of which were copied from the originals at the National Archives and Records Administration in College Park, Maryland.

Andy

The material in this chapter was drawn from the author's interviews with Mr. Andrews, as well as from a detailed account he wrote about the Stuttgart mission after the war. The written account provided the author with many of the premission details, including the 306th's briefing and Mr. Andrews's concern about the lack of Tokyo tanks in his Fortress for what would be the longest mission up to that point in the war.

Mr. Andrews's accounts of his earlier missions, including the July 4 raid on Nantes, France, that precipitated his nightmares, as well as the recollections of his boyhood in Milwaukee, Wisconsin, were drawn from interviews.

Mr. Andrews also gave the author a copy of an oral history that he taped in 1990, describing all the aircraft he flew throughout the war, including their respective flying characteristics. The oral history supplied valuable details that were incorporated into the segment dealing with his flight training, as well as his months as a flight instructor before joining the Eighth Air Force.

The interviews also provided the author with the story of Mr. Andrews's romantic relationship, the naming of his Fortress *Est Nulla Via Invia Virtuti* and the peace of mind he derived from reading the "Choric Song" from Alfred, Lord Tennyson's melancholy poem *The Lotos-Eaters*.

Bob

For the opening section of this chapter, in which Brigadier General Robert F. Travis was introduced to the flight crews of the 303rd Bomb Group at the pre-dawn briefing for the Stuttgart mission, the source was Wilbur "Bud" Klint, who flew the mission that day as the copilot of *Old Squaw*.

Bud Klint was also the source for the statement made by Lieutenant Colonel Kermit Stevens, the 303rd's commander, prior to the Schweinfurt mission on August 17, in which Stevens told his pilots that if they dove their planes with full bomb loads into the center of the Schweinfurt target area, he would consider the mission a success. This briefing scene was also re-created in *Half a Wing, Three Engines and a Prayer: B-17s Over Germany*, an outstanding book about the 303rd Bomb Group written by Brian D. O'Neill.

Over the course of numerous interviews with the author, Bud Klint displayed vivid memories of General Travis at the briefing, including the physical impression he made that morning, the way he presented himself in his brief talk, and the substance of his remarks.

In describing the personality of General Robert Travis, the author relied on a number of different sources, including Don Stoulil and William Eisenhart, themselves veteran pilots of the 303rd Bomb Group, who flew with the general over the course of their combat tours. In addition, the author was able to find useful insights into his personality in the general's personal correspondence, which is archived in the Robert Jesse Travis Collection at the Manuscript, Archives, & Rare Book Library, Emory University, Atlanta, Georgia, along with many other family letters that shed light on his life before the war.

The general's burning desire to succeed in the army is revealed in the letters he wrote to his father, retired Major General R. J. Travis, both during and after World War II, in some of which he did not hesitate to disparage the lackluster performance of his peers when he felt he deserved promotion ahead of them.

That General Travis was a stickler for regulations is revealed in his letters to his father. The source for the anecdote in which the general walked the flight line with a tape measure looking for men smoking within fifty feet of an aircraft was found in an account of his life on the Arlington National Cemetery Web site.

Two different sources confirmed the general's love of poker, and his predilection to play with junior officers, both sources being officers who played poker with the general on several occasions at Gowen Field in Boise, Idaho, before leaving to join the Eighth Air Force. One was Andy Andrews, who recalled the general taking more than five minutes to call one hand in their game, which irritated the other players, all of whom were lieutenants, and none of whom said anything as they waited. Creighton Carlin, the navigator in Jimmy Armstrong's crew, also recalled playing poker with the general, and claimed in an interview that he won $2,000 from him in a single game.

The details about General Travis's extraordinary father, Major General Robert Jesse Travis, were found in the Travis collection at Emory University. The younger general's admiration for his father is evident in all his letters to him. The letters between father and son also reveal that the younger Travis hesitated to call on his father for help when dealing with issues that impacted his future in the army. The letters reflect the elder Travis's great pride in his son's accomplishments.

General Travis's caustic observations about fellow Brigadiers Kissner and Thatcher, among others, can be found in a letter to his father. The letter to Pop Arnold is part of the file related to Ira Eaker's official reprimand of Travis, and it is in the Carl A. Spaatz papers at the Library of Congress, Washington, D.C.

The source for the description of Major Lewis Lyle, who flew with General Travis on the Stuttgart mission, was Brian D. O'Neill's *Half a Wing, Three Engines and a Prayer: B-17s Over Germany.*

Ted

The principal source of information for this chapter was Braxton Wilken Robinson, the widow of Ted Wilken. Ted wrote v-mail letters to her almost every day after his crew arrived in England. Within censorship guidelines, he would update her on his personal activities, as well as those of the men whom he had trained with and whom Braxton knew well.

The information about Ted Wilken's life before the war was culled from a number of sources, including family scrapbooks that were provided to the author, along with letters and newspaper articles about his early achievements. The author was also given copies of award citations and other documents that underscore his extraordinary athletic achievements at Choate School.

The story of how Ted met Braxton, as well as the narrative describing their falling in love, was provided to the author by Braxton Wilken Robinson in a series of interviews at her home in Oregon in 2009. She also described the events related to Ted's training courses, and what it was like to be newly married and following her husband from base to base across the country. The letter in the middle of the chapter from Braxton to Ted's mother, in which she eloquently sums up the "live for the moment" nature of wartime marriages, was provided to the author by Braxton.

The sources for the events and incidents that took place in Spokane, Washington, after Ted's crew first came together for their final training exercises before going overseas were Braxton Wilken Robinson and Warren P. Laws, Ted's copilot, who shared these stories with his fiancée, Elizabeth.

Jimmy

The primary source for the events that unfolded in this chapter was retired Lieutenant Colonel James E. Armstrong, who granted interviews to the author at his home in Georgia. Mr. Armstrong also provided most of the background on the men who served in his crew.

The accounts of the missions flown in *Sad Sack II* were drawn from the interviews with Mr. Armstrong, along with the records of the missions flown by the 384th Bomb Group, and Mr. Armstrong's wonderful book, *Escape!*, which is an account of his participation in the Stuttgart mission, and his subsequent adventures trying to escape from occupied Europe and reach England.

The description of the Schweinfurt mission and its impact on the morale of his crew came from author interviews. The description of the *Yankee Raider* was drawn from interviews with Mr. Armstrong and Olen Grant. Its maintenance history was found on the 384th Bomb Group Web site.

The events surrounding the first meeting between Mr. Armstrong and Mr. Grant, when Mr. Grant arrived to join the crew in a military police vehicle, and their subsequent activities as they prepared to take off for Stuttgart were drawn from author interviews with both men, as well as the unpublished written account of the mission by Mr. Grant.

The Mission

Juggernaut

The incident in which two members of Andy Andrews's crew were involved in a vehicular accident prior to takeoff, necessitating their last-minute replacement, was drawn from an interview with Mr. Andrews, and was supplemented with his written account of the premission events at Thurleigh.

In describing the vast and complex two-hour assemblage of the 338-plane air armada on the morning of September 6, the author relied on official records, including the Frag orders for each group and the postmission group reports that documented what actually occurred.

The description of the combat box formation, including its origins and development under the leadership of General Curtis LeMay, was drawn from Wilbur H. Morrison's *The Incredible 305th: The "Can Do" Bombers of World War II*, and Martin Bowman's *USAAF Handbook 1939–1945*.

To demonstrate how the sixteen bomb groups that flew the mission were each choreographed into their positions within the bomber train, the author utilized the Frag order to the 388th group.

The sections of this chapter that revealed the relationship between Ted Wilken and Warren Laws, as well as the details of Mr. Laws's personal background, were drawn from Mr. Laws's written account of the mission and author interviews with Mr. Laws's widow, Elizabeth Laws, and Mr. Laws's son, Warren P. Laws, Jr.

The order of takeoff, takeoff times, and order of formation in the 388th Bomb Group was taken directly from the takeoff plan and formation sketch found in the 388th's mission report. The events that transpired aboard the *Patricia* as it formed up with the rest of the 388th over southern England were recorded in Mr. Laws's written account of the mission.

The actual times that the groups finally came together in the sky over England, culminating in the final formation of the bomber train before heading for the enemy coast, were taken from the postmission group reports.

The exodus of aborting aircraft from the Fourth and First Bombardment Wings as the bomber train neared France was observed by Mr. Andrews,

Mr. Karnezis, and Mr. Armstrong. The specific numbers of Fortresses that were forced to abort the mission from each group, as well as the individual aircraft, were found in the postmission group reports, along with the stated reasons for their departure.

According to the Eighth Bomber Command's final narrative of the operation, forty-four Fortresses aborted the mission prior to reaching the French coast. Another thirty-two turned back prior to reaching Germany due to bad weather, mechanical problems, or navigation error. They represented 22 percent of the original attacking force.

The Golden Eagle

The author relied on a number of sources in describing the events in this chapter. Most of the information about Jagdgeschwader 2 was drawn from John Weal's fine book, *Jagdgeschwader 2 "Richthofen."*

Egon Mayer's combat record, including a list of his victories in the air, was found at Kacha's Luftwaffe Page (www.luftwaffe.cz/index.html). Additional information about his background and personality was gleaned from the Luftwaffe Archives & Records Reference Group (www.lwag.org/forums/index.php).

Mayer's role in conceiving the frontal attack strategy against the Flying Fortress that changed the course of the air war was documented in Robert Forsyth's *Fw 190 Sturmbocke vs B-17 Flying Fortress*, as well as *The Luftwaffe Over Germany: Defense of the Reich* by Donald Caldwell and Richard Muller, and Donald Miller's *Masters of the Air: America's Bomber Boys Who Fought the Air War Against Nazi Germany*. A copy of the circular in which General Adolf Galland, commander of all fighter forces in the Luftwaffe, embraced Mayer's frontal attack strategy can be found in Mr. Forsyth's book.

Egon Mayer's fighting prowess was already legendary among the air warriors in the Luftwaffe, and he was becoming well known by reputation to the Eighth Air Force. Caldwell and Muller described one of Mayer's sorties in *The Luftwaffe Over Germany* that astonished the American bomber crews who witnessed it. On July 14, the 305th Bomb Group had been returning from a bombing run near Paris when two Fw 190s appeared ahead of them. Ed Burford, one of the B-17 navigators, recalled what happened next in an interview with Mr. Caldwell. "Whoever it was gave a riveting display of aerobatics in front of our entire 102nd Combat Wing before slashing in to fatally damage the leading ship of the 422nd Squadron in the low slot. . . . I had never seen such a tremendous volume of tracer go after that one plane with a wingman in tow. Downright discouraging to hit nothing but air."

The Fw 190 pilot was Egon Mayer.

The deployment strategy by the Luftwaffe of the fighter staffeln in France and Germany in September 1943, as well as the Luftwaffe's tactics in attempting to destroy the B-17 bomber trains, is covered in depth in Caldwell and Muller's *The Luftwaffe Over Germany*. The author also found useful information in Cajus Bekker's *The Luftwaffe War Diaries*.

In describing the deployment of the staffeln of Jagdgeschwader 2 to meet the threat of the diversionary raids mounted by the Eighth Air Force along the Dutch coast and at Rouen northwest of Paris, among other sorties, the author relied on the German air force defensive activity report for September 6, 1943, which chronologically detailed all fighter movement in France on the morning of September 6, and the "Y" Service Report, which was a compilation of all enemy radio transmissions, including the German fighter staffeln, monitored minute by minute by tracking stations in southern England.

Into the Valley

The report of the early loss of two Fortresses to flak shortly after the combat box formation that included the 306th, the 92nd, and the 305th groups crossed into French airspace was found by the author in the postmission group reports, as well as a crew interrogation report.

The surprisingly few, desultory attacks by enemy fighters while the Stuttgart bomber stream was crossing France were noted in the crew interrogation reports from most of the groups. All the developments within individual B-17s came from interviews with the pilots mentioned or crew interrogation reports.

In depicting the first attacks by the scores of enemy fighters that broke through the cloud cover as the combat wings were approaching southern Germany, the author relied on the descriptions contributed by Mr. Karnezis, Mr. Andrews, Mr. Armstrong, Mr. Laws, and Major Ralph Jarrendt in his crew interrogation report.

The author's account detailing the level and intensity of the Luftwaffe attacks on the American bomber train was drawn from the crew interrogation reports, the postmission group reports, the Luftwaffe Archives, the Eighth Air Force's narrative of the mission, and the confidential report sent by Ira Eaker to Hap Arnold on September 10, 1943.

The account of Mr. Andrews's actions after one of his bomber's engines was shot out in the first wave of fighter attacks was drawn from his written narrative of the mission, as well as his interviews with the author.

The Blind Leading the Blind

The ferocity of the attacks by German fighters on the low squadron of the 388th was documented in the crew interrogation reports of the men who returned from the mission, and in the Missing Air Crew Reports (MACRs) of those planes that were lost. The MACRs were continually updated during the war as new information became available. Mr. Laws also wrote in detail about these attacks in his postwar account. In addition, the author found valuable information in the Escape and Evasion Reports written by the men who survived and then escaped occupied Europe after their Fortresses were shot down. The Escape and Evasion Reports were particularly useful in determining what happened aboard each lost plane in its last moments. The author also utilized this material in attempting to establish the order in which the eleven Fortresses in the 388th were lost that day.

The section of this chapter dealing with the insurmountable challenges that faced First Lieutenant Henry Dick, the lead bombardier of the 388th Bomb Group, in trying to get a fix on the primary target over Stuttgart was evoked in detail in the lengthy postmission report that he filed on September 8, 1943. The subsequent movements of the 388th in maintaining formation with the 96th Bomb Group can also be found in Dick's report, as well as the postmission report filed by Major R. B. Satterwhite, the group leader of the 388th.

A Ride in the Whirlwind

The author's account of the events that transpired after the First Bombardment Wing arrived over Stuttgart at 0949 on the morning of September 6, 1943, were reconstructed from the postmission reports filed by the nine groups within the First Bombardment Wing. In addition to the reports filed by the group leaders, the author reviewed the reports filed by the nine lead navigators and the nine lead bombardiers.

For the events that transpired inside *Satan's Workshop*, the lead plane in which General Travis was flying, the author relied on the postmission reports filed by Major Lyle, the group leader, First Lieutenant Norman Jacobsen, the lead navigator, and First Lieutenant Jack Fawcett, the lead bombardier. The report filed by Lieutenant Fawcett was particularly valuable. He wrote at length about what occurred aboard the plane while he tried to acquire the primary target with his bombsight.

To the author's knowledge, General Travis never explained his decision to circle over Stuttgart three times before the bomb load in *Satan's Workshop* was accidentally toggled by Lieutenant Fawcett, thus signaling the other bombardiers to release their own payloads. The author drew his conclusions on the decision based on the general's actions and decisions on the missions he led after Stuttgart, and the testimony of other pilots he flew with, including Don Stoulil and Bill Eisenhart, both of whom were interviewed by the author. The appendix in this book provides some insight into the general's determination to complete a mission as it was ordered.

The impact of the general's decision was felt by most of the pilots and crewmen the author interviewed, including Bud Klint, Jimmy Armstrong, and Andy Andrews, all of whom vividly remembered the challenge of attempting to stay in a tight formation as they flew three times over the flak batteries surrounding Stuttgart. For those on the outer rim of the formation, it was particularly difficult. Mr. Armstrong likened it to the child's game of crack the whip, but it had deadly consequences. After draining gas at an accelerated rate, many of those Fortresses without Tokyo tanks could not make it back to England. In addition, the tight combat boxes soon lost their integrity, and the ragged formations that headed homeward were easier targets for the German fighters.

Another description of the confused maelstrom of Fortresses over Stuttgart can be found in Brian D. O'Neill's *Half a Wing, Three Engines and a Prayer: B-17s Over Germany,* a book in which he closely tracked the combat careers of many of the flight crews in the 303rd Bomb Group as they attempted against the odds to complete their combat tours in 1943 and 1944.

The paragraphs in *To Kingdom Come* that describe the increasing frustration and anger of pilot David Shelhamer, eventually leading him to order the salvoing of his plane's bomb load through the clouds, was drawn from Mr. Shelhamer's account to Brian O'Neill.

The accidental release of the bomb load in *Satan's Workshop* was described by the chagrined Lieutenant Fawcett in his postmission report, along with his honest admission that he had no idea where the bombs had landed.

The experiences of Andy Andrews, Jimmy Armstrong, Olen Grant, and Bud Klint as they continued to circle the target were drawn from the author's interviews with them, along with Mr. Armstrong's book, *Escape!*

And the Sky Rained Heroes

The description of the events leading up to the Fourth Bomb Wing's attack of its secondary target at Strasburg, including the specific movements of the 388th and 96th Bomb Groups, were drawn from the postmission reports of lead bombardiers Henry Dick and Thomas Hines.

Mr. Karnezis described the resumption of German fighter attacks on the 388th Bomb Group, and the loss of his friend Earl Melville's plane, *Shedonwanna?*, in an author interview. The details of what happened aboard *Shedonwanna?* in its last moments were drawn from surviving crew members' accounts in the plane's Missing Air Crew Report. MACRs also provided valuable information in helping the author describe the destruction of *Impatient Virgin* and *Shack Up*. Additional details were supplied by Major Jarrendt's crew, among others, in their crew interrogation reports after returning to Knettishall.

The events leading to the loss of three more Fortresses in the 388th's low squadron, including Lew Miller's unnamed bomber, *Lone Wolf*, and *In God We Trust*, were drawn from the Missing Air Crew Reports for each bomber, the Escape and Evasion Reports filed later in the war by survivors of the doomed planes, the Escape and Evasion Reports submitted by Warren Laws and Joe Schwartzkopf, and the written account of the mission by Mr. Laws.

Est Nulla Via Invia Virtuti

The description of the actions taken by Mr. Andrews in attempting to save his plane and crew after losing an engine on their approach to Stuttgart, and then losing a second one after leaving Stuttgart, followed by the attacks of four German fighters and the subsequent landing of *Est Nulla Via Invia Virtuti* in Switzerland after being intercepted by a Swiss fighter plane, was drawn largely from the account of Mr. Andrews's combat experiences that he wrote after the war. Additional details were drawn from author interviews with Mr. Andrews.

Another source of information about these events from the Swiss perspective, including information about the Swiss pilot who intercepted Mr. Andrews's bomber, as well as the actions of Allen Dulles, the head of the American spy network in Europe, can be found in an account by the American Swiss Foundation at the Web site www.americanswiss.org/index.php?option=com_content&task=view&id=36&Itemid=78.

Theirs Not to Reason Why

The descriptions of the incidents that occurred in the final minutes before *Slightly Dangerous II* crashed into the French countryside, including the ultimately successful attacks by German fighters, the scene of copilot Jack George firing his .45-caliber pistol at one of the Fw 190s, the struggle in the cockpit after the steering cables were shot out, and Mr. Karnezis's signaling the rest of the crew to bail out, were based on interviews with Mr. Karnezis at his home in California, along with the Escape and Evasion Reports filed by Mr. Karnezis and Mr. George after they reached freedom.

The subsequent account of Mr. Karnezis's exiting the plane with the slashed parachute, his injuries after hitting the ground, his escape from the German search party, and his rumination on the famous line from "The Charge of the Light Brigade" while he struggled to escape across the forest was drawn from author interviews.

To the Last Beat of the Heart

The source for confirming Egon Mayer's first aerial victory of the day, the destruction of a Flying Fortress ten miles northeast of Troyes, France, was Kacha's Luftwaffe Page.

The final moments aboard Ted Wilken's plane before it went down, including the description of the frontal attacks that set the nose on fire while killing the bombardier, navigator, and top turret gunner, and wounding Ted Wilken, Warren Laws, and John Eicholtz, were drawn from Mr. Laws's written account of the Stuttgart mission. The author also relied on the Escape and Evasion Reports of Mr. Laws and Mr. Schwartzkopf, both of which provide descriptions of the plane's last minutes, culminating in their bailing out of the stricken bomber.

The account of Ted Wilken's death following his attempt to keep the plane in the air until the rest of his crew was clear was provided by Olivier Mauchamp, a young French farmworker at the time of the crash. Mr. Mauchamp's full statement, which includes the description of how Lieutenant Wilken's parachute was snagged by the spinning bomber as it plunged to earth, can be found at the 388th Bomb Group Database.

The author is firmly convinced that *Patricia* was shot down by Egon "Connie" Mayer, who claimed a victory over a Flying Fortress at 12:17 p.m. on September 6, approximating the location it crashed as "six kilometers west of Troyes." The crash site of *Patricia* was seven kilometers from the western edge of Troyes. Radio operator Joe Schwartzkopf reported that *Patricia* was shot down at twenty minutes past the hour, only a three-minute discrepancy. Warren Laws reported that he landed in his parachute at thirty minutes past the hour. No other Fortresses went down that day in proximity to *Patricia*.

The events that occurred after Warren Laws and Joe Schwartzkopf safely parachuted out of the stricken *Patricia* were drawn from the Escape and Evasion Reports filed by the two men, as well as the written account of the mission and its aftermath by Warren Laws.

Hard Landings

In relating the events leading up to the ditching of *Old Squaw* in the English Channel, copilot Bud Klint provided the author with an account of the mission in his interviews. Another account of these events from the perspective of the entire crew can be found in Brian D. O'Neill's *Half a Wing, Three Engines and a Prayer: B-17s Over Germany*.

The description of the return of General Robert Travis in *Satan's Workshop* to the 303rd Bomb Group's air base at Molesworth accompanied by four other aircraft was drawn from the postmission reports filed by Major Lewis Lyle, and squadron leaders Captain George Stallings and First Lieutenant Donald Gamble. The quoted statements made by General Travis and Major Lyle after the mission can be found on the Web site of the 303rd Bomb Group (303rd BG [H] Combat Mission No. 67).

The Last One Left

Yankee Raider may well have been the last Fortress in the original bomber train of 338 planes still heading for England at the time it was shot down. It was certainly one of the last stragglers still airborne.

In describing *Yankee Raider*'s last minutes in the air, the author drew on his interviews with crew members James Armstrong, Olen Grant, Clifford Hammock, and Wilbert Yee. In particular, Mr. Grant had indelible recollections of *Yankee Raider* heading toward earth with him being the last man still aboard.

In the course of writing his own book, *Escape!*, Mr. Armstrong recorded his own interviews with many of the surviving crew members, including Olen

Grant, Eldore Daudelin, Creighton Carlin, Walter House, and Wilbert Yee, garnering their own impressions of the mission. These were also helpful to the author in reconstructing the minute-by-minute narrative.

Slipstreams

Remains of the Day

The opening scene of this chapter, in which Colonel Budd Peaslee, the 384th's group commander, witnessed the return of his group from the mission, including his shock at realizing that only two out of the eighteen bombers that had been dispatched that morning were returning to the base, is drawn from Colonel Peaslee's narrative of this event in his book, *Heritage of Valor: The Eighth Air Force in World War II.*

The growing anxiety of General Frederick Anderson, head of Eighth Air Force Bomber Command, as he waited for the first Flash Reports to arrive during the afternoon of September 6 is documented in General Anderson's confidential diary for that day, which is in his collected papers at the Hoover Institution Archives, Stanford University, Stanford, California (Box 2, Folder 8).

The account of Robert Artaud, the young French ambulance driver who rescued Mr. Grant from his crashed bomber and drove him to the local hospital, was provided to the author by Mr. Grant's daughter, who visited Mr. Artaud in his French village long after the war to thank him for saving her father's life.

The description of how General Arnold spent the daylight hours of September 6 was drawn from his diary entries, which detailed his activities from early that morning until his return from the shopping expedition with General Eaker in the late afternoon.

The formal dinner at Claridge's Hotel in General Arnold's honor on the evening of September 6 required substantial planning. There were more than sixty invited guests, including every senior British and American war leader in England at that time. A complete file folder on preparations for the dinner, including copies of the invitations, acceptances, declinations, the menu, the seating arrangements around the fifty-foot-long table, and follow-up correspondence from the guests after the dinner, is archived in the Eaker papers at the Library of Congress.

In describing the events leading to Mr. Karnezis's decision to seek help at the farm of Marcelle Andre, and her subsequent tending of his injuries along with her daughter, Marie Therese, the author relied on his interviews with Mr. Karnezis.

Eventide

The reference to General Anderson's ascension to Eighth Air Force Bomber Command was drawn from James Parton's *Air Force Spoken Here*. The accounting of the disastrous Stuttgart mission results, including the stark fact that not one of the 262 bombers that reached Stuttgart hit one of the principal targets while sustaining a loss of 45 Fortresses, was compiled at Eighth Air Force Bomber Command headquarters in High Wycombe from the Flash Reports submitted by each group after the collation of the individual crew interrogation reports. A preliminary narrative of the complete operation was provided to General Eaker on the evening of September 6.

The account of Mr. Armstrong's first night as an escapee in France was provided to the author in an interview. It was supplemented by additional details included by Mr. Armstrong in his own book, *Escape!*

There were numerous sources for the author's recounting of the dinner held in General Arnold's honor at Claridge's Hotel on the night of September 6. General Arnold's diary provided many details, and he also wrote about the evening expansively in his book, *Global Mission*. Air Marshal Sir Trafford Leigh-Mallory recorded his own observations in a letter to General Eaker after the dinner, including his admiration of General Arnold's personality and the high quality of General Eaker's cigars, among other details. This letter is archived in the Eaker papers, along with the correspondence received from other guests. The seating details were extracted from a commemorative folio that was signed by every guest at the dinner. Their signatures appear next to their places at the table.

General Anderson's trepidation at what he would tell Arnold if asked about the success of the Stuttgart mission is fully documented in his confidential diary entries for September 6, which were drafted by his closest aide. Excerpts include, "Today's mission was hell.... The bombs were scattered all over hell's half acre.... The target was not destroyed and probably the only gains we could claim are some destruction of unimportant buildings in cities and towns.... The general was placed in a particularly tough spot in attending this dinner party tonight. It wasn't easy for him to have to face the questioning of General Arnold . . . on a day when he had just lost 46 bombers and crews without any tangible gains. The general feels badly enough without having to make an accounting at the moment to any higher-ups."

According to General Arnold in his book, *Global Mission*, General Anderson informed him at the Claridge's dinner that "the bombing results on Stuttgart 'had been excellent.'" This would explain Arnold's anger when he learned differently a few days later, resulting in his branding the mission "a complete failure" after receiving Eaker's subsequent report.

As of September 8, General Anderson still hadn't recovered from the subterfuge of two days earlier. In the general's daily diary, his aide recorded, "General Anderson seemed pretty much whipped today, the strain of the past few days seeming to catch up with him."

The Day After

The meeting between Andy Andrews and Allen Dulles was recounted by Mr. Andrews to the author. It is also detailed in his written narrative of the Stuttgart mission. Another version of their first meeting appears in an account written by the American Swiss Foundation.

The first series of misadventures of Jimmy Armstrong, from the morning he woke up on September 7 in a French briar patch to his arrival in Paris on September 20, were told to the author by Mr. Armstrong. After the war, he fulfilled his promise to return to France to thank the people who had protected him from arrest by the Gestapo, and the accounts of those who survived the war are included in his book, *Escape!*

The Back of the Tiger

The September 10 confidential memorandum sent by General Eaker to General Arnold in response to Arnold's insistence on a personal report from Eaker on the Stuttgart mission, entitled *Further information on Stuttgart mission as requested your A3517 September 9th*, is archived in the Eaker papers at the Library of Congress.

The renewed demands by General Arnold in September to resume the air offensive against Germany in the wake of the Stuttgart failure, and General Eaker's subsequent actions limiting the Eighth Air Force to raids within France while replacement crews arrived to make up the Stuttgart losses, are documented by James Parton in *Air Force Spoken Here* and Thomas Coffey in *HAP*.

The sources for the author's description of the events surrounding the official reprimand of General Travis by Generals Eaker and Anderson were the official military records that included the charges against Travis of having made a "base slander" against the Eighth Air Force, the exhibits of several letters written by

Travis that were included with the charges, General Travis's response to the reprimand, and the final adjudication of the matter. The folder is archived in the papers of General Carl A. Spaatz in the Library of Congress.

Interlude

In describing the morale and fighting condition of the Luftwaffe fighter command in September 1943, the author relied on Caldwell and Muller's *The Luftwaffe Over Germany: Defense of the Reich*.

In chronicling the continued success of Egon "Connie" Mayer that September in combat against the Eighth Air Force, the author drew from the record of his victories in Kacha's Luftwaffe Page and the Luftwaffe Archives & Records Reference Group.

Paris Blues

The narrative related to Olen Grant's stay in the German military hospital in Paris was provided by Mr. Grant to the author in interviews. Additional details can be found in Mr. Grant's unpublished war reminiscence, *For You the War Is Over*.

The account of Mr. Karnezis's journey from La Chapelle–Champigny to Paris, as well as the story of his weeks at the home of the Maraceaux family, his encounter with a German Wehrmacht officer, and his witnessing of the attack on Paris by the Eighth Air Force was related to the author by Mr. Karnezis.

The makeup of the crews and aircraft from the 388th Bomb Group that participated in the September 15, 1943, raid on Paris was found in Ed Huntzinger's *The 388th at War*.

Hitting the Road

In relating the story of Warren Laws's and Joe Schwartzkopf's first days on the run, and their being sheltered by Marcel Vergeot and Monsieur Nelle, among other families, while Warren developed his proficiency in French, the author relied on his interviews with Warren P. Laws, Jr., himself a former air force pilot, who traveled to France several times to meet and interview the people who had helped his father escape from occupied Europe, including the Vergeot family, the Nelle family, the LeDantecs, the Bonnards, and the Dorés, all of whom protected or sheltered Warren and Joe during their time in France. Warren and Joe were staying at the LeDantecs' when Warren saw the wrecked *Patricia* being hauled back to Germany. The accounts of the French families were related to the author by Warren Laws, Jr., and Elizabeth "Libby" Laws. She also provided the author with the details of their courtship that were included in this chapter.

Eclipse

The description of the events surrounding the notification of Braxton Wilken that Ted Wilken was missing in action was drawn from author interviews with Braxton Wilken Robinson. She also provided the author with copies of the telegrams and letters excerpted in this chapter.

The account of the steps taken by her stepfather, Chester "Red" McKittrick, to ascertain Ted's fate, and her reactions to the letter from Gene Cordes, one of Ted's former crew members, were related to the author in an interview.

Greek Holiday

All the material in this chapter, including Mr. Karnezis's final days with the Maraceaux family, his journey to Brittany and then Brest, the reconnection with other fliers shot down on the Stuttgart mission, his five days aboard the French fishing boat with fifteen other escapees, and their voyage to England, was recounted to the author in interviews with Mr. Karnezis. Another perspective on the escapees' time aboard the French fishing boat can be found in the Wikipedia encyclopedia entry for Wing Commander John Checketts.

Friends and Enemies

The decision by General Arnold in the wake of the Stuttgart mission to make the delivery of long-range P-51 fighters and jettisonable gas tanks to England a top priority is documented by both James Parton in *Air Force Spoken Here* and Thomas Coffey's *HAP*.

The increasing frustration of General Arnold at the perceived failure of Ira

Eaker to utilize all the assets Arnold was sending him is covered in significant detail by Mr. Parton. The account of Arnold's tirade to Air Marshal Portal in Cairo over Eaker's handling of the Eighth Air Force is recounted in both the above biographies.

Eaker's humiliation at the way he was removed, and his subsequent anger at Arnold, was drawn from Miller's *Masters of the Air: America's Bomber Boys Who Fought the Air War Against Nazi Germany*.

The cables between Eaker, Arnold, and Eisenhower after Arnold informed Eaker that he was being "promoted" to his new assignment in the Mediterranean were reviewed by the author at the National Archives and Records Administration in College Park, Maryland.

Desperate Journey

The account of Warren Laws's first thwarted attempts to escape from France was provided to the author by Warren Laws, Jr., who interviewed two of the American escapees who were with Mr. Laws in Paris when their underground contact was arrested by the Gestapo. Mr. Laws, Jr., also interviewed Abbé Bonnard, the Catholic priest who related the account of Mr. Laws's mission with the S.A.S. to resupply the local Maquis unit.

The narrative of Mr. Laws's perilous journey over the Pyrenees in December 1943, including his efforts to save the life of his comrade who asked to be left behind in the mountains, was related to the author by Warren P. Laws, Jr., who had read the written account of his father. In 2009, Mr. Laws, Jr., retraced his father's steps by making the same climb over the Pyrenees. The author chose to change the name of Mr. Laws's fellow escapee to Henry Krueger to avoid any embarrassment to his family.

The account of Mr. Laws's time in the Spanish prison at Girona, as well as his subsequent release to an American military attaché, was drawn from interviews with Mr. Laws, Jr., and Elizabeth Laws.

The Telegram

The copies of the telegrams Braxton Wilken received from the War Department, along with the other letters excerpted in this chapter, were provided to the author by the recipient. The section related to her actions in the wake of the devastating news was related in interviews.

On the Run

The narrative of Mr. Armstrong's remarkable adventures as an escapee in France, including the many occasions when his plans were thwarted by bad luck, unreliable contacts, inclement weather, German collaborators, a failed rendezvous, snowdrifts in the Pyrenees, and German foot patrols, culminating in a harrowing voyage by boat to England in the middle of a vicious storm, was related to the author in his interviews with Mr. Armstrong. Additional details were supplied by Mr. Armstrong in his book, *Escape!*

After the war, Mr. Armstrong also interviewed many of the French people who assisted him, and their own accounts are included in his book.

Against All Odds

The author's observations on the diminished fighting strength of Luftwaffe fighter command in March 1944, as well as the relative training experience of the American and German pilots after attrition cost the Luftwaffe many of its more experienced pilots, were drawn from *The Luftwaffe Over Germany* and Weal's *Jagdgeschwader 2 "Richthofen."*

The details of Egon Mayer's final combat mission were based on *Jagdgeschwader 2 "Richthofen,"* Kacha's Luftwaffe Page, the Eighth Air Force Fighter Command Report on Active Operations for that day, and Norman Fortier's book, *An Ace of the Eighth: An American Fighter Pilot's Air War in Europe*, in which Mr. Fortier, himself a decorated fighter pilot, states that based on gun camera footage, it was Lieutenant Walter Gresham who shot down Egon Mayer.

Cloak and Dagger

The final episode in Andy Andrews's wartime career in Europe was related to the author in interviews. The narrative of his months in the temporary holding camp in the Jura Mountains, which details his efforts to raise the men's morale by teaching several academic courses, and his own demoralization after his crew's transfer to the former ski resort at Adelboden, Switzerland, were also drawn from interviews, as well as the account researched and written by the American Swiss Foundation. Additional material about Mr. Andrews's time at Adelboden can be found in the excellent book *Refuge from the Reich: American Airmen and Switzerland During World War II*, by Stephen Tanner.

The story of the recruitment of Andy Andrews by OSS Station Chief Allen Dulles to become a courier of top secret intelligence information was provided to the author by Mr. Andrews in their interviews. Mr. Andrews also described his experiences with Mr. Dulles in an account he wrote after the war. This subject is also covered in the American Swiss Foundation account, as well as by Stephen Tanner in *Refuge from the Reich*. The details of Mr. Andrews's trip across wartime Germany, and his subsequent debriefing at OSS Headquarters in Virginia, were recounted to the author in interviews.

The End of a Tour

In summing up the outstanding combat career of General Robert F. Travis, the author relied principally on official documents, as well as the letters written by General Travis. A complete list of his combat decorations was found in the National Archives and Records Administration in College Park, Maryland.

The general's evident pride in his awards is evident in the letters he wrote to his father during his wartime service with the Eighth Air Force. After he was reprimanded by General Eaker for security breaches, General Travis was careful in his letters to avoid censorship concerns. Many of his letters to his father are archived in the Manuscript, Archives, & Rare Book Library (MARBL) at Emory University, Atlanta, Georgia.

In writing about General Travis's role in the Eighth Air Force's mission to Oschersleben, Germany, on January 11, 1944, the author relied on the mission report of the 303rd Bomb Group (303rd BG [H] Combat Mission No. 98), which is archived at their Web site. The nearly five-thousand-word letter written by General Travis to the widow of copilot William Fisher after the battle is also published on the same Web site. This letter never mentions the recall order issued by General Jimmy Doolittle that General Travis said afterward he never received.

The details of General Travis's mission to Berlin, Germany, on April 29, 1944, during which he was wounded, was related to the author by pilot Don Stoulil, who was with General Travis in the cockpit at the time.

In describing General Travis's last mission to the marshaling yards at Mainz, Germany, on September 21, 1944, the author relied on his interview with Captain William Eisenhart, who was the lead pilot of the entire Eighth Air Force that day, and flew with the general. The account of the incident in which Mr. Eisenhart's urine accidentally sprayed the general's face, leading to a dressing-down of him by General Travis after the mission was over, was also related to the author by Mr. Eisenhart, who added that following the mission, his navigator and bombardier were each awarded the Distinguished Flying Cross for leading the successful mission. Mr. Eisenhart, the lead pilot, said that he received no award at all.

Reb

In chronicling Olen Grant's many months of captivity at Stalag 17 in Krems, Austria, the author relied on his interviews with Mr. Grant, in which Mr. Grant recalled the deprivations of life faced by every Allied POW in a German prisoner-of-war camp. Mr. Grant also supplied the author with copies of the letters he wrote home while he was a prisoner.

The sources for the narrative of Mr. Grant's extended recuperation period in the German military hospital in Paris, followed by his arrival by train at Frankfurt, which had been bombed shortly before his arrival, his escape from a German mob intent on killing him, and his time in solitary confinement before being transferred to Stalag 17 were provided in interviews with Mr. Grant, although some additional material was drawn from Mr. Grant's unpublished reminiscence, *For You the War Is Over.*

The account of Mr. Grant's subsequent exchange for a wounded German soldier in Marseille, France, followed by his voyage home aboard the ocean liner *Gripsholm,* was drawn from interviews, as well as the story of his whirlwind courtship and marriage to Priscilla Hutchinson that appeared in the *New York Daily News* six days after his return to the United States.

Epilogue

In describing the air bases from which the men in this story took off for Stuttgart in 1943, the author relied on the memories of his own visits to them. Donald Miller's *Masters of the Air* was the source for the casualty figures.

The narrative on the subsequent life of Martin "Andy" Andrews after the war came from author interviews, as well as letters Mr. Andrews wrote detailing his participation in the production of the newsreels about President Truman and the Hungarian Revolution.

The Armstrong segment was drawn from interviews.

Part of the account of General Arnold's final years was derived from official sources, but most of the factual material was presented by Thomas Coffey in his biography *HAP.*

The Eaker segment came from official sources, as well as *Air Force Spoken Here*, the biography of General Eaker written by his former aide, James Parton.

The two segments on Reb Grant and Demetrios Karnezis were drawn from interviews. The narrative related to Bud Klint also came from interviews, along with material in Brian D. O'Neill's *Half a Wing, Three Engines and a Prayer: B-17s Over Germany.*

The material on Warren Laws came from interviews with his widow and son.

The narrative on Ted Wilken's widow and daughter came from author interviews.

The section related to General Travis's possible demotion, and the steps he took to avoid it, are documented in nine letters archived in the Manuscript, Archives, & Rare Book Library (MARBL) at Emory University, Atlanta, Georgia.

The account of Mr. Schwartzkopf's life after the war was drawn from an interview with his daughter, Lori Sarnese.

The account of General Travis's death came from the official Air Force Accident Summary. The description of the dedication ceremony at Travis Air Force Base, as well as the ensuing mutilation of his painting, can be found at the Arlington National Cemetery Web site (www.arlingtoncemetery.net/rftravis.htm).

BIBLIOGRAPHY

Books

Armstrong, Lt. Col. James E. *Escape!* Spartanburg, S.C.: Altman Printing Company, 2000.

Arnold, General H. H. *Global Mission.* New York: Harper and Brothers, 1949.

Astor, Gerald. *The Mighty Eighth: The Air War in Europe as Told by the Men Who Fought It.* New York: Dell, 1997.

Bekker, Cajus. *The Luftwaffe War Diaries.* Garden City, N.Y.: Doubleday, 1968.

Bendiner, Elmer. *The Fall of Fortresses.* New York: G. P. Putnam's Sons, 1980.

Biddle, Tami. *Rhetoric and Reality in Air Warfare: The Evolution of British and American Ideas About Strategic Bombing, 1914–1945.* Princeton, N.J.: Princeton University Press, 2002.

Bowers, Peter M. *Boeing B-17 Flying Fortress.* Seattle: Museum of Flight, 1985.

Bowman, Martin. *Great American Air Battles of World War II.* Shrewsbury, UK: Airlife, 1994.

———. *B-17 Flying Fortress Units of the Eighth Air Force (Part 2).* Westminster, Md.: Osprey Publishing, 2002.

———. *USAAF Handbook 1939–1945.* Mechanicsburg, Penn.: Stackpole Books, 1997.

Caidin, Martin. *Black Thursday.* New York: Bantam, 1987.

———. *Flying Forts: The B-17 in World War II.* New York: Bantam, 1990.

Caldwell, Donald, and Richard Muller. *The Luftwaffe Over Germany*. London: Greenhill Books, 2007.

Coffey, Thomas M. *Decision Over Schweinfurt*. New York: David McKay Company, 1977.

———. *HAP: The Story of the U.S. Air Force and the Man Who Built It*. New York: Viking Press, 1982.

Crosby, Harry H. *A Wing and a Prayer: The "Bloody 100th" Bomb Group of the U.S. Eighth Air Force in Action Over Europe in World War II*. New York: HarperCollins, 1993.

Davis, Richard G. *Carl A. Spaatz and the Air War in Europe*. Washington, D.C.: Center for Air Force History, 1993.

Fisher, Charles A. *Mission Number Three: Missing in Action*. Latrobe, Penn.: Publications of the St. Vincent College, 1997.

Forsyth, Robert. *Fw 190 Sturmbocke vs B-17 Flying Fortress*. New York: Osprey Publishing, 2009.

Fortier, Norman. *An Ace of the Eighth: An American Fighter Pilot's Air War in Europe*. New York: Presidio Press, 2003.

Freeman, Roger A. *The Mighty Eighth: A History of the Units, Men and Machines of the U.S. 8th Air Force*. London: Cassell and Co., 2000.

———. *The Mighty Eighth: War Manual*. London: Cassell and Co., 2001.

Gobrecht, Harry D. *Might in Flight: Daily Diary of the Eighth Air Force's Hells Angels, 303rd Bombardment Group (H)*. San Clemente, Calif.: 303rd Bomb Group Association, 1997.

Griffith, Charles. *The Quest: Haywood Hansell and American Strategic Bombing in World War II*. Montgomery, Ala.: Air University Press, 1999.

Hansell, General Haywood S., Jr. *The Strategic Air War Against Germany and Japan: A Memoir*. Washington, D.C.: Office of Air Force History, 1986.

Harris, Sir Arthur. *Bomber Offensive*. Barnsley, England: Pen & Sword Military Classics, 2005.

Hastings, Max. *Bomber Command*. London: Pan Books, 1999.

Huntzinger, Edward J. *The 388th at War*. Privately printed, 1979.

Huston, General John W. *American Airpower Comes of Age: General Henry H. "Hap" Arnold's World War II Diaries*. Montgomery, Ala.: Air University Press, 2002.

———. *American Airpower Comes of Age: General Henry H. "Hap" Arnold's World War II Diaries* (Vol. 2). Montgomery, Ala.: Air University Press, 2002.

Jablonski, Edward. *Double Strike: The Epic Air Raids on Regensburg-Schweinfurt, August 17, 1943*. Garden City, N.Y.: Doubleday and Company, 1974.

LeMay, Curtis E., and MacKinlay Kantor. *Mission with LeMay: My Story*. Garden City, N.Y.: Doubleday, 1965.

Levine, Alan J. *The Strategic Bombing of Germany, 1940–1945*. New York: Praeger, 1992.

Middlebrook, Martin. *The Schweinfurt-Regensburg Mission*. London: Cassell Military Paperbacks, 2000.

Miller, Donald L. *Masters of the Air: America's Bomber Boys Who Fought the Air War Against Nazi Germany*. New York: Simon & Schuster Paperbacks, 2006.

Morrison, Wilbur H. *Fortress Without a Roof: The Allied Bombing of the Third Reich*. New York: St. Martin's Press, 1982.

——. *The Incredible 305th: The "Can Do" Bombers of World War II*. New York: Jove Books, 1962.

Parton, James. *Air Force Spoken Here: General Ira Eaker and the Command of the Air*. Bethesda, Md.: Adler & Adler, Publishers, 1986.

O'Neill, Brian D. *Half a Wing, Three Engines and a Prayer: B-17s Over Germany*. New York: McGraw-Hill, 1999.

Overy, Richard J. *Bomber Command, 1939–1945: Reaping the Whirlwind*. New York: HarperCollins, 1997.

Peaslee, Col. Budd J. *Heritage of Valor: The Eighth Air Force in World War II*. New York: J. B. Lippincott Company, 1964.

Probert, Henry. *Bomber Harris: His Life and Times*. Mechanicsburg, Penn.: Stackpole Books, 2003.

Rooney, Andy. *My War*. New York: Times Books, 1995.

Schaffer, Ronald. *Wings of Judgment: American Bombing in World War II*. New York: Oxford University Press, 1985.

Smith, John N. *Airfield Focus 44: Grafton Underwood*. Peterborough, England: GMS Enterprises, 2001.

Smith, Starr. *Jimmy Stewart: Bomber Pilot*. St. Paul, Minn.: Zenith Press, 2005.

Spick, Mike. *Luftwaffe Bomber Aces: Luftwaffe at War*. London: Greenhill Books, 2001.

——. *Aces of the Reich: The Making of a Luftwaffe Fighter-Pilot*. London: Greenhill Books, 2006.

Strong, Russell A. *First over Germany: A History of the 306th Bombardment Group*. Winston-Salem, N.C.: Hunter, 1982.

Tanner, Stephen. *Refuge from the Reich: American Airmen and Switzerland During World War II*. Rockville Centre, N.Y.: Sarpedon, 2000.

Verrier, Anthony. *The Bomber Offensive*. New York: Macmillan, 1969.

Weal, John. *Jagdgeschwader 2 "Richthofen."* Oxford: Osprey Publishing, 2000. Rockville Centre, N.Y.: Sarpedon, 2000.

Military Sources

The most important sources of information for the author's reconstruction of the principal events that occurred during the mission to Stuttgart on September 6, 1943, were found in the official reports submitted by the bomb wings, groups, and squadrons that fought in the battle. The author secured a complete set of these reports from the National Archives and Records Administration in College Park, Maryland, and the Air Force History Support Office at Bolling Air Force Base in Washington, D.C.

Sixteen bomb groups participated in the attack on Stuttgart. They were the 91st, 92nd, 94th, 95th, 96th, 100th, 303rd, 305th, 306th, 351st, 379th, 381st, 384th, 385th, 388th, and 390th. Seven of these groups were part of the Fourth Bombardment Wing, and nine were in the First Bombardment Wing.

On the evening of September 5, 1943, Eighth Air Force Bomber Command issued the field order for the Stuttgart mission to the First and Fourth wings. A subsequent field order was issued by the two wings to the sixteen bomb groups. These field orders, called "Fragmentation orders," or Frags, were specific to each group's role in the overall mission.

As an example, the 388th Bomb Group, which absorbed the highest losses on the Stuttgart mission, received its first Frag at 2240 on the night of September 5, 1943. This order was revised several times by the operations staff at the Fourth Bombardment Wing before takeoff in the early hours of the following morning.

Another important set of military records utilized by the author were the briefing notes prepared by the operations staff of each bomb group for the flight crews. They provided the takeoff times, order of takeoff, rendezvous instructions, weather reports, target importance data, a sketch of the group formation, and in some cases excerpts of the actual statements made by the group leaders at the briefing.

Additional group reports detailed the actual takeoff time of each crew and the landing times for those that returned. The most valuable tool for reconstructing what occurred on a mission were the firsthand accounts of the men who flew it, beginning with the crew interrogation reports they submitted upon returning to their bases. These debriefing notes detailed what happened to each crew on the mission, including the level of enemy fighter attacks, their own claims of enemy aircraft destroyed, any problems or unusual events crew members might have experienced, and their firsthand observations of how, when, and where other bombers in their squadron and group were lost.

Within hours of a group's return, a preliminary group action report, or Flash Report, was submitted to bomb wing headquarters. These Flash Reports provided the author with extensive summaries of the mission, including how many aircraft aborted and the reasons why, how many enemy fighters were encountered and how many claimed, the intensity of flak over the target, actual bombing results, and a compilation of those crews that were lost.

Each group leader who flew the strike also filed a postmission report, along with the lead navigator and the lead bombardier. A final comprehensive group report on the mission, with all the collated statistical data, was prepared at wing headquarters. Utilizing the data compiled by the wings, Eighth Air Force Bomber Command then completed a comprehensive narrative of the mission, which itemized the total number of planes dispatched by all the groups, the number that aborted the mission or failed to reach the target, overall claims of enemy planes destroyed, numbers of personnel lost or missing, actual bombing results, the total numbers of enemy aircraft encountered, and the tactics they employed.

Of vital importance to telling this story, and particularly the descriptions of what occurred aboard those aircraft that were lost on the mission, were the missing crew reports filed after the battle. These included the personal accounts from the returning crews' interrogation reports, which often provided a good picture of how, when, where, and why a Fortress went down, as well as whether any parachutes were observed before it disappeared or crashed. These missing crew reports were updated throughout the war whenever any new information was secured that shed light on the fate of individual crew members.

Of equal value to the author were the Escape and Evasion Reports filed by those men who survived the downing of their bombers and were successful in escaping from occupied Europe in the weeks and months after the battle. These detailed narratives were generated after an escapee reached England or the United States, and often provided additional information on what happened to other members of that particular crew.

In addition to the official reports cited above, other military sources utilized by the author included:

Daily Diary of Major General Frederick Anderson, Jr., Frederick Lewis Anderson Papers, Hoover Institution Archives, Stanford University, Stanford, California.

Eighth Air Force Fighter Command Report on Active Operations: Sunrise to Sunset—6th September 1943. National Archives and Records Administration (NARA), College Park, Maryland.

"General Ira Eaker's No Win Situation." Article by Brigadier General Richard Baughn in the *Wright Stuff*, Air Force Research Institute, Maxwell Air Force Base, Alabama (June 25, 2009).

German Air Force Day Defensive Activity. Dawn 6-9-43—Dawn 7-9-43. Air Force History Support Office, Bolling Air Force Base, Washington, D.C.

Menu, Seating Chart, and Relevant Correspondence Related to the Dinner Given in Honor of General Arnold at Claridge's Hotel, September 6, 1943. General Henry H. Arnold Papers, Library of Congress, Washington, D.C.

Negative Damage Report K.M. 208. Photographs taken by 540 Squadron on 6.9.1943. SORTIE: E/144. Locality: Stuttgart. Damage Assessment. Air Force History Support Office, Bolling Air Force Base, Washington, D.C.

Number 11 Group Synopsis of Operations, 24 Hours ended 0600 Hours, 7 September. Air Force History Support Office, Bolling Air Force Base, Washington, D.C.

Official Reprimand of Brig. General Robert F. Travis by Major General Ira C. Eaker (11 September, 1943), with accompanying documents and exhibits. Carl Andrew Spaatz Papers, Library of Congress, Washington, D.C.

"Some Observations of War and Warriors." Speech by Ira Eaker to Squadron Officers' School, September 23, 1974. Air Force Historical Research Agency, Maxwell Air Force Base, Alabama.

Statement on the Success of Strategic Bombing by General Henry H. Arnold at London Press Conference, September 4, 1943. General Henry H. Arnold Papers, Library of Congress, Washington, D.C.

Strategic and Tactical Mission Analysis. Mission of 6 September 1943. Air Force History Support Office, Bolling Air Force Base, Washington, D.C.

The Case for Day Bombing. Ira Eaker. 1943. General Ira C. Eaker Papers, Library of Congress, Washington, D.C.

"Y" Service Report. Operation serial number 35. 6-9-43. 14 pages. Air Force History Support Office, Bolling Air Force Base, Washington, D.C.

423rd Bomb Squadron, 306th Bomb Group Daily Diary, September 6, 1943. Air Force History Support Office, Bolling Air Force Base, Washington, D.C.

Private Diaries/Personal Letters (Unpublished)

The following written material provided valuable information in illuminating the personal lives and adventures of the men featured in this book.

Martin Andrews. A detailed written account of the Stuttgart mission, as well as the experiences associated with Mr. Andrews's service as an unofficial agent of the Office of Strategic Services (OSS) in 1944. Also letters and journals of various activities in England in 1943. (118 pages)

James E. Armstrong. Letters, telegrams, and notes related to his escape from France, including an unpublished manuscript revealing what happened to several other escapees. (182 pages)

Olen Grant. An unpublished reminiscence of his experiences in the war entitled *For You the War Is Over*, which includes his detailed recollections of the Stuttgart mission, and the events surrounding his survival after going down with his plane. Fifteen letters to his family in Arkansas written during his imprisonment in Stalag 17. (136 pages)

Warren P. Laws. An unpublished narrative of his experiences on the Stuttgart mission, including a very detailed description of the events that took place in the cockpit of his plane prior to its being shot down.

Robert F. Travis. Personal letters to and from his family during his service with the Eighth Air Force in England and afterward, providing candid assessments of many of the men he served with during his tour as commander of the Forty-first Combat Wing. (34 pages)

Ray T. Wilken. Letters, telegrams, and personal notes detailing his experiences during his courtship and marriage to Braxton Nicholson, his training days, and his service with the 388th Bomb Group at Knettishall, England. (17 pages)

Author Interviews

Martin "Andy" Andrews: **2008** (7/14, 7/29, 7/30, 10/31, 11/13, 12/12, 12/13, 12/14, 12/15); **2009** (1/20, 8/6, 11/6); **2010** (2/4, 2/6, 2/17)

James E. Armstrong: **2008** (11/6); **2009** (1/12, 1/13, 1/14, 1/19, 1/29, 1/31, 6/28, 7/1, 7/24)

Richard Baughn: **2010** (7/19)

Tami Davis Biddle: **2009** (1/26)

William Eisenhart: **2010** (6/4)

Olen Grant: **2009** (2/7, 5/14, 5/20, 5/28, 6/4, 7/1, 8/25, 8/26, 10/22, 10/29); **2010** (2/5, 2/11, 3/29, 4/3)

Clifford Hammock: **2009** (1/14)

Richard Henggeler: **2008** (6/26, 11/11)

Demetrios "Jim" Karnezis: **2008** (11/1, 11/13); **2009** (1/20, 1/31, 2/1, 2/20, 2/21, 2/22); **2010** (1/12, 1/31, 2/17, 3/22)

Wilbur "Bud" Klint: **2009** (2/4, 3/25, 3/26, 5/14, 5/19, 7/13, 7/14)

Warren Laws: **2009** (2/10, 2/11); **2010** (4/15, 5/16)

Elizabeth "Libby" Laws: **2009** (2/10, 2/11)

Gary Moncur: **2009** (1/31, 2/1)

Brian D. O'Neill: **2009** (1/29, 1/30, 2/6)

Braxton Wilken Robinson: **2009** (1/22, 1/31, 2/5, 2/22, 2/23, 3/25); **2010** (3/29, 5/6, 5/9)

Donald Stoulil: **2010** (2/25, 4/1, 5/21)

Wilbert Yee: **2009** (1/14)

Other Important Interviews

Interviews with General Ira C. Eaker by Lieutenant Joe B. Green in Conjunction with the Senior Officer Debriefing Program at the Army War College at Carlisle Barracks, February 11, 1967, January 28, 1972. Courtesy of Tami Davis Biddle.

Interview with General Ira Eaker by Dr. Charles H. Hildreth and Dr. Alfred Goldberg, May 1962. U.S. Air Force Archives.

Interview with General Ira Eaker by Arthur K. Marmor, January 1966. U.S. Air Force Archives.

Memoir/Unpublished

Lieutenant Colonel Richard D. Hughes served on the staff of General Frederick Anderson and was a senior member of the "Enemy Objectives Unit" that recommended which strategic targets should be attacked in 1943. In the book, he makes strikingly candid comments about many of the senior commanders in the Eighth Air Force, including Ira Eaker, and offers his perceptions of why the air offensive against Germany was suspended in the wake of the Stuttgart and Schweinfurt raids. It is archived at the Air Force Historical Research Agency, Maxwell Air Force Base, Alabama.

Papers/Collections

Of significant value to the author in understanding the internal conflicts between the senior commanders of the U.S. Army Air Forces in 1943 were the confidential diaries, correspondence, and cables found in their papers, including those of:

General Henry H. Arnold, Library of Congress, Washington, D.C.

General Ira C. Eaker, Library of Congress, Washington, D.C.

General Carl A. Spaatz, Library of Congress, Washington, D.C.

General Frederick Anderson, Jr., Hoover Institution Archives, Stanford University, Stanford, California.

General Curtis E. LeMay, Library of Congress, Washington, D.C.

General Robert Jesse Travis Collection, Manuscript, Archives, & Rare Book Library, Emory University, Atlanta, Georgia.

Web Sites

The following Web sites were particularly useful in researching different parts of the story. The Luftwaffe Archives site is extraordinarily helpful as a resource for researching the personal backgrounds and tactics of the fighter pilots who proved to be such a nemesis to the Eighth Air Force in 1943. Another site that provided important information about the Luftwaffe pilots, including Egon "Connie" Mayer, was Kacha's Luftwaffe Page. The author was able to utilize the user-friendly Footnote Web site to access all the Missing Air Crew Reports of the Eighth Air Force.

Most of the Eighth Air Force Bomb Groups now enjoy a Web site dedicated to their contributions to winning the air war against Germany. Due to the focus of this story on a limited number of squadrons and groups, the author was especially grateful for the information found at the Web sites of the 303rd, 306th, 384th, and 388th bomb groups.

American Swiss Foundation: www.americanswiss.org/index.php?option=com_content&task=view&id=36&Itemid=78

Kacha's Luftwaffe Page: www.luftwaffe.cz/index.html

Luftwaffe Archives & Records Reference Group: www.lwag.org/forums/index.php

Missing Air Crew Reports: www.footnote.com/index.php

303rd Bomb Group: www.303rdbg.com/missionreports/000menu.pdf

306th Bomb Group: www.306thbw.org/306thBmbGrp/306thBG.htm

384th Bomb Group: www.384thbombgroup.com

388th Bomb Group: www.388thbg.org/index/index.htm

388th Bomb Group Database: www.388bg.org

ADDITIONAL PHOTO CAPTIONS AND CREDITS

1. (Page 2)   General Henry H. "Hap" Arnold shortly after the war (U.S. Air Force).
2. (Page 14)   General Ira Eaker, 1942 (U.S. Air Force).
3. (Page 24)   Olen "Reb" Grant, 1943 (Courtesy of Olen Grant).
4. (Page 34)   Demetrios Karnezis, 1943 (Courtesy of Demetrios Karnezis).
5. (Page 42)   Martin "Andy" Andrews, 1942 (Courtesy of Martin Andrews).
6. (Page 51)   Robert Falligant Travis, 1943 (U.S. Air Force).
7. (Page 58)   Ray Theodore Wilken, 1941 (Courtesy of Braxton Wilken Robinson).
8. (Page 67)   James Edwin Armstrong, 1943 (Courtesy of James Armstrong).
9. (Page 78)   B-17 Contrails over Europe, 1943 (U.S. Air Force).
10. (Page 91)   Egon "Connie" Mayer, 1943 (Photo by H. Hoffmann, 1943).
11. (Page 99)   B-17 on fire, falling earthward (U.S. Air Force).
12. (Page 106)   B-17 with tail sheared off plunges toward the clouds (U.S. Air Force).
13. (Page 113)   B-17 falling with wing blown off (U.S. Air Force).
14. (Page 124)   B-17 in flames, heading down (U.S. Air Force).
15. (Page 131)   Andy Andrews (standing, far right) with crew, 1943 (U.S. Air Force).
16. (Page 138)   *Slightly Dangerous*, 1943 (U.S. Air Force).
17. (Page 146)   Two B-17s exploding in midair (U.S. Air Force).
18. (Page 154)   Official bailout procedures for the B-17 (U.S. Air Force).
19. (Page 161)   James Armstrong (standing, far right) with crew, 1943. Sergeant James Redwing is kneeling, second from right (U.S. Air Force, courtesy of James Armstrong).

Photograph by Carolyn R. Mrazek

Robert J. Mrazek is a military historian, novelist, former U.S. congressman, and Navy veteran. His books include *A Dawn Like Thunder: The True Story of Torpedo Squadron Eight*, which was named a *Washington Post* "Best Book of 2009" (American History), as well as *Stonewall's Gold*, which was the winner of the Michael Shaara Prize for Best Civil War Novel of 1999. As a congressman, Mrazek wrote the law that saved Manassas battlefield from being developed into a shopping mall.

INDEX